W9-AVI-433

The Disney Queue Line Survival Guidebook

Activities to Cure
Queue Line Boredom at
the Walt Disney World® Resort

Kimberly Button

Copyright © 2006 by Kimberly Button

ISBN 0-7414-3268-4

Every effort has been made to ensure the accuracy of information in this book, however, the publisher and author assume no responsibility for errors or omissions. Prices, attractions, schedules, etc. are constantly changing so readers should always verify information before making final travel plans. The author and publisher cannot be held responsible for the experiences of readers while traveling. *The Disney Queue Line Survival Guidebook* is not affiliated with, authorized by, endorsed by or officially associated in any way with the Walt Disney Company, Disney Enterprises, Inc. or any of their affiliates.

Cover design, interior design and maps by J. Daniel Jenkins.

Printed in the United States of America

Published December 2010

INFINITY PUBLISHING
1094 New DeHaven Street, Suite 100
West Conshohocken, PA 19428-2713
Toll-free (877) BUY BOOK
Local Phone (610) 941-9999
Fax (610) 941-9959
Info@buybooksontheweb.com
www.buybooksontheweb.com

Trademarks

This book makes reference to various fictional characters, product names, companies and other works that are trademarks, registered marks or service marks of their various creators and owners, including Disney copyrighted characters, trademarks, marks and registered marks owned by The Walt Disney Company and Disney Enterprises, Inc.

All references to these properties are used in this book solely for editorial purposes. Neither the author nor the publisher makes any commercial claim to their use.

For Mom and Dad, who have always believed in me.

For Carrie, the Enchanted Tiki Birds and Flights of Wonder are dedicated to you.

For Daniel, who shared my dream and helped make it a reality. This book would not have been possible without you. I love you.

About the Author

Kimberly Button is a former Walt Disney World® Resort cast member and Disney Cruise Line® crew member. Having logged hundreds of visits to the Disney theme parks, she shares her expert knowledge of how to enjoy your time at Florida's Walt Disney World® Resort, even the hours spent waiting in queue lines. For 15 years, Button has been widely published in national magazines, newspapers and websites such as *Arthur Frommer's Budget Travel*, Woodall's publications, *Family Motor Coaching,* and *The Dollar Stretcher.* She is also the Budget Travel Editor of www.BellaOnline.com. Visit www.kimbutton.com for more information on Button's work.

Table of Contents

Introduction

If there is one thing that every visitor dreads about visiting the theme parks of the Walt Disney World® Resort, it is waiting in queue lines. After spending a fortune on admission tickets you want to feel like every minute that you spend in the theme park is time well spent, but when the queue line for Space Mountain is an hour long for a two and a half minute ride, you start to lose that "magical" feeling. That's where *The Disney Queue Line Survival Guidebook* comes in.

The Disney Queue Line Survival Guidebook is a unique collection of hints and tips to reduce your wait times for Disney theme park attractions combined with scavenger hunts, trivia questions, word puzzles, and hidden Mickey searches tailored to each theme park attraction that will entertain every member of your party during the times that you do have to wait in line. No more idly staring at the backside of the guests in front of you for an hour. No more anxious parents trying to amuse their bored children. No more tempers flaring from the sheer frustration of doing nothing. *The Disney Queue Line Survival Guidebook* is the answer that every Disney theme park guest has been looking for.

For first time visitors to the Walt Disney World® Resort, the collection of activities for each attraction and theme park will give you an eye opening education of the incredible "show" that Disney has created in even the smallest of details throughout their parks. For visitors who have been to the Disney theme parks countless times before, you can test your knowledge of the trivia and history behind Disney's attractions. Almost every member of your party, from young to old, can play along with a wide assortment of activities.

You'll notice that *The Disney Queue Line Survival Guidebook* is a little different than most Disney guidebooks because it is tailored specifically to the four theme parks. Many Disney visitors purchase Disney guidebooks that list information on how to get the best airline flight, where to go fishing, how to plan a Disney wedding, etc. along with the theme park information. For many visitors, much of this information isn't necessary and you certainly don't want to be carrying around pages of useless information throughout the theme parks. Though there are a wonderful array of activities to enjoy at the Walt Disney World® Resort, let's face it, you're going to Disney to visit the theme parks and that's where you'll spend most of your time just standing around waiting in queue lines.

The Disney Queue Line Survival Guidebook is solely designed to help you maximize your time and find the most enjoyment in the attractions and shows in each theme park. I won't tell you what attractions and shows you MUST see because your preferences and mine are sure to be different. I also don't present itineraries that tell you what to do every minute of the day in each theme park. If you need someone whom you don't know telling you how to enjoy *your* vacation, this book isn't for you.

What I do realize is that most visitors to Disney theme parks just want to have as much fun as possible in a limited amount of time. If you're starving and desperately need a quick bite to eat, you're not going to take the time to look up a theme park's dining options in a guidebook…you're just going to grab a hamburger and continue enjoying the attractions. If your kids really want to climb the Swiss Family Treehouse but it's only given two out of five stars in a guidebook, are you really going to tell them no? *The Disney Queue Line Survival Guidebook* gives you only the essential, straightforward information that you need to simply enjoy Disney's theme park attractions along with plenty of entertaining fun and games so that your entire day, even the time spent in queue lines, can be purely magical.

How to Use
The Disney Queue Line Survival Guidebook

The Disney Queue Line Survival Guidebook is unique because it is the first book to focus solely on Disney's theme park attractions as well as how to best utilize your time while standing in the always dreaded queue line. Even on the slowest of days at Disney theme parks you will have to stand in a queue line before boarding many attractions or wait in a theater for a show to start. Each listing in this book will provide helpful information on how to best experience that attraction or show along with activities to keep your party amused and entertained, beginning with the easier activities and ending with the more challenging.

Each Walt Disney World® (WDW) Resort theme park is given its own chapter. Within the chapter, the theme park's attractions and shows are divided into appropriate groupings and listed alphabetically. For instance, the Magic Kingdom attractions and shows are divided among the lands that they occupy, such as Fantasyland. In the Disney-MGM Studios chapter, the listings are divided between attractions and shows. In each theme park's chapter you will also find bonus activities that can be enjoyed while waiting for parades and fireworks as well as general trivia about the theme park that can be played anytime, such as waiting in line for an attraction, waiting to order food at a quick service counter, or waiting for transportation back to your hotel.

Each attraction and show (collectively referred to as attractions) for which you can typically expect a wait time will have the following information listed:

Overview: A brief description of the attraction as well as the guest capacity. Note: Many attraction descriptions mention Audio-Animatronics. Audio-Animatronics is a technology that Disney Imagineers (think of them as architects that design fun) developed to give life-like movement to animal and human

3

characters, sort of like robots that look and behave exactly like human beings.

Thrill Time: The time duration of the attraction.

Be Aware of: In this section, you will find details of the queue line and the attraction which will help you make a determination of whether or not to experience the attraction. Steps in the queue line, strobe lights, and moments of pitch darkness or enclosed spaces can all be problems for many people yet are not plainly obvious before experiencing the attraction. Other concerns, such as attractions and queue lines in direct sun with no shade, are also pointed out so that you can decide when to experience an attraction.

Helpful Hints: These insider tips will help you have the most enjoyable experience at each attraction, from when is the best time to ride an attraction to which seating area is the best. The Parent/Guardian Switch option will also be listed if it is available. (See "Hints and Tips on Surviving Disney Queue Lines" for more information on the Parent/Guardian Switch option.)

Disabled Access: This section states wheelchair accessibility, whether guests must transfer from their wheelchair or motorized scooter, and lists assistive devices available. Some assistive devices need to be rented from Guest Relations before boarding the attraction so visit Guest Relations upon entering the theme park to obtain any equipment needed.

The following information might also be listed with each attraction:

FASTPASS AVAILABLE: If you see this designation with an attraction listing, you're able to utilize FASTPASS, Disney's unique system of allowing guests to enjoy some of their most popular attractions with a minimal wait. Above each FASTPASS ticket kiosk located outside of selected attractions is a clock stating a time frame that you would be able to come back to the attraction and bypass the standard queue line if you utilize the FASTPASS option. To use the FASTPASS system, simply insert your theme park ticket into the kiosk (every member of your party with an admission ticket must have their own FASTPASS) and you will be given a FASTPASS ticket (along with the return of your theme park ticket) with the appointed time for you to come back to the attraction and enjoy a reduced wait time (usually 5-10 minutes). Pay careful attention to the time span that is listed on your ticket so that you don't miss your return time.

Warning: Look on your FASTPASS ticket to find the time that you can receive another FASTPASS for a different attraction. Often, you must wait until your return time for one attraction before you can receive a FASTPASS ticket for another attraction. On the busiest of days, the allotted amount of FASTPASS tickets for the entire day can be claimed rather quickly so be sure to visit the most popular attractions early in the day or claim a FASTPASS time for later in the day.

Restrictions: Disney's official cautions and guidelines to ensure the safety of its guests.

👁 ***Look For*** or 🔊 ***Listen For***: This section points out unusual objects or sounds that are part of the Disney "show" that guests might normally miss, such as decorations with hidden meanings or a unique audio soundtrack.

☆ ***Hidden Mickey Hunt***: These clues will help you find hidden Mickeys, Mickey Mouse shapes that have been cleverly inserted into some Disney attractions by Disney's Imagineers. Searching for hidden Mickeys has become a popular pastime among Disney enthusiasts and this section points out where you can locate easy to find Mickeys while waiting within attraction queue lines.

👣 ***Scavenger Hunt***: A fun list of items to find throughout the queue line. Some are easy and some are difficult, but all of the items can be found in the decorations or artwork in the standard queue line.

Hints and Tips on Surviving Disney Queue Lines

- When you enter a theme park, be sure to pick up a current guide map as well as a "Times Guide and New Information" insert. The Times Guide is essential so that you will know when stage shows and parades will be held, what attractions are currently closed, and the operating hours of attractions and restaurants which might be different from the regular theme park operating hours.

- The Guest Information Board is an invaluable source of information on the wait times of attractions within each theme park. The board lists the wait times of attractions as well as updates on any attraction closings. With this information, you can make preliminary decisions on what to do for your first hour in the park and enlist the help of the Information Board cast members for their expert knowledge of how to navigate the theme park. The location of each park's Guest Information Board is listed on the front page of the theme park chapter.

- Wait times are usually prominently displayed outside of the queue area so that guests know how long they will be in line. The posted times are often padded by 5-10 minutes in case the wait is longer than predicted. However, you might want to ask cast members if the wait time displayed is accurate. The front line cast members can become so busy attending to guests that they might not have enough time to update the display. Cast members can easily look at the line and accurately judge the wait time with their knowledge of how many vehicles are running that day, any expected maintenance delays, etc.

- Always consider the FASTPASS option if it is available and the attraction is experiencing a very long wait time. (See "How To Use *The Disney Queue Line Survival Guidebook*" for more information about FASTPASS.)

- The best time to experience the most popular attractions, especially the thrill attractions, are first thing in the morning, later in the evening and during parade and fireworks times. If you can, arrive early at a theme park, leave the park and take a break during the afternoon, and then return later in the evening in order to avoid lengthy queue lines.

- Do not go to an attraction that is located near a parade viewing site after the parade is over. For instance, avoid going to the Haunted Mansion after watching the afternoon parade from Liberty Square in the Magic Kingdom. With such a large amount of people suddenly converging on one attraction, these "parade dumps," as cast members call them, make queue lines swell and can add 20 minutes or more to your wait time. Your best bet is to head to an attraction in a section of the park away from the parade route or stop and get a bite to eat and let the queue lines dwindle.

- If an attraction that you wanted to experience was temporarily shut down during the day (it went "101" in cast member terms), ask a cast member at any attraction entrance or any manager (they will be in plain clothes and wearing a name tag) with a radio to contact the Guest Information Board to see if it is operating. Cast members can sometimes access hidden phones for attraction information park-wide.

- If you're traveling with small children, don't let their inability to ride an attraction deter the adults from enjoying the thrill rides of the park. Disney offers a "Parent/Guardian Switch" option on many attractions which allows one adult to stay with the kids while the other rides the attraction. When the adults switch places, there is no need to wait in an additional line as cast members will immediately board the second adult onto the attraction. Parent/Guardian Switch availability is listed in the *Helpful Hints* section of each attraction if it is available, but always ask cast members what your options are before entering the queue line. The cast members may give you special instructions regarding their Parent/Guardian Switch policy or may be able to handle special requests.

- If only some members of your party want to experience an attraction but your party doesn't want to split up while waiting in the queue line, keep in mind that nearly all of Disney's theme park attractions have exits near the boarding areas. For instance, a guest can stay in the queue line and enjoy the pre-show of The Twilight Zone Tower of Terror and still be able to exit the attraction before guests board the elevators. All of the thrill attractions have "chicken exits" and many of the tamer attractions have exits, as well. If you plan on staying in the queue line and not boarding the attraction, though, be sure to double check with a cast member before entering the queue line to make sure an exit is available and where it is located.

- Many parties try to maximize their time by having one person stand in the queue line while others go get food or shop. While this plan works in theory, it's also full of pitfalls. Most queue lines are sectioned off by ropes or poles and by trying to cross these barriers you'll soon find yourself in the "Queue Line Olympics," a challenging and embarrassing feat of grown adults trying to squeeze themselves through two feet wide openings, hurling their legs over ropes and squeezing past sweaty strangers in tight queue areas. You'll also run the chance of never catching up with your party. For your safety and enjoyment, stick together and leave the eating and shopping for later.

- If you have any medical disabilities or language impairments that might prevent you from enjoying attractions, contact Guest Relations when entering the theme park or a cast member at each attraction. Guest Relations has booklets available which details the restrictions and requirements for each attraction within the park, lists options for those with medical disabilities and includes detailed park information on accessible restrooms, service animal break areas, etc. For visitors who cannot understand English, a device is available at Guest Relations which can translate the audio of certain attractions into several different languages. Whatever your concern might be, ask a cast member if the attraction is suitable for you.

- Think the only way to enjoy a theme park's parade is to line up for an hour beforehand to get a good viewing spot? Not necessarily. Because the parades travel down major guest thoroughfares which become blocked off, crosswalks must be set up to allow for the flow of traffic. However, even these crosswalks get roped off before parade time. Ask the cast members patrolling the area when they will allow guests to stand in the crosswalk sections and you could still get a front row seat without a long wait. The areas at parade step off and step down (where the parade actually enters and exits the park) are also little known areas where fewer guests congregate.

- Central Florida is known for its afternoon showers that appear out of nowhere, drench theme park guests, and then disappear quickly. If you do not want to be caught in the rain while waiting in an outside queue line or while riding an outdoor attraction, plan to visit indoor attractions or those with cover in the mid-afternoon. This game plan will also protect you from the Florida heat and humidity which peaks in the afternoon and wilts theme park guests.

When most people think about the Walt Disney World® Resort, they envision the Magic Kingdom. Cinderella Castle rises tall above seven lands of fantasy and fun where Disney's animated characters take center stage and guests still flock to experience classic attractions created with Walt Disney's personal touch over 40 years ago. As the original theme park which spurred the development of the entire Walt Disney World® Resort, no trip to Disney is complete without a visit to this magical land.

Guest Information Board Location: Across from Casey's Corner on the left hand side of Main Street heading towards Cinderella Castle.

Magic Kingdom

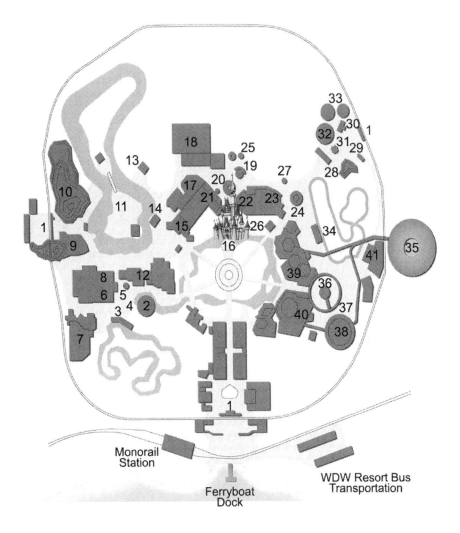

Monorail
Station

Ferryboat
Dock

WDW Resort Bus
Transportation

Magic Kingdom

1 Walt Disney World
Railroad Stations

Adventureland

2 Swiss Family Treehouse
3 Jungle Cruise
4 Shrunken Ned's Junior
Jungle Boats
5 The Magic Carpets of Aladdin
6 The Enchanted Tiki Room
Under New Management
7 Pirates of the Caribbean

Frontierland

8 Country Bear Jamboree
9 Splash Mountain
10 Big Thunder Mountain Railroad
11 Tom Sawyer Island
12 Frontierland Shootin' Arcade

Liberty Square

13 The Haunted Mansion
14 Liberty Square Riverboat
15 The Hall of Presidents

Fantasyland

16 Cinderellabration
17 Peter Pan's Flight
18 "it's a small world"
19 Dumbo the Flying Elephant
20 Cinderella's Golden Carrousel
21 Mickey's PhilharMagic
22 Snow White's Scary Adventures
23 The Many Adventures of
Winnie the Pooh
24 Mad Tea Party

25 Ariel's Grotto
26 Storytime with Belle
27 Pooh's Playful Spot

Mickey's Toontown Fair

28 The Barnstormer at Goofy's
Wiseacre Farm
29 Donald's Boat
30 Mickey's Country House
31 Minnie's Country House
32 Toontown Hall of Fame Tent
33 Judge's Tent

Tomorrowland

34 Tomorrowland Indy Speedway
35 Space Mountain
36 Astro Orbiter
37 Tomorrowland Transit Authority
38 Walt Disney's
Carousel of Progress
39 Stitch's Great Escape!
40 Buzz Lightyear's Space
Ranger Spin
41 Tomorrowland Arcade

Magic Kingdom Tips

- Allow for more transportation time to arrive at the Magic Kingdom than for any other Walt Disney World® Resort theme park. Guests driving personal vehicles will park at the Transportation and Ticket Center from which you will need to travel by monorail or ferry to reach the Magic Kingdom. The monorail takes approximately five minutes to travel to the Magic Kingdom and the ferry takes approximately seven minutes.

- There are two monorails with service from the Magic Kingdom - a monorail with direct service to the Transportation and Ticket Center and a resort monorail with stops at Disney's Contemporary Resort, Disney's Polynesian Resort and Disney's Grand Floridian Resort and Spa as well as the Transportation and Ticket Center. At the end of the night when the queue lines are long, you might consider utilizing the Resort monorail which usually has a shorter queue line but makes more frequent stops.

- The most crowded parade and fireworks viewing sites are along Main Street, U.S.A. and near Cinderella Castle. Consider viewing the parade from the less crowded locations of Frontierland. To view the Wishes fireworks show, consider standing along the bridge leading to Tomorrowland or find a spot to relax in Fantasyland.

ADVENTURELAND

The jungles, wild animals and intriguing stories of exotic lands come to life in this tropical paradise.

The Enchanted Tiki Room Under New Management

Overview: This show has literally gone to the birds as Iago (from *Aladdin*) plans to introduce a new act at the Enchanted Tiki Room against the better wishes of Zazu (from *The Lion King*). After the Tiki gods teach Iago a lesson, a flock of birds celebrate with a rousing song and dance show that is guaranteed to bring the 340 guests in the theater to their feet.

Thrill Time: 9 ½ minutes

Be Aware of: This attraction has shorter operating hours than the rest of the Magic Kingdom. Consult your Times Guide for operating hours.

Portions of this show are dark with lightning and thunder and many bright, flashing lights. The Tiki poles surrounding the room will start talking at the end of the show which might frighten some younger children.

Helpful Hints: This attraction typically has one of the shortest wait times of all Magic Kingdom attractions. It's especially important to choose a seat in a good location in this show. Because most of the action will be taking place on the ceiling, you'll have to bend your neck back for nearly 10 minutes. Choose a seat in the back rows to minimize your neck discomfort.

This is an attraction where it doesn't pay to be first in the queue line. Iago, who has the starring role in the show, is positioned at the far right of the theater as you enter. The first guests into the theater will be seated directly under Iago and will have a hard time seeing the character as well as having bright lights shining into their eyes for most of the show. Try to sit in the center of the theater if possible.

Disabled Access: Guests may remain in their wheelchair or motorized scooter. Disney's assistive listening devices interact with this attraction. Disney's handheld captioning devices interact with this attraction.

• • • • • • • • • • • • • • • • • • • •

☆ **Hidden Mickey Hunt**: Clusters of berries carved into the wooden doors leading into and out of the theater form hidden Mickeys.

1. What type of bird is thought to deliver babies to expectant moms and dads?
A. Flamingo
B. Stork
C. Ostrich

2. When birds migrate, what do they do?
A. Build a nest for their young
B. Eat a lot of food in preparation for winter
C. Fly to warmer climates

3. Match the following birds with their description:

Hummingbird   A bird who likes to peck holes in wood
Cardinal   A pink bird with long legs
Woodpecker   A bird who likes the cold
Bluebird   A bird who likes to come out at night
Dove   A red bird often associated with winter
Flamingo   A tiny bird whose wings flap very fast
Owl   A bird associated with the symbol of peace
Peacock   A bird whose feathers appear blue
Penguin   A bird with brightly colored feathers

4. Which type of bird is not mentioned in the Christmas song "Twelve Days of Christmas"?
A. Partridge
B. Turtle dove
C. Lark

5. Which comedian supplied the voice of Iago in the Disney animated film *Aladdin*?
A. Eddie Murphy
B. Gilbert Gottfried
C. Andy Rooney

6. Which type of bird was trained to carry war messages through the air?
A. Eagle
B. Pigeon
C. Owl

7. Which bird was almost chosen as the United States' national bird before the Bald Eagle won the honor?
A. Cardinal
B. Dove
C. Turkey

8. What is the state bird of Florida?
A. Chickadee
B. Mockingbird
C. Robin

9. Which Disney film has a song titled "Feed the Birds" which was reportedly a favorite of Walt Disney's?
A. *Cinderella*
B. *Snow White and the Seven Dwarves*
C. *Mary Poppins*

10. In the Disney animated film *The Three Caballeros*, the main characters were a duck, a rooster and what other type of bird?
A. Parrot
B. Blackbird
C. Toucan

Jungle Cruise

Overview: Enjoy a fun-filled boat ride through the jungle with a tour guide whose bad jokes and puns are as much a beloved part of the attraction as the Audio-Animatronic animals that represent the rivers of three continents. Each open-air boat accommodates 40 guests.

Thrill Time: 10 minutes

FASTPASS AVAILABLE

Be Aware of: This attraction usually opens later than the rest of the Magic Kingdom. Consult your Times Guide for operating hours.

This attraction and queue line are located outdoors, however both are covered. This attraction closes during inclement weather such as thunder and lightning.

There are gunshots along the ride, as well as a giant snake which guests will see on the left side of the boat. One scene has lions eating a zebra, although the scene is not gory. There is a dark tunnel which might frighten small children and those with claustrophobia.

Helpful Hints: It's best to visit the Jungle Cruise during the daylight when you are able to see more of the jungle. Though the attraction is illuminated at night, you will miss some of the atmosphere of the daytime cruises.

There are fans and a water fountain in the queue line. Guests sitting on the left hand side of the boat are more likely to be sprayed by some of the water elements.

Parent/Guardian Switch option is available.

Disabled Access: Guests may remain in their wheelchair or motorized scooter. The disabled queue line is located to the left of the standard queue. Disney's assistive listening devices interact with this attraction. Disney's handheld captioning devices interact with this attraction.

• • • • • • • • • • • • • • • • • • •

Scavenger Hunt: Find a bike with a wicker basket, a picture of elephants, a butterfly species chart and a case of arachnid sedative.

Listen For: The music in the queue line is from the 1930s, including the Cole Porter tune "You're the Top" with the lyrics "You're a Bendel bonnet, a Shakespeare sonnet, you're Mickey Mouse!"

1. What is a group of elephants called?

2. In the Disney animated film *The Jungle Book*, the young boy Mowgli is sent to live in the man village after being raised by what type of animals?
A. Apes
B. Wolves
C. Elephants

3. In *The Jungle Book*, is Mowgli happy to be sent to the man village?

4. Which character from Disney's *The Jungle Book* had his own 1990s cartoon series?
A. Baloo
B. King Louie
C. Mowgli

5. Find the following characters from *The Jungle Book* in the word search below: Mowgli, Kaa, Baloo, Shere Khan, King Louie, Bagheera and Colonel Hathi.

```
B N G A P J B L F A I H D C K G
J S I H B W K I N G L O U I E J
R H D E R A M G S L U K Q N F B
A E F B M T G R K B J T A E G O
E R Q J F D Y H P W C Y I A S A
L E K C O L O N E L H A T H I M
H K C H L G A J W E O L C G P I
B H G M O W G L I M R H F J B Q
M A A P F E N K D B T A H E R D
D N Q C K I A S C G B A L O O F
```

6. In the Disney animated film *Tarzan*, what is the name of the woman who visits the jungle and falls in love with Tarzan?

7. What is the name of Tarzan's ape friend in Disney's *Tarzan*?
A. Terk
B. Tonto
C. Tantor

8. What famous comedian starred as the father of a boy who leaves the jungle to go on a quest in New York City in Disney's 1997 film *Jungle 2 Jungle*?
A. Steve Martin
B. Robin Williams
C. Tim Allen

9. Which 1997 Disney film starred Brendan Fraser as a man who had been raised by apes in the jungle?

10. In what year was Disney's animated film *The Jungle Book* released?
A. 1954
B. 1960
C. 1967

11. Disney's *The Jungle Book* is based on a novel of the same name written by what author?
A. Rudyard Kipling
B. Sir Arthur Conan Doyle
C. Daniel Defoe

12. Disney's *Tarzan* was inspired by the novel *Tarzan of the Apes* written by which author?
A. George Orwell
B. Richard Brown
C. Edgar Rice Burroughs

13. Which famous woman, inspired by the stories of *Tarzan of the Apes* as a child, lived with chimpanzees in Africa?

14. What is the name given to male elephants and rhinos? What are female elephants and rhinos called?

15. According to a menu in the boat boarding area, what does the Crew Mess serve on Thursdays?

The Magic Carpets of Aladdin

Overview: Hop aboard a magic carpet and fly through the air just like Aladdin and Jasmine did in the Disney animated film *Aladdin*. Each of the 16 magic carpets has two rows which each hold two adults or a combination of three adults and kids.

Thrill Time: 1 ½ minutes

Be Aware of: This entire queue line and attraction are located outdoors. This attraction closes during inclement weather such as thunder and lightning.

Children under 7 must be accompanied by an adult and must sit on the inside of the row. It's ironic, then, that the adults sitting on the outside rows are more likely to get spit on by the camel as you go flying past him! If you're afraid of heights, be aware that at the end of the ride your carpet will rise to the highest point of the attraction before bringing you back down to exit.

Helpful Hints: To avoid being sprayed with water as the camel "spits," fly your carpet as high as it will go. Flying high will also give you a smoother ride and a great view of Adventureland. Guests sitting in the front row control how high the magic carpet flies, while guests in the back row can tilt the carpet forward or backward.

Parent/Guardian Switch option is available.

Disabled Access: Guests must transfer from a motorized scooter to a wheelchair provided at the attraction. Guests may remain in their wheelchair.

● ● ● ● ● ● ● ● ● ● ● ● ● ● ● ● ● ●

☆ ***Hidden Mickey Hunt***: After you enter the main queue line, on the upper level ramp to your right about five feet into the queue you will see two blue round stones and a half circle stone embedded in the walkway which form the image of a Mouse Ears hat.

𝓠 ***Scavenger Hunt***: Find the Genie's lamp, clay pots and jewels.

1. How many Genies can you count on the attraction? How many Abus? How many camels can you see?

2. In the Disney animated film *Aladdin*, can Aladdin fly?

3. In *Aladdin*, what does the Sultan feed Jafar's parrot?
A. Moldy crackers
B. Caviar
C. Sunflower seeds

4. In *Aladdin*, when Jasmine visits the marketplace and gives an apple to a hungry child she nearly gets her hand cut off. What other Disney princess got into a lot of trouble when she ate an apple?
A. Cinderella
B. Ariel
C. Snow White

5. In *Aladdin*, what type of animal does Jafar turn into when he becomes the most powerful sorcerer in the world?
A. Snake
B. Dragon
C. Eagle

6. When Aladdin is turned into a prince, what is he known as?
A. Ali Zabba
B. Prince Ali Ababwa
C. The Handsome One

7. Unscramble the following names and places that are in the Disney film *Aladdin*:

BAGRAAH   (Hint: The city where the movie takes place)
VEAC FO NDERSOW   (Hint: Where the lamp was hidden)
SMEINAJ   (Hint: The princess Aladdin falls in love with)
BUA   (Hint: Aladdin's monkey)
JAAHR   (Hint: Jasmine's pet tiger)
ETH LTNUSA   (Hint: Jasmine's father)
OAIG   (Hint: Jafar's bird)
RTTSEE TAR   (Hint: What the guards nicknamed Aladdin)

8. Which of the following wishes can the Genie perform?
A. Kill someone
B. Make someone wealthy
C. Bring people back from the dead

9. Which of the following was not one of Aladdin's wishes?
A. To be a prince
B. To be saved from drowning
C. To escape from the demolished treasure cave

10. If the Genie in *Aladdin* were given one wish, what does he say he would wish for?
A. Fortune
B. Freedom
C. Fame

11. In *Aladdin*, why does Aladdin think he can never be with Jasmine, even though he loves her?
A. Because Jasmine won't give him the time of day
B. Because Jasmine's father doesn't like Aladdin
C. Because the princess can only marry a prince

12. Which famous comedian supplied the voice of the Genie in the movie *Aladdin*?
A. Steve Martin
B. Ray Romano
C. Robin Williams

13. Which television show featured a female genie whose master was an astronaut?
A. *Bewitched*
B. *I Dream of Jeannie*
C. *The Munsters*

14. *Aladdin* won an Academy Award for Best Song for which song in the film?
A. "Arabian Nights"
B. "A Whole New World"
C. "A Friend Like Me"

Pirates of the Caribbean

Overview: Take a leisurely boat ride through an 18th century seaport under siege by pirates. Your 20-passenger boat (six rows each hold approximately four adults and children) sails through comical scenes of 125 Audio-Animatronic pirates invading the town and searching for treasures.

Thrill Time: 7 ½ minutes

Be Aware of: There is one small drop in the pitch dark with a mild splash at the beginning of the ride. There are periods of darkness as well as gunshot and fire elements.

The queue line has slight inclines and declines. At the end of the attraction, the boats sometimes bump together while you are waiting to exit. After disembarking the boat, guests exit the attraction via a steep, inclined moving walkway.

Helpful Hints: This dark ride with cool breezes is the perfect attraction for hot and humid days.

Disabled Access: Guests must transfer from a motorized scooter to a wheelchair. Guests must transfer from a wheelchair and step down into the ride vehicle. Disney's handheld captioning devices interact with this attraction.

• • • • • • • • • • • • • • • • • •

Scavenger Hunt: In the queue line, find: a cannon, people playing chess and a barrel of explosives.

Do you want to know how to talk like a pirate? Here are some pirate words and their meanings so you can speak like a pirate today:

Pirate word	Meaning
ahoy	hello
arrr	yes or I'm happy
avast	to notice something
aye	yes
aye aye	okay, I'll do that
land ho	I see land
shiver me timbers	an expression of surprise

1. What type of bird are pirates famous for having as their pets?
A. Mockingbird
B. Seagull
C. Parrot

2. On treasure maps, what letter is said to "mark the spot"?
A. M
B. X
C. T

3. According to the famous saying, "Dead men tell no _____."

4. The Jolly Roger is the name given to the most famous pirate flag. The flag is black with what symbols?
A. Skull and crossbones
B. Pirate ship
C. Gold coins

5. Who played Captain Jack in Disney's live action film *Pirates of the Caribbean: The Curse of the Black Pearl*?
A. Russell Crowe
B. Johnny Depp
C. Will Smith

6. In *Pirates of the Caribbean: The Curse of the Black Pearl*, what is the Black Pearl?
A. A cursed pearl necklace
B. A violent storm
C. A ship

7. What is the name of the 2006 sequel to *Pirates of the Caribbean: The Curse of the Black Pearl*?
A. *Pirates of the Caribbean: Dead Man's Chest*
B. *Pirates of the Caribbean: Here We Go Again*
C. *Pirates of the Caribbean: Mutiny on the Bay*

8. What was the infamous pirate Blackbeard's actual name?
A. Edward Teach
B. Francis Drake
C. Anne Bonny

9. To terrorize his enemies, Blackbeard would appear to set what part of his body on fire?
A. Arm
B. Beard
C. Foot

10. Unscramble the following pirate terms and words:

LKAW TEH NKAPL   (Hint: Step off a ship and into the ocean)
EIGHW CHONRA   (Hint: Haul up the anchor and set sail)
VYAD NESOJ CKLOER   (Hint: The bottom of the sea)
NDAL BBREUL   (Hint: Someone who doesn't like the sea)
TINUMY   (Hint: When crew members turn on their captain)
GNOELLA   (Hint: A large sailing ship)
RREESUAT STHEC   (Hint: Where riches are stored)
AOCNNN   (Hint: A large gun mounted on wheels)
YVCSRU   (Hint: A disease caused by lack of Vitamin C)
OOONLBDU   (Hint: A Spanish gold coin)
EYAGLL   (Hint: The kitchen on a ship)

11. Disney's first live action film, *Treasure Island*, featured another pirate, Long John Silver. For what reason did the 1950 film, which is set in the West Indies, actually have to be entirely shot in England?
A. The main actor would not leave his home country
B. The production costs were less expensive in England
C. Walt Disney had income from his cartoons which couldn't be spent outside of England.

12. Which author wrote the classic novel *Treasure Island*?
A. Laura Ingalls Wilder
B. Jules Verne
C. Robert Louis Stevenson

Swiss Family Treehouse

Overview: Journey through one of the biggest tree houses you'll ever see as you peek inside the life of the family from Disney's film *Swiss Family Robinson*.

Thrill Time: Average of 15-20 minutes.

Be Aware of: This entire attraction is located outdoors. This attraction closes during inclement weather such as thunder and lightning.

Guests climb up 62 steps and down 66 steps in this attraction. There is only one small area with limited seating throughout the treehouse.

Helpful Hints: This attraction typically has one of the shortest wait times of all Magic Kingdom attractions. It's best to enjoy the Swiss Family Treehouse early in the day when you have plenty of physical energy and the temperatures are cooler.

Disabled Access: There is no disabled access for this attraction.

● ● ● ● ● ● ● ● ● ● ● ● ● ● ● ● ● ● ●

1. On average, how many trees are planted at the Walt Disney World® Resort each year?
A. 1,000
B. 6,000
C. 10,000

2. Approximately how many plastic leaves can be found on the Swiss Family Treehouse tree?
A. 300,000
B. 719,000
C. 1 million

3. What ABC hit television show premiered in 2004 featuring people stranded on an island after a plane crash?
A. *Lost*
B. *Survivor*
C. *The Amazing Race*

4. The cast of the *Gilligan's Island* television show was stranded on an island after a tour that lasted how long, according to the theme song?
A. Two hours
B. Three hours
C. Five hours

5. In the Disney film *Swiss Family Robinson*, what happens after the Robinson family is found on their deserted island?
A. They go on to write a book and become very famous
B. They chose not to leave the island
C. They build a resort on the island

6. In what month is Arbor Day, the holiday that encourages tree planting?
A. April
B. May
C. November

7. What kind of tree is the Swiss Family Treehouse supposed to represent?
A. Oak
B. Spruce
C. Banyan

8. Unscramble the following species of trees:

PPAEL
EINP
RCBHI
ALTNUW
RIF
MEL
PCERSU
PPLORA

FANTASYLAND

Children of all ages will enjoy this fairy tale inspired land packed with attractions inspired by Disney's famous animated characters.

Ariel's Grotto

Overview: Meet Ariel from Disney's *The Little Mermaid* in her grotto under the sea.

Thrill Time: Just enough time for an autograph and picture.

Be Aware of: Ariel's Grotto opens later and closes earlier than the Magic Kingdom's normal operating hours. Consult your Times Guide for operating hours.

The queue line for this attraction is entirely outdoors with no shade. This attraction closes during inclement weather such as thunder and lightning.

Helpful Hints: There is a fun play area with a soft surface and squirting fountains for kids to play in while their parents wait in line. A large portion of the queue has a ledge that guests can sit on while waiting.

Disney photographers will take your picture with Ariel for you to view later in the day at Town Square Exposition Hall. There is an additional fee for Disney's professional photographs.

Disabled Access: Guests may remain in their wheelchair or motorized scooter.

● ● ● ● ● ● ● ● ● ● ● ● ● ● ● ● ● ●

1. In Disney's *The Little Mermaid*, how old is Ariel?
A. 10 years old
B. 16 years old
C. 25 years old

2. What is the name of the talking bird in *The Little Mermaid*?
A. Scuttle
B. Flounder
C. Zazu

3. What is the name of Ariel's fish friend in *The Little Mermaid*?
A. Nemo
B. Flounder
C. Goldie

4. In *The Little Mermaid*, King Triton orders who to supervise Ariel?
A. Scuttle
B. Sebastian
C. Ursula

5. What is the name of Ariel's prince in *The Little Mermaid*?
A. Aaron
B. Stefan
C. Eric

6. In *The Little Mermaid*, what is in the sea shell that hangs around Ursula's neck?
A. Ariel's voice
B. A map to treasure hidden under the sea
C. Pocket change

7. In *The Little Mermaid*, Scuttle tells Ariel that what type of utensil is called a "dinglehopper"?
A. Knife
B. Spoon
C. Fork

8. All of Ariel's sister's names begin with what letter of the alphabet?

9. What wooden Disney animated character also dreamed of being human like Ariel does?
A. Pinocchio
B. The Beast
C. Bambi

10. Where in the Walt Disney World® Resort can you watch fish and dolphins and other creatures of the sea swimming around in an extremely large aquarium?
A. Epcot
B. DisneyQuest
C. Blizzard Beach

11. Where in the Walt Disney World® Resort can you swim with sharks and tropical fish?

Cinderella's Golden Carrousel

Overview: Carrousels have been a theme park classic for many generations and Cinderella's Golden Carrousel, inspired by the classic Disney animated film *Cinderella*, won't disappoint either young or old. Located in the shadow of Cinderella Castle, hop aboard one of 87 elaborately carved horses and spin to the sounds of classic Disney songs played on an organ.

Thrill Time: 2 minutes

Be Aware of: This attraction is located outdoors, however, it is covered. Cinderella's Golden Carrousel stops operating shortly before scheduled fireworks displays.

Helpful Hints: This gentle attraction is wonderful for smaller children and anyone who doesn't enjoy the fast paced thrill rides of the park. The horses on the outside of the platform are larger, taller and move higher off of the ground. The horses on the inside of the platform close to the motor are much smaller, shorter and don't move as high off of the ground as the others.

Each horse has a safety harness that can be secured around younger children. One stationary chariot is available for guests who don't want to ride upon a moving horse, since all of the horses move up and down.

Refer to the Times Guide to see when the Sword in the Stone Ceremony will be held just outside of the carrousel throughout the day. This fun, interactive ceremony features Merlin from the Disney animated film *The Sword in the Stone* as well as children from the audience who are selected to help pull the sword out of the stone. The stone is located behind the carrousel facing the castle. There are lots of great picture taking opportunities at this small show.

Parent/Guardian Switch option is available.

Disabled Access: Guests must transfer from their wheelchair or motorized scooter and walk a very short distance to the circular platform, step up onto the platform and climb aboard a carrousel horse or sit inside the stationary chariot. The disabled queue line is located at the attraction exit. Guests with service animals should check with a host or hostess at this attraction.

• • • • • • • • • • • • • • • • • • •

 Scavenger Hunt: On the carrousel, find: gold eagles, the Fairy Godmother, a scene with Cinderella trying on her pink dress, a scene of Cinderella running down steps, a horse with a gold sheep's head on its saddle, a horse with a sword, a horse with a Bald Eagle and flag pendant on its saddle and a horse with feathers on its saddle.

1. In the Disney animated film *Cinderella*, Cinderella sings that "A dream is a wish your _____ makes."
A. Soul
B. Love
C. Heart

2. In *Cinderella*, the Fairy Godmother's spell ends at what time?
A. When the sun sets
B. At eleven o'clock
C. At midnight

3. In *Cinderella*, what phrase is Cinderella's Fairy Godmother famous for saying?
A. Ta Ta For Now
B. Bibbidi Bobbidi Boo
C. Supercalifragilisticexpialidocious

4. In *Cinderella*, Cinderella's coach for the ball turns back into what at midnight?
A. Pumpkin
B. Horse
C. Mouse

5. In Disney's *Cinderella*, why is the royal ball held?
A. To celebrate a national holiday
B. To find a wife for the prince
C. It is the annual winter ball

6. In *Cinderella*, who makes Cinderella's dress for the ball because she is so busy doing her chores?
A. Her horse
B. Bruno
C. The mice and birds

7. What is the name of the evil cat in *Cinderella*?
A. Lucifer
B. Kitty
C. Cheshire

8. What was not the name of one of Cinderella's mice in the Disney animated film?
A. Gus
B. Bob
C. Jaq

9. From which foot does Cinderella lose her glass slipper as she runs away from the party?

10. Which of the following was not the name of one of
Cinderella's stepsisters in Disney's *Cinderella*?
A. Drizella
B. Druella
C. Anastasia

11. Cinderella's prince is always called by the name Prince
Charming, but what was his real name in Disney's *Cinderella*?
A. Alfred
B. Henry
C. He was never given another name

12. In *Cinderella*, which of the following is not one of the reasons
why Cinderella almost didn't get to try on the glass slipper and
marry her prince?
A. Her stepmother locked her in her room
B. Her stepmother broke the glass slipper
C. Her stepmother sent Cinderella on an errand

13. Which other Walt Disney World® Resort theme park has a
famous carrousel horse on display?
A. Epcot
B. Disney MGM-Studios
C. Disney's Animal Kingdom

14. True or False: The restaurant in Cinderella Castle used to be
named after a character from Sleeping Beauty.

15. In which U.S. state did Disney designers find the carrousel
before bringing it to the Magic Kingdom?
A. New York
B. New Jersey
C. Pennsylvania

16. Carrousels were originally designed for what purpose?
A. To teach knights how to fight on horses
B. To teach women how to climb on a horse
C. To teach children about different kinds of animals

Cinderellabration

Overview: If you've ever wondered how the story ends after Cinderella falls in love with her prince in the Disney animated film *Cinderella*, you'll want to see Cinderellabration. The show invites guests to Cinderella's coronation where the Fairy Godmother and several other characters from the film help Cinderella get ready to become a princess. Cinderella's princess friends (Sleeping Beauty, Snow White, Jasmine and Belle) make an appearance in their finest costumes, as well, creating an extravagant display of beautiful ball gowns and fairy tale endings.

Thrill Time: 16 ½ minutes

Be Aware of: This attraction closes during inclement weather. The entire viewing area is in direct sunlight with no cover.

There is no seating for this show unless you want to sit on the ground in the very front of the viewing area. There are fireworks during the show which produce smoke and a lot of ash that lands on guests who are close to the stage.

Helpful Hints: Consult your Times Guide for performance times.

This is a great show to enjoy while you're munching on a snack or eating a meal because food is allowed in the viewing area. Because the viewing area is elevated, it's easy to walk up to the crowd just before the show starts and still have a decent viewing location without the wait.

Though guests are allowed to sit in the very front of the viewing area, this isn't necessarily the best place to view the show. If you don't mind standing throughout the show, pick a place at least 10 feet from the stage (usually where the first rows of standing guests are located) for better views without straining your neck.

Cinderella's coronation will take place on the right side of the stage and since the entire show is about Cinderella, you'll want to make sure that you have a good view of this area. Standing in the center of the viewing area will give you the best all around views.

Disabled Access: Guests may remain in their wheelchair or motorized scooter. Disney's assistive listening devices interact with this attraction. Disney's handheld captioning devices interact with this attraction.

• • • • • • • • • • • • • • • • • • •

ℙ *Scavenger Hunt*: On Cinderella Castle, find a gargoyle, a family crest, a lion and flags.

1. How many towers are on Cinderella Castle?

2. How tall is Cinderella Castle?
A. 150 feet
B. 189 feet
C. 210 feet

3. During Walt Disney World's 25th Anniversary Celebration, what was Cinderella Castle decorated as?
A. A pink birthday cake
B. A giant diamond
C. A spaceship

4. The 125 costumes used in Cinderellabration required how many hours of labor to create?
A. 4,000
B. 25,000
C. 100,000

5. Some of the material used for the costumes in Cinderellabration was created especially for the show in which country?
A. France
B. Japan
C. Norway

6. Cinderella Castle was built using how many bricks?
A. None
B. 27,986
C. 156,900

7. The castles at each of Disney's theme parks around the world are named after either Cinderella or Sleeping Beauty. Which other Disney theme park has a Cinderella Castle?
A. Disneyland Paris
B. Tokyo Disneyland
C. Hong Kong Disneyland

8. When Walt Disney designed the castles in Disneyland and the Magic Kingdom, he was inspired by the Neuschwanstein castle in which country?
A. Germany
B. France
C. Italy

Dumbo the Flying Elephant

Overview: Fly through the air just like Dumbo, from the Disney animated film *Dumbo*, when you climb aboard one of these 16 loveable elephants with oversized ears. Parties of two (or three with a very small child) control a lever to fly their elephant as high in the sky or as low to the ground as they like while getting a fantastic glimpse of Fantasyland.

Thrill Time: 1 ½ minutes

Be Aware of: This entire queue line and attraction are located outdoors. This attraction closes during inclement weather such as thunder and lightning.

Children under seven years of age must be accompanied by an adult. If you are afraid of heights, be aware that at the end of the ride your elephant will rise to the highest point of the attraction before bringing you back down to exit.

If you plan on riding Dumbo the Flying Elephant just before the fireworks presentation, consult a cast member to make sure the attraction won't be closed.

Helpful Hints: This popular attraction usually has very long lines because of the slow loading and unloading process. It is best to try to ride Dumbo the Flying Elephant as early in the day as possible or during parade times.

There are some game-like diversions located throughout the queue line that will amuse very young children. Pushing the lever to fly as high as possible will give you a smoother ride.

Parent/Guardian Switch option is available.

Disabled Access: Guests must transfer from a wheelchair or motorized scooter and step down into the ride vehicle. The disabled queue line is located to the right of the standard queue line.

• • • • • • • • • • • • • • • • • •

Scavenger Hunt: Find elephants standing on top of each other, Timothy Mouse, pinwheels and a stork carrying a baby in a blanket.

1. What are circus clowns famous for wearing on their nose?
A. A big red ball
B. A piece of tissue
C. An earring

2. Which one of the following animals would you probably not see in a circus?
A. Elephant
B. Tiger
C. Whale

3. Which one of the following circus animals has stripes?
A. Bear
B. Tiger
C. Horse

4. What color do clowns usually paint their faces?
A. White
B. Black
C. Red

5. A famous circus trick is to stuff clowns into what tiny object?
A. A car
B. A suitcase
C. A piano

6. Complete the following phrase: "Lions and tigers and _____, oh my!"

7. In the Disney animated film *Dumbo*, what "helps" Dumbo fly?
A. Praying
B. A feather
C. A special hat

8. In *Dumbo*, what color elephants does Dumbo see after accidentally drinking some "bubbly"?
A. Blue
B. Yellow
C. Pink

9. Unscramble the following words of things that you might find in a circus:

TABROCA   (Hint: Someone who performs amazing stunts)
GIB OPT   (Hint: Where the circus takes place)
NLIO   (Hint: A scary animal)
TTNOOC ANYDC   (Hint: Something sweet you can eat)
GGLJUING   (Hint: You have your hands full with this trick)
GHIH RIWE   (Hint: Don't look down from this place)
ANTSUPE   (Hint: A type of nut)
NIGR STRAEM   (Hint: The person in charge of the circus)
PZEEART   (Hint: This helps you fly through the air)

10. True or False: Dumbo never speaks in the Disney film.

11. According to the famous phrase, what does an elephant never do?
A. Forget
B. Eat fish
C. Swim

12. The elephant is the symbol of which U.S. political party?
A. Democrats
B. Republicans
C. Independents

13. True or False: Elephants flap their ears to speak to one another.

14. How much can an elephant's ear weigh?
A. Up to 110 pounds (50 kg)
B. Up to 200 pounds (91 kg)
C. Up to 250 pounds (113 kg)

15. Which of the following items does not have the nickname "Elephant Ear"?
A. A plant
B. A fried pastry
C. A sneaker

16. Walt Disney World® Resort has a unique type of "circus" show on property. Which of the following Cirque du Soleil shows is performed in the West Side at Downtown Disney?
A. *La Nouba*
B. *Quidam*
C. *"O"*

17. Which Florida city is the home base of many circuses and was the winter home of the *Ringling Bros. and Barnum & Bailey Circus*?
A. Miami
B. Sarasota
C. Tampa

"it's a small world"

Overview: Take a boat ride through the countries of the world as hundreds of Audio-Animatronic children dressed in their national costumes sing the infamous tune "it's a small world" in five different languages.

Thrill Time: 10 ½ minutes

Be Aware of: Guests must step up and over the side of the boat to get into the bench seating which is extremely low to the ground. At the end of the attraction, the boats sometimes bump together while you are waiting to exit.

Helpful Hints: The best seats are in the front row of the boat and the second row isn't too bad depending on how tall the guests in front of you are. These seats will give you a panorama of the scenes that you sail through instead of just being able to see what's on one side of the boat.

Parent/Guardian Switch option is available.

Disabled Access: Guests may remain in their wheelchair. The disabled queue line is located at the attraction exit to the left of the standard queue. Disney's handheld captioning devices interact with this attraction.

• • • • • • • • • • • • • • • • • • •

 Scavenger Hunt: In the mural behind the boarding area, find: the Eiffel Tower, the Leaning Tower of Pisa, a windmill, a Greek temple and Big Ben.

"it's a small world" represents the many cultures and languages of the world. The following words are examples of how people around the world say hello in their native language:

Language	Word for hello	Pronunciation
Arabic	salam	sah-lahm
Danish	davs	darvs
German	guten tag	goo-ten targ
Hindi	namaste	nar-mars-te
Italian	ciao	chow
Russian	privyet	pree-vyet
Swedish	hej	hay
Turkish	merhaba	mer-ha-ba
Vietnamese	xin chao	sin chow

1. "it's a small world" is often referred to as the "_____ cruise that ever sailed."
A. Most colorful
B. Happiest
C. Saddest

2. Fill in the blanks of the "it's a small world" theme song:
"It's a world of _____, a world of _____ ;
It's a world of hopes and a world of _____;
There's so much that we _____,
That it's time we're aware
It's a small world after all!"

3. How many Audio-Animatronic dolls are in the "it's a small world" attraction?
A. 173
B. 239
C. 289

4. Which of the following languages is the "it's a small world" theme song not sung in throughout the attraction?
A. Swedish
B. Italian
C. French

5. Did you know that guests can use a Disney device to translate the narration of many Walt Disney World® Resort attractions into a language other than English? Guests can also get guide maps and restaurant menus in a language other than English. Can you guess

which five languages Disney currently uses for its foreign language guide maps and translation devices?

6. Approximately how many Walt Disney World® Resort cast members are multilingual?
A. 500
B. 2,900
C. 7,000

7. How can you tell if a Disney cast member speaks a language other than English?
A. They will have a foreign flag attached to their nametag
B. There's no way to know for sure
C. They will be wearing a specially designed costume

8. On what continent is it common to greet people with a kiss on both cheeks?

9. In what country is it common to greet others by bowing at the waist with your hands on your thighs?

10. "it's a small world" was originally designed by Walt Disney for the 1964-65 New York World's Fair. There have been many World's Fairs held over the years since the mid-nineteenth century. In which country was Expo 2005, the most recent World's Fair, held?
A. Japan
B. Belgium
C. Australia

11. "it's a small world" was originally designed to benefit UNICEF which protects children's rights in how many countries around the world?
A. 58
B. 103
C. 157

12. How many garment pieces are worn by all of the Audio-Animatronic children in "it's a small world"?
A. 789
B. 2,296
C. 10,863

Mad Tea Party

Overview: This dizzying attraction has groups of up to four people spinning in colorful teacups in a delightful party atmosphere to celebrate the famous Mad Hatter's Unbirthday party scene from the Disney animated film *Alice in Wonderland*. Not only does the platform with the 18 teacups spin around and around, but each teacup spins on top of the platform, too.

Thrill Time: 1 ½ minutes

Be Aware of: This attraction and queue line are located outdoors, however, both are covered. This should go without saying, but do not ride this attraction after eating unless you want to feel sick. Anyone who experiences motion sickness should think twice before riding this attraction.

Helpful Hints: To reduce the dizzying effects of the Mad Tea Party, don't spin your teacup and just let the moving platform spin you around.

Characters from *Alice in Wonderland* frequently appear outside of the attraction throughout the day. Ask any character escort or Mad Tea Party cast member when the *Alice in Wonderland* characters will appear.

Parent/Guardian Switch option is available.

Disabled Access: Guests must transfer from their wheelchair or motorized scooter to board this attraction. The disabled queue line is located to the right of the standard queue.

Anyone who has difficulty maintaining an upright posture should not ride this attraction.

• • • • • • • • • • • • • • • • • • • •

♀ *Scavenger Hunt*: Find the Dormouse.

1. How many pink lanterns can you find hanging from the ceiling of the Mad Tea Party? How many green lanterns?

2. In the Disney animated film *Alice in Wonderland*, the White Rabbit sings that he is late for what?
A. Picking up carrots
B. Tea
C. A very important date

3. In the Disney film, who does Alice follow into Wonderland?
A. Cheshire Cat
B. Tweedledee and Tweedledum
C. The White Rabbit

4. The Queen of Hearts is famous for saying what phrase?
A. "Who's the fairest one of all?"
B. "Off with their heads!"
C. "Supercalifragilisticexpialidocious"

5. In the Disney film *Alice in Wonderland*, Alice grows very large and shrinks very small after she does what?
A. Wishes to be big or small
B. Eats or drinks specially marked items
C. Says a magic spell

6. In Disney's *Alice in Wonderland*, what type of jewelry is the White Rabbit famous for carrying?
A. A pocket watch
B. A gold necklace
C. An 18 "carrot" gold ring

7. What is the name of the cat that Alice meets in Wonderland in Disney's *Alice in Wonderland*?
A. Dinah
B. Felix the Cat
C. The Cheshire Cat

8. According to the Mad Hatter, how many Unbirthdays do you get a year?
A. 1
B. 12
C. 364

9. According to the Mad Hatter in *Alice in Wonderland*, why is the White Rabbit always running late?
A. He didn't have a battery in his watch
B. His watch was 2 days slow
C. He couldn't walk fast enough

10. The Queen of Hearts is named after one of the four types of suits that occur in a deck of playing cards. What are the other three suits of cards?

11. When someone asks you if you want one lump or two with your tea, what are they really asking?
A. How many hits over the head you would like
B. How many sugar cubes you would like
C. How many lumps of clotted cream you would like

12. In *Alice in Wonderland*, the Mad Hatter's hat has a tag in it with 10/6 written upon it. What do those numbers represent?
A. His birthday
B. The price tag of 10 shillings and 6 pence
C. His hat size

13. When Alice plays croquet with the Queen of Hearts in *Alice in Wonderland*, what type of birds do they use as mallets?
A. Ostriches
B. Penguins
C. Flamingos

14. The film premiere of Disney's *Alice in Wonderland* was held in which country?
A. England
B. France
C. Canada

15. *Alice in Wonderland* was based on the book *Alice's Adventures in Wonderland* written by which famous author?
A. The Brothers Grimm
B. Lewis Carroll
C. Jane Austen

16. In what year was the Boston Tea Party in which chests of tea were thrown into the Boston harbor to protest British monopoly of the tea trade?
A. 1773
B. 1783
C. 1883

17. One of Walt Disney's big breaks early in his career (before he created Mickey Mouse) was the success of his short films which combined a live action girl in an animated world. The films were loosely based on *Alice's Adventures in Wonderland*. What was the name of this collection of short films produced in the 1920s?
A. Alice's Adventures
B. Alice Comedies
C. Alice's Antics

The Many Adventures of Winnie the Pooh

Overview: Journey through the storybook world of Winnie the Pooh as you ride in oversized "hunny" pots (each pot has two rows which each accommodate two adults or a combination of three adults and children) through scenes such as Winnie the Pooh's dream of Heffalumps and Woozles, Tigger's love of bouncing and Piglet's scary encounter with a rain storm.

Thrill Time: 3 minutes

FASTPASS AVAILABLE

Be Aware of: The "hunny" pots do a lot of twisting and turning, including some gentle bouncing, throughout the ride. This attraction has thunder and lightning elements.

Helpful Hints: Though not a thrill ride, this highly popular attraction usually has very long lines. It's best to try to ride the attraction as early in the day as possible or during parade times, or utilize FASTPASS.

Parent/Guardian Switch option is available.

Disabled Access: Guests must transfer from a motorized scooter to a wheelchair that is provided at the attraction. Guests may remain in their wheelchair. Disney's handheld captioning devices interact with this attraction.

• • • • • • • • • • • • • • • • • •

Scavenger Hunt: In the queue line, find pictures of Eeyore and Tigger.

1. What color is Winnie the Pooh's shirt?
A. Yellow
B. Red
C. Blue

2. Where does Winnie the Pooh live?
A. France
B. The Hundred Acre Wood
C. A National Park

3. What is Winnie the Pooh's favorite food?
A. Ice cream
B. Honey
C. Carrot cake

4. According to the Winnie the Pooh theme song, what is Winnie the Pooh stuffed with?
A. Cotton batting
B. Wool
C. Fluff

5. Tigger likes to say "T.T.F.N.!" to all of his friends. What does "T.T.F.N.!" stand for?

6. What does Tigger like to do more than anything?
A. Bounce
B. Eat honey
C. Sleep

7. What does Eeyore always lose?
A. His tail
B. His memory
C. His shirt

8. What color is Piglet?
A. Grey
B. Green
C. Pink

9. Match the following Hundred Acre Wood characters with their descriptions:

Winnie the Pooh	Sometimes stammers when talking
Rabbit	She is a mother
Piglet	Likes to say "Thanks for noticing"
Tigger	He always sorts things out
Roo	Likes to say "Oh, bother"
Kanga	Very smart with lots of stories
Eeyore	His nickname is Long Ears
Owl	Made out of rubber and springs
Christopher Robin	Kangaroo who plays with Tigger

10. Which grumpy character likes to tend to the vegetables he plants?
A. Kanga
B. Roo
C. Rabbit

11. Who is the creator of Winnie the Pooh?
A. Walt Disney
B. Hans Christian Andersen
C. A.A. Milne

12. Which is not a popular nickname of Winnie the Pooh?
A. Silly Old Bear
B. Bear of Very Little Brain
C. Hungry Bear

13. What is written on the sign that hangs above Winnie the Pooh's door?
A. Welcome
B. Pooh's Thotful Spot
C. Mr. Sanders

14. What creatures does Winnie the Pooh have nightmares about?
A. Frogs and snakes
B. Zoo keepers
C. Heffalumps and Woozles

15. What was Winnie the Pooh's original name in his early appearances?
A. Edward Bear
B. Ted. E. Bear
C. He had no name

16. Which of the following is not a type of honey?
A. Clover
B. Pekoe
C. Orange

17. Where is the original stuffed toy bear that inspired the creation of Winnie the Pooh?
A. The Smithsonian
B. New York Public Library
C. Museum of London

18. According to *Forbe's* "Top Earning Fictional Characters List," where did Winnie the Pooh and his Hundred Acre Wood friends rank in 2003?
A. First with $5.9 billion in retail sales
B. Second with $4.7 billion in retail sales
C. Third with $2.4 billion in retail sales

Mickey's PhilharMagic

Overview: Mickey's PhilharMagic might be named after the famous mouse but its star is definitely Donald Duck. After Mickey asks Donald to help him set up the orchestra, Donald spies Mickey's Sorcerer's hat, puts it on, and mayhem ensues. Follow Donald's brilliantly animated 3-D adventures through the scenes of recent Disney animated films such as *The Lion King*, *Aladdin*, *Beauty and the Beast* and *The Little Mermaid* as he tries to capture the wayward Sorcerer's hat and return it to Mickey. The theater seats 500 guests.

Thrill Time: 10 minutes

FASTPASS AVAILABLE

Be Aware of: Like all 3-D shows, the theater will be very dark and certain larger-than-life effects might scare small children. The show is also filled with loud noises. Expect to be misted with water. Guests must wear 3-D glasses for the best experience.

Helpful Hints: Sit in the front, center of the theater for the best effects or to the left of center for the best view of the ending. Be sure to turn around and look behind you when the film has ended. When entering the theater from the queue line, the doors to your left will lead to the front and middle section of the theater and the doors to your right will lead to the rear. If you're at the beginning of the line when entering the theater, hang back for a little bit before entering a row as you will be required to go to the very end of the row which is not the best seating.

Children who might be bothered by the 3-D effects can still enjoy the attraction without wearing the 3-D glasses.

Disabled Access: Guests may remain in their wheelchair or motorized scooter. Disney's assistive listening devices interact with this attraction. Reflective captioning is available.

• • • • • • • • • • • • • • • • • • • •

Scavenger Hunt: In the indoor queue line, find: artwork donated by Minnie Mouse, a seashell bathing suit top, the Three Little Pigs, umbrellas, a penguin, a skeleton microphone, a trumpet, a harp and music notes.

1. What color shirt and hat does Donald Duck always wear?
A. Green
B. Yellow
C. Blue

2. What are the names of Donald Duck's three nephews?
A. Hal, Al and Pal
B. Huey, Dewey and Louie
C. The Three Musketeers

3. What color pants does Donald Duck usually wear?
A. Blue
B. Green
C. He doesn't wear pants

4. Who is Donald Duck's girlfriend?
A. Darcy
B. Daisy
C. Daphne

5. Donald Duck is known for quickly losing his what?
A. Car keys
B. Temper
C. Remote control

6. Which is not one of the phrases that Donald Duck is famous for saying?
A. "Aww….phooey!"
B. "What's up, Doc?"
C. "Hiya, toots!"

7. Which Disney animated cartoon series followed the adventures of Donald Duck's nephews in the town of Duckburg?
A. *Duckburg Detectives*
B. *Naughty Nephews*
C. *Ducktales*

8. What is Donald Duck's middle name?
A. Fauntleroy
B. Fitzgerald
C. Don

9. Find the following musical instruments in the word search below: guitar, harp, violin, trumpet, trombone, flute, clarinet, saxophone, piano, drum, cello, oboe and cymbal.

```
N F L U T E X D H Y G D R U M A
M U I S V C G L S A I T Z H D Y
N J C L A R I N E T R U M P E T
G K L U P X T W I R V P E I Z F
B U V F A I O K M O C G C A P Y
D A I T S V B P G M F Y L N F R
R M O T C I O Z H B J K M O R F
B Y L U A C E L L O K D C B O I
V C I T E R M P Z N N Q R T A M
R S N I A P V R T E G E A L P L
```

10. Mickey's PhilharMagic has one of the world's largest movie screens without what?
A. Seams
B. Paint
C. Rips and tears

11. Mickey's PhilharMagic is loosely based on the popular animated film *Fantasia* in which Mickey gets in trouble by trying on the Sorcerer's hat and doesn't know how to control the power that the hat gives him. In *Fantasia*, a famous scene shows Sorcerer Mickey failing to control what when he has the Sorcerer's power?
A. Pink elephants
B. The sun and the moon
C. Water-toting brooms

12. What celestial symbols decorate Mickey's famous Sorcerer's hat?
A. Stars and moons
B. Suns
C. Comets

13. Sorcerer Mickey can be found successfully controlling the waters in what other Walt Disney World® Resort theme park attraction?
A. IllumiNations at Epcot
B. Fantasmic! at the Disney MGM-Studios
C. Primeval Whirl at Disney's Animal Kingdom

Peter Pan's Flight

Overview: Take a night time flight above London and Never Land in a pirate galleon that gives you a bird's eye view of scenes from the Disney animated film *Peter Pan* and the London skyline. This attraction, which seats three adults or a combination of four adults and kids, is unusual because guests look down on the action from their vantage point in the ships that sail above.

Thrill Time: 2 ½ minutes

FASTPASS AVAILABLE

Be Aware of: This attraction is somewhat dark because of the night time setting, but the lit up scenes will probably alleviate any fear of the darkness. Guests fly through the night aboard ships that are suspended from the roof and look down over the city below. If you suffer from a fear of heights, you might want to think twice about this ride. Guests must pass through turnstiles in the standard queue.

Helpful Hints: This attraction is notorious for always having an extremely long wait (roughly 45 minutes or more) even though it's not a thrill ride. Be sure to utilize FASTPASS or come early or late in the day.

Parent/Guardian Switch option is available.

Disabled Access: Guests must transfer from a motorized scooter to a wheelchair that is provided at the attraction. Guests must transfer from a wheelchair, step onto a moving walkway and board the vehicle. The moving walkway cannot be stopped at this attraction. The disabled queue line is to the left of the standard queue. Disney's handheld captioning devices interact with this attraction. Service animals are not permitted on this attraction.

• • • • • • • • • • • • • • • • • • •

1. In the Disney animated film *Peter Pan*, which of the following does not help Wendy, John and Michael fly?
A. Faith, trust and pixie dust
B. Thinking of happy thoughts
C. A magical spell

2. In *Peter Pan*, what is so special about Never Land?
A. Everyone who lives there has magical powers
B. It's a place where you never have to grow up
C. It's full of gold and treasures

3. In *Peter Pan*, why did Peter Pan banish Tinker Bell from Never Land?
A. Because she tried to have Wendy killed
B. Because she was a girl
C. Because the rest of the group voted her off the island

4. True or False: In *Peter Pan*, Tinker Bell is jealous of Wendy.

5. Fill in the blanks on the location of Never Land according to the Disney animated film *Peter Pan*: "_____ star to the right and straight on 'til _____."

6. In *Peter Pan*, why does the crocodile which follows Captain Hook make a tick tock sound?
A. Because he is nervous
B. Because he was cursed by the spirits of Skull Rock
C. Because he swallowed a clock

7. In *Peter Pan*, what is the name of the Darling children's nursemaid dog?
A. Rover
B. Nana
C. Spot

8. Which Darling child carries an umbrella and wears a top hat in *Peter Pan*?
A. Wendy
B. Michael
C. John

9. Which Darling child carries a teddy bear in the Disney film?
A. Wendy
B. Michael
C. John

10. In *Peter Pan*, what is unusual about the Lost Boys?
A. They all look alike
B. They are dressed in animal costumes
C. None of them can speak

11. What type of fish does Peter Pan call Captain Hook in the Disney film?
A. Blowfish
B. Codfish
C. Catfish

12. Does Tinker Bell ever speak in Disney's *Peter Pan*?

13. Which character in *Peter Pan* has the word 'Mother' tattooed on his chest?
A. Mr. Smee
B. Captain Hook
C. Peter Pan

14. In *Peter Pan*, on which arm is Captain Hook's hook located?

15. How did Captain Hook lose his hand?
A. Peter Pan cut it off
B. He was born without a hand
C. His hand was cut off when he stole a treasure chest

16. Kathryn Beaumont was the voice of Wendy in *Peter Pan*. Which other animated character did she also supply the voice for?
A. Alice in *Alice in Wonderland*
B. Cinderella in *Cinderella*
C. Snow White in *Snow White and the Seven Dwarves*

17. Approximately how many years was *Peter Pan* in the works before being released in theaters?
A. Five
B. Ten
C. Twenty

18. The original author of the play *Peter Pan*, James M. Barrie, bequeathed the play rights to whom?
A. His dog
B. Walt Disney
C. The Great Ormond Street Hospital in London

19. True or False: The Disney animated film is the first time that Peter Pan was portrayed by a boy.

20. Which 1991 movie, featuring Robin Williams and Julia Roberts, follows an adult Peter Pan's quest to rescue his children from Captain Hook?
A. *Hook*
B. *Return to Never Land*
C. *Finding Neverland*

21. Which 2004 movie tells the tale of James M. Barrie and his inspiration to create the play *Peter Pan*?
A. *Beyond the Sea*
B. *Peter Pan*
C. *Finding Neverland*

22. Which one of the following women hasn't portrayed Peter Pan?
A. Mary Lou Retton
B. Sandy Duncan
C. Cathy Rigby

23. Which of the following humorists collaborated on the 2004 book *Peter and the Starcatchers* which is supposed to be the prequel to *Peter Pan*?
A. Dave Barry
B. Bill Bryson
C. Jerry Seinfeld

Snow White's Scary Adventures

Overview: Board a three-row mining car (each row seats two adults or a combination of three adults and kids) for a ride through scenes from the Disney animated film *Snow White and the Seven Dwarves*.

Thrill Time: 3 minutes

Be Aware Of: This attraction can be frightening to small children because of the many scenes which include the evil witch.

The attraction is dark and the mining cars twist and turn through the Enchanted Forest in jerky movements. Guests must pass through turnstiles in the standard queue.

This attraction closes early before scheduled fireworks displays. Consult a cast member for operating times during the fireworks display.

Helpful Hints: Parent/Guardian Switch option is available.

Disabled Access: Guests must transfer from a wheelchair or motorized scooter to board this attraction. Guests must be able to step up into the attraction vehicle. The disabled queue line is located at the attraction exit to the right of the standard queue. Disney's handheld captioning devices interact with this attraction.

• • • • • • • • • • • • • • • • • • •

◉ Look for: The mining cars are each named after one of the seven dwarves. See if you can spot a car with each of the dwarves' names.

☆ **Hidden Mickey Hunt**: On the large mural behind the loading area, find the cottage located near the center of the mural. On the chimney, just below the bluebirds, three stones form a hidden Mickey shape.

Also, look for the clothesline with shorts hanging from it. One of the pairs of shorts is decorated with many Mickey Mouse ears.

⚲ Scavenger Hunt: In the large mural behind the loading area, find: a deer, a bluebird, mushrooms and the Evil Queen.

1. What are the names of the seven dwarves in the Disney animated film *Snow White and the Seven Dwarves*?

2. In the Disney film, where do the seven dwarves live?
A. In a treehouse
B. In a cave
C. In a cottage deep in the woods

3. In *Snow White and the Seven Dwarves*, what type of poisoned fruit does the Old Witch give Snow White to eat?
A. Orange
B. Apple
C. Pear

4. What happens when Snow White eats the poisoned apple?
A. She falls into a deep sleep and can't wake up
B. She forgets who she is
C. She turns into a pig

5. According to a song that Snow White sings in *Snow White and the Seven Dwarves*, what should you do while you are working?
A. Whistle
B. Sing
C. Exercise

6. Fill in the blank of the jealous Queen's famous saying: "Magic mirror on the wall, who is the _____ one of all?"
A. Prettiest
B. Fairest
C. Richest

7. In *Snow White and the Seven Dwarves*, why does Snow White have to run away from her home and hide?

8. The seven dwarves sing "Heigh Ho, Heigh Ho" as they head off to work in the gem mines. Unscramble the following words to reveal the names of gemstones:

REAEMLD   (Hint: A green stone)
ELRAP   (Hint: You can find it in an oyster)
UYBR   (Hint: A red stone)
AERISHPP   (Hint: A blue stone)
AOPL   (Hint: A white stone with different colors inside)
IAOMNDD   (Hint: It's in engagement rings)

9. In the Disney film, which dwarf is the only one with blue eyes?
A. Happy
B. Doc
C. Dopey

10. In the Disney film, which dwarf wears glasses?
A. Bashful
B. Sleepy
C. Doc

11. In *Snow White and the Seven Dwarves*, why can't Dopey talk?
A. He was born without a voice
B. He stutters so he refuses to talk
C. He has never tried

12. Does Grumpy ever smile in *Snow White and the Seven Dwarves*?

13. In the Disney film, what was Snow White's prince's name?
A. Prince Edward
B. Prince Phillip
C. Prince

14. An apple a day will keep what away, according to the popular saying?
A. Dentist
B. Doctor
C. Disease

15. What was so unusual about the 1939 Academy Award that Walt Disney received for *Snow White and the Seven Dwarves?*
A. The award broke while he was on stage
B. The award was encrusted with jewels in honor of the Seven Dwarves' mine
C. There was one full size award and seven mini Oscars to represent the Seven Dwarves

16. True or False: *Snow White and the Seven Dwarves* was the world's first full length animated feature film.

17. When *Snow White and the Seven Dwarves* was originally released in theaters, in which country was the film considered too scary for children and anyone under the age of 16 had to be accompanied by a parent?
A. England
B. France
C. Germany

18. *Snow White and the Seven Dwarves* was the highest grossing movie of all time until it was surpassed by which movie that debuted two years later, also another film classic?
A. *Casablanca*
B. *Gone with the Wind*
C. *Cinderella*

19. Approximately how many varieties of apples are there in the world?
A. 750
B. 2,500
C. 7,500

Storytime with Belle

Overview: Belle helps her guests recreate the story of Disney's animated film *Beauty and the Beast* in this intimate outdoor theater where selected members of the approximately 150 guest audience become part of the show.

Thrill Time: 10 ½ minutes

Be Aware of: This attraction closes during inclement weather such as thunder and lightning. There is limited bench seating in this small theater area which is outside and uncovered. The front row is generally reserved for children.

Helpful Hints: Consult your Times Guide for performance times. Arrive early for a chance to have seating during the show.

Six children will be chosen from the audience to act out the parts of characters from *Beauty and the Beast* and one adult male will be chosen to play the Beast. Belle asks for volunteers for some of the characters so tell your kids to be ready to raise their hand if they would like to be in the show.

This is a wonderful opportunity to meet Belle who signs autographs and poses for pictures after the show. The lengthy queue line will form to the right of the stage after the show.

Disabled Access: Guests may remain in their wheelchair or motorized scooter.

• • • • • • • • • • • • • • • • • • •

⚲ Scavenger Hunt: Find a rose, a lion's head spitting water and carved lions in stone.

1. Belle is a Disney princess because she married a prince. Who else is a Disney princess?

2. What color is Belle's beautiful ball gown in Disney's *Beauty and the Beast*?
A. Red
B. Blue
C. Gold

3. In the Disney film, what is Belle's favorite hobby?
A. Reading
B. Sewing
C. Cooking

4. According to a song in *Beauty and the Beast*, what does Belle's name mean?
A. Intelligent
B. Beauty
C. Princess

5. In *Beauty and the Beast*, what section of the castle is Belle forbidden to visit?
A. Library
B. Kitchen
C. West wing

6. In *Beauty and the Beast*, who is in love with Belle, but Belle is not in love with him?
A. Gaston
B. Lumiere
C. Maurice

7. How does Belle end up a prisoner of the Beast in *Beauty and the Beast*?
A. She exchanges places with her father who was held prisoner
B. Beast captures her in the forest
C. She is being punished for not marrying Gaston

8. In *Beauty and the Beast*, what is Belle's father's occupation?
A. Sculptor
B. Inventor
C. Chef

9. In *Beauty and the Beast*, what object allows Belle and the Beast to see what is happening in the world outside of the castle?
A. Crystal ball
B. Mirror
C. Snow globe

10. In which other Disney theme park can you find a stage show featuring Belle?
A. Disney's Animal Kingdom
B. Epcot
C. Disney-MGM Studios

11. In 1997, Disney released an animated sequel to *Beauty and the Beast* in which Belle is getting ready for which holiday?
A. Easter
B. Halloween
C. Christmas

12. Which Broadway singer supplied the voice for Belle in *Beauty and the Beast*?

A. Paige O'Hara

B. Jodie Benson

C. Angela Lansbury

FRONTIERLAND

Enjoy the thrilling adventures of the Wild West in the wilderness-themed attractions of Frontierland.

Big Thunder Mountain Railroad

Overview: Hop aboard an ore car on the Big Thunder Mountain Railroad, one of the three "mountain" thrill rides of the Magic Kingdom. At speeds of up to 33 miles per hour, this ride is faster than Space Mountain and at 197 feet above sea level, it is taller than Space Mountain or Splash Mountain. Travel through the town of Tumbleweed, home to the Big Thunder Mining Company, and experience the "wildest ride in the wilderness" as you speed past waterfalls, land slides and the Southwestern landscape of a flooded mining town. Each of the 15 rows in the ore cars can accommodate two adults or two adults and a child.

Thrill Time: 3 ½ minutes

FASTPASS AVAILABLE

Restrictions: Passengers must be at least 40 inches (102 cm) tall. Guests should be in good health and free from high blood pressure, heart, back or neck problems, motion sickness and other conditions that could be aggravated by the ride. Expectant mothers should not ride.

Be Aware of: Most of this ride is outside and uncovered. This attraction closes during inclement weather such as thunder and lightning. There are periods of darkness and bats during the ride.

Helpful Hints: There are fans and water fountains located in the queue line. For the wildest ride, sit in the back of the ore cars.

This attraction is surprisingly fun in the rain because the trains travel a bit faster on the wet tracks.

If you have the time, ride Big Thunder Mountain Railroad once during the day and again at night. During the day, guests can see the Audio-Animatronics that portray the story of the attraction. At night, the attraction takes on a different atmosphere with beautiful lighting effects on the landscape.

Be sure to secure your hats, glasses and other personal items that are likely to fly off during the ride.

Parent/Guardian Switch option is available.

Disabled Access: Guests must transfer from their wheelchair or motorized scooter to board this attraction. The disabled queue line is located at the attraction exit to the right of the standard queue line. Service animals are not permitted on this attraction.

• • • • • • • • • • • • • • • • • • •

👁 👂 **Look and Listen for**: The mining equipment scattered around the attraction is real antique equipment that Disney Imagineers found in ghost towns in the western U.S. In the queue line, you will hear the classic songs "Turkey in the Straw," "Oh, My Darling Clementine" and "Home on the Range."

Scavenger Hunt: Find a barrel labeled "Explosive Assemblies."

1. Big Thunder Mountain Railroad is set in the time period of the gold rush. Find the following words in the word search below that are related to mining for gold: gold dust, prospector, pick, pan, axe, shovel, nugget, ore, sediment, fortune, gulch, vein, stream and sluice box.

```
P L A A G O L D D U S T E S V
I P R O S P E C T O R E S E T
H I C R O P B D F G N L Z P U
D C M E S S T V X P U R D I A
L K F S H O V E L I G E P M I
Q G N O O B V C C Q G G J E R
E U I C X A X E A H E K M N R
A L T T G G B R I L T O P T I
P C B M F O R T U N E U X A U
S H V E X S T R E A M U I S N
```

2. Which American landscape inspired the setting for Big Thunder Mountain Railroad?
A. Monument Valley in Arizona
B. The Grand Canyon
C. South Dakota's Badlands

3. Monument Valley is famous for being the setting of a variety of films, especially Westerns. Which famous actor known for starring in Western films is nicknamed "The Duke"?
A. John Wayne
B. Clint Eastwood
C. Gary Cooper

4. The cost of building Big Thunder Mountain Railroad was the same as the cost of building the entire Disneyland theme park in 1955. Approximately how much did each project cost?
A. $17 million
B. $30 million
C. $33 million

5. In which state was the first gold discovery in America in 1799?
A. California
B. Nevada
C. North Carolina

6. When was gold found at Sutter's Mill in California, starting the California Gold Rush?
A. 1810
B. 1848
C. 1905

7. Though people had already been panning for gold in California for several months in 1848, which event got the entire United States in a gold rush fever?
A. President Polk's State of the Union Address
B. An Associated Press newspaper story
C. A film star mentioning the gold they found in their backyard

8. What were the prospectors called who came to California to search for gold?
A. '49ers
B. Fools
C. Golden Boys

9. Where does the United States keep its Bullion Depository (the government's gold reserve)?
A. The U.S. Mint in Philadelphia
B. Fort Knox, Kentucky
C. The White House

10. How heavy is a standard gold bar which measures 7 inches by 3 5/8 inches by 1 ¾ inches?
A. 2 pounds
B. 15.6 pounds
C. 27.5 pounds

11. The U.S. Bullion Depository holds approximately 147.3 million ounces of gold at a book value of $42.22 per ounce. What is the approximate value of this gold?
A. $3 billion
B. $4.7 billion
C. $6.2 billion

12. Most gold jewelry is classified by how many carats (also spelled karats) it is. What does this carat classification mean?
A. The ratio of man-made gold to naturally occurring gold
B. The ratio of Australian gold to American gold used
C. The ratio of actual gold to the amount of other metals used

13. Which of the following types of gold jewelry is pure gold?
A. 9K
B. 18K
C. 24K

14. Which wedding anniversary is considered the "Golden Anniversary"?
A. 25th
B. 50th
C. 60th

15. Which 1975 Disney film starring Don Knotts and Tim Conway features Wild West outlaws who help three orphan children hide the gold they discovered from the greedy townspeople?
A. *The Apple Dumpling Gang*
B. *No Deposit, No Return*
C. *The Happiest Millionaire*

16. Which 1971 Disney film featured a duck who laid golden eggs?
A. *The Mighty Ducks*
B. *Million Dollar Duck*
C. *Freaky Friday*

Country Bear Jamboree

Overview: Singing Audio-Animatronic bears of all shapes and sizes perform a comical spoof of old-fashioned country songs in this stage show which features Disney characters Big Al, Teddi Beara and Liverlips McGrowl who lead the 175-guest audience in an interactive singing, clapping and foot stomping good time.

Thrill Time: 16 minutes

Be Aware of: When entering the building through the standard queue line, guests must pass through turnstiles. There is very limited seating in the indoors queue area. The theater seating is on benches with back rests.

Helpful Hints: A digital countdown outside of the building tells you exactly how long it will be before the next show starts, a great idea for when everyone is impatient with queue line waits. This show is an excellent choice when you want to rest and sit down for a while. It's also great for kids because they can clap, sing and be loud without getting in trouble.

When entering the theater, the door on the far left will lead to the front rows, the doors to the far right will lead to the rear of the theater. During the Christmas holiday season, a special show is staged at the Country Bear Jamboree.

Disabled Access: Guests may remain in their wheelchair or motorized scooter. The disabled queue line is located to the left of the standard queue. Disney's assistive listening devices interact with this attraction. Reflective captioning is available.

• • • • • • • • • • • • • • • • • • •

♀ **Scavenger Hunt**: In the indoor waiting area, find: claw marks on the floor, a bear playing a banjo, a bear dressed in a tutu, a raccoon, a bear on a swing and a bear with angel wings.

1. Which really tall bear has friends named Ojo and Pip and Pop and also has his own attraction at the Disney-MGM Studios?
A. Bear in the Big Blue House
B. Winnie the Pooh
C. Big Al

2. Which type of bear likes to swim in icy water?
A. Polar bear
B. Panda bear
C. Sloth bear

3. What type of food are bears famous for liking?
A. Honey
B. Spaghetti and sauce
C. Pancakes

4. What is a baby bear called?
A. Cub
B. Baby
C. Short stuff

5. Which type of bear likes to eat bamboo?
A. Grizzly bear
B. Panda bear
C. Honey bear

6. What do bears do when they hibernate in the winter time?
A. Sleep
B. Do their Christmas shopping
C. Diet so they can be slim for spring

7. True or False: Bears can swim.

8. Which famous cartoon bear family who has been featured in countless children's books includes Papa Q. Bear, Mama Bear and Brother and Sister?
A. The Berenstain Bears
B. The Hillbilly Bears
C. The Bungling Bears

9. Which cartoon bear is famous for searching for pic-a-nic baskets in Jellystone Park?
A. Paddington Bear
B. Yogi Bear
C. Griz Lee Bear

10. What is the name of the Muppets bear whose favorite saying is "Waka, Waka, Waka!"?
A. Gonzo
B. Rizzo
C. Fozzie

11. Which group of colorful bears have pictures on their stomachs and include Birthday Bear, Goodluck Bear and Cheer Bear?
A. The Cabbage Patch Kids
B. The Gummi Bears
C. The Care Bears

12. What is the name of the bear that replaced Bambi as the symbol of forest fire prevention?
A. Ash
B. Smokey
C. Teddy

13. What is the name of the 2003 Disney animated film in which an Inuit hunter is changed into a bear and must discover the true meaning of brotherhood?
A. *Bearly Brothers*
B. *Brother Bear*
C. *Band of Bears*

14. Which former U.S. President is partly responsible for the name "Teddy Bear"?
A. Franklin Delano Roosevelt
B. Theodore Roosevelt
C. George Washington

Splash Mountain

Overview: Splash Mountain is one of the Magic Kingdom's three "mountain" thrill rides. This peaceful water ride floats through Audio-Animatronic scenes inspired by the Disney film *Song of the South*, featuring Brer Rabbit, before becoming an exhilarating thrill ride with a five story drop. The hollowed out logs, with four rows each holding two people, descend down the face of Splash Mountain at a speed of 40 mph, making this the fastest attraction in the Magic Kingdom.

Thrill Time: 11 ½ minutes

FASTPASS AVAILABLE

Restrictions: Passengers must be at least 40 inches (102 cm) tall. Guests should be in good health and free from high blood pressure, heart, back or neck problems, motion sickness and other conditions that could be aggravated by the ride. Expectant mothers should not ride.

Be Aware of: Major portions of Splash Mountain are located outside. This attraction closes during inclement weather such as thunder and lightning.

You will get wet on this attraction! There are three smaller drops, two of which are in the dark, before the five story drop. There are no compartments to store loose items.

The queue line has flights of stairs. If you are unable to climb stairs, contact a cast member for assistance. Guests must step up and over the log for boarding. At the end of the attraction, the logs sometimes bump together while you are waiting to exit.

Helpful Hints: There are many theories as to where the driest spot in the logs might be. Though guests sitting in the front rows have always gotten soaked, the attraction has been recently tweaked to soak the guests in the back rows, too. If your log is stopped next to the waterfall after the five story drop, the guests on the right side of the log can expect to get drenched again.

To brace yourself for the five story drop, pay attention to when you start traveling up a darkened incline with Audio-Animatronic buzzards along the ceiling. During the day you'll be able to see daylight peeking in at the top of the hill before the five story plunge.

During the hot weather months, everyone decides to experience Splash Mountain in the afternoon to get a break from the heat, creating extremely lengthy queue lines. Regardless of the weather, be sure to experience this attraction in the early morning or as close to park closing as possible to avoid long queue lines.

The Laughin' Place playground at the attraction exit is a great place for young children to play while you wait for the rest of your party.

Parent/Guardian Switch option is available.

Disabled Access: Guests must transfer from their wheelchair or motorized scooter and step down to board this attraction. Service animals are not permitted on this attraction.

• • • • • • • • • • • • • • • • • • •

Look and Listen For: Listen for the sounds of birds and squirrels throughout the outdoor queue line. In the indoor queue line, listen for Brer Frog who begins telling the tale of Splash Mountain.

At the boarding area, look for the light post at the far left. The light blinks when the logs are being loaded and the light goes out when the logs are in motion.

Scavenger Hunt: How many birdhouses can you find in the outdoor queue line?

1. In the Disney song "Zip-a-dee-do-dah," which type of bird is on the singer's shoulder?
A. Bluebird
B. Robin
C. Sparrow

2. What type of food are rabbits famous for liking?
A. Carrots
B. Turnips
C. Asparagus

3. What is the name of the Disney rabbit who is friends with Bambi?
A. Dale
B. Flower
C. Thumper

4. Besides *Bambi*, what other Disney animated film featured a main character that was a rabbit?

5. Which Warner Brothers rabbit is famous for saying, "What's Up, Doc?"
A. Sylvester
B. Lucky Bunny
C. Bugs Bunny

6. Which 1922 book tells the tale of a stuffed rabbit who longs for a child to love him so that he can become real?
A. *Peter Cottontail*
B. *The Velveteen Rabbit*
C. *The Raggedy Rabbit*

7. Who is the author of *The Tale of Peter Rabbit* which tells the story of a bunny going into Mr. McGregor's garden?
A. Beatrix Potter
B. A. A. Milne
C. Laura Ingalls Wilder

8. What type of rabbits, which can be found in the desert, have long ears that point upwards?
A. South American rabbits
B. Jack rabbits
C. No rabbits have ears that point upwards

9. What type of rabbit has really long ears that hang down?
A. Snowshoe Hare
B. Lop-eared Rabbit
C. American Short Tail

10. What is the name of the underground homes that rabbits dig and then live in?
A. Shelters
B. Burrows
C. Dungeons

11. What is the name of the 1988 Disney film which combines live action with animated cartoons to tell the story of a rabbit who is accused of murder?

12. How many words can you make from the letters in SPLASH MOUNTAIN?

13. What is the official name of the area in Splash Mountain from where guests plunge five stories down into a river of water?
A. Chick-a-pin Hill
B. Too-Late-Now Cliff
C. Soaker Mountain

14. Name the Walt Disney World® Resort's two water parks.

15. Name the five other Magic Kingdom attractions in which you board a vehicle that moves on water.

16. For the ultimate water-based thrill ride, you will want to experience one of the world's tallest and fastest water park speed slides which is located on the Walt Disney World® Resort property. What is the name of this attraction which shoots you down a 120 foot hill at 55 mph?
A. Summit Plummet
B. Crush 'n' Gusher
C. Downhill Double Dipper

17. What does the word brer mean?

18. What is the name of the uncle in the Disney film *Song of the South* who tells the stories of Brer Rabbit and his friends?
A. Uncle Joe
B. Uncle Remus
C. Uncle Johnny

19. Why were the tales of Uncle Remus once banned from libraries and schools?
A. They were thought to be racist
B. They were thought to promote violence
C. The author was thought to be a Communist

20. *Song of the South* is based on the Uncle Remus character that which author created in the late 19th century?
A. Laura Numeroff
B. Johnny Gruelle
C. Joel Chandler Harris

21. Walt Disney created another popular cartoon character before he created Mickey Mouse. What was the name of the cartoon rabbit that he created in the late 1920s?
A. Roger the Rabbit
B. Oswald the Lucky Rabbit
C. Mortimer the Mousy Rabbit

Tom Sawyer Island

Overview: Hop aboard a 55-passenger river raft and float across the Rivers of America to Tom Sawyer Island, inspired by Mark Twain's Tom Sawyer stories. On the rustic island, which is truly a kid's giant playground, you'll find plenty of old-fashioned activities to keep the whole family entertained, from rickety suspension and barrel bridges to scary caves and Fort Langhorn.

Thrill Time: The raft ride is 2 minutes. Allow approximately 30 minutes to explore the island.

Be Aware of: This attraction opens later than the rest of the Magic Kingdom and closes at dusk. Consult your Times Guide for operating hours.

The activities on Tom Sawyer Island are physically demanding and guests must do plenty of walking on the island. Guests with mobility issues or parents with children too tired to play might not want to experience this attraction.

The rafts will not cross the river during inclement weather such as thunder and lightning. If you are on the island when a lightning storm starts, you will not be able to leave the island until the storm has passed.

Helpful Hints: This is a great place for kids to burn off some energy by running and playing throughout the island. Adults can expend some energy, too, or just enjoy the surprisingly peaceful natural setting while playing a game of checkers or sitting in a rocking chair.

Aunt Polly's Dockside Inn located on the island has snacks and refreshments available for purchase. The food stand is only open seasonally so be sure to check your Times Guide for operating hours. Restrooms are provided on the island.

If you find a large whitewash paint brush on the island, bring it to the raft captain for a special surprise.

Disabled Access: Most aspects of Tom Sawyer Island are not accessible to guests with disabilities. Wheelchairs are allowed on the rafts, however, motorized scooters are not.

● ● ● ● ● ● ● ● ● ● ● ● ● ● ● ● ● ● ●

1. Which *Home Improvement* actor starred as Tom Sawyer in the 1995 Disney live action film *Tom and Huck*?
A. Jonathan Taylor Thomas
B. Zachery Ty Bryan
C. Taran Noah Smith

2. One of the famous scenes in *The Adventures of Tom Sawyer* features Tom painting a fence for his Aunt Polly. What color did he paint the fence?
A. Black
B. Red
C. White

3. Where else at the Walt Disney World® Resort can you explore the wilderness and enjoy rustic adventures such as horseback riding, wagon rides and an outdoor campfire?

4. Mark Twain also wrote a famous short story about what kind of animal that jumps?
A. Frog
B. Kangaroo
C. Cat

5. Mark Twain wrote which children's book about a beggar and a prince who switch places?
A. *The Prince and the Pauper*
B. *Country Mouse, City Mouse*
C. *The Princess and the Pea*

6. What was Mark Twain's real name?
A. Samuel Clemens
B. Jake Spat
C. Tom Sawyer

7. Which Missouri town was the birthplace of Mark Twain?
A. St. Louis
B. Dexter
C. Hannibal

8. In nautical terms, the word twain is a measurement of river depth. A twain is how many feet deep?
A. 4 feet
B. 8 feet
C. 12 feet

9. Which of the following books was published first: *The Adventures of Tom Sawyer* or *The Adventures of Huckleberry Finn*?

Walt Disney World Railroad

Overview: Relive one of Walt Disney's fondest past times and take an old-fashioned, open-air train ride around the outskirts of the Magic Kingdom. Guests can board the 365-passenger train (each bench accommodates five guests) at any of the three stations (Main Street, U.S.A., Frontierland, and Mickey's Toontown Fair) and disembark at any location. The entire trip circles 1½ miles of the Magic Kingdom at a leisurely 10 mph.

Thrill Time: For a roundtrip ride, the train is in motion for a total of 18 minutes, not including the time it takes to load and unload passengers at each stop.

Be Aware of: This attraction closes during inclement weather such as lightning.

During parade times, the trains have to hold their position for approximately seven minutes to allow for parade floats to cross the train tracks. The Walt Disney World Railroad also stops operating during fireworks displays. Depending on the time of the fireworks, the train either stops operating about an hour before park closing or will stop traveling for about 40 minutes during the fireworks presentation. Consult your Times Guide for operating hours or ask a WDW Railroad cast member for the evening operating hours of the day of your visit.

Guests boarding at the Frontierland station must climb a flight of steps to the train platform. If you are unable to climb stairs, use the disabled queue line located at the attraction exit to the right.

Helpful Hints: This is a great attraction for when you need to sit down and rest or if you need transportation to destinations within the Magic Kingdom.

The queue lines tend to be shorter for this attraction because the trains arrive approximately every 6-7 minutes and two or three trains run each day.

If you don't want to ride the train around the entire Magic Kingdom, the best portion of the trip to take is from Frontierland to Mickey's Toontown station. Along this route you will see a portion of the Big Thunder mountain ride as well as an Indian village with Audio-Animatronics. On the Main Street, U.S.A. to Frontierland portion of the trip you can see some of the Audio-Animatronics inside Splash Mountain.

For guests who have rented strollers from the Magic Kingdom and who only want to travel a portion of the Railroad, you can leave your Disney stroller behind at one location and pick up a replacement at the next station. For guests with personal strollers, the stroller must be able to fold up and be placed in the seating bench with you if you want to travel with the stroller.

Guests are allowed to ride in the caboose of the train. Ask a cast member at the train station if this is possible on your trip.

The Frontierland station exits at the entrance to Splash Mountain.

Disabled Access: Guests must transfer from a motorized scooter to a vehicle seat or a wheelchair that is provided at the attraction. Guests may remain in their wheelchair. Disney's handheld captioning devices interact with this attraction.

• • • • • • • • • • • • • • • •

♀ ***Scavenger Hunt***: In the Frontierland station, find a wooden leg and a cuckoo clock.

1. What type of noise do trains make?

2. What is the last car on a train called?

3. What children's book features a little train with a big positive attitude who says "I think I can, I think I can" while trying to pull a cargo of toys over a very large mountain?
A. *Chugga-Chugga Choo-Choo*
B. *The Little Engine That Could*
C. *Casey Jr. Saves the Day*

4. In Marian Potter's classic book *The Little Red Caboose*, why is the caboose sad?
A. Because he is red
B. Because he always comes last and no one waves to him
C. Because the engineer forgets to bring him along for the ride

5. Which popular children's book series by Reverend W. Awdry features a train with friends named Percy, Anabel and Clara?
A. *Thomas the Tank Engine*
B. *Budgie*
C. *Curtis the Caboose*

6. Which children's book features a young boy who journeys on a train to the North Pole and receives a special gift from Santa?
A. *The Christmas Train*
B. *The Polar Express*
C. *Starlight Express*

7. Which famous Disney train debuted in the animated film *Dumbo*?
A. Casey Jr.
B. Dumbo Express
C. Toot, Toot

8. Find the following words related to trains in the word search below: engineer, station, steam, smoke, freight, boxcar, caboose, signal, track, coal, horn, locomotive, conductor and tunnel.

```
A B S I G N A L Q M E T C R D E
R S T E A M I D E V S B L M S N
W T R C X Y P D I U M F G A E G
B A A P O X X T H B O X C A R I
G T C H I A O V Q N K L A F I N
M I K S T M L N B R E G B K L E
K O H G O N O N A O O C O I H E
B N D C S F R E I G H T O U O R
R M O P A A S L H C O M S E R H
A L B C O N D U C T O R E I N W
```

9. Where were the vintage steam-powered locomotive trains of the Walt Disney World Railroad discovered?
A. The Mexican Yucatan
B. San Diego, California
C. Boston, Massachusetts

10. At his home in California, Walt Disney built a half mile, 1/8 scale model railway in his backyard which was an inspiration to create Disneyland. What was the name of his railroad?
A. Mickey Mouse Express
B. Carolwood Pacific Railroad
C. Disney's Dream Depot

11. Which man is primarily responsible for building a railroad that linked the entire east coast of Florida, from Jacksonville to the Florida Keys, thus bringing in more visitors and changing the state from an uninhabited frontier to a popular vacation destination?
A. John D. Rockefeller
B. Henry Flagler
C. George Vanderbilt

12. Which of the following is not a railroad property on a standard Monopoly board game?
A. B&O Railroad
B. Pennsylvania Railroad
C. Union Pacific Railroad

85

LIBERTY SQUARE

Colonial America is featured in this historic land where old-fashioned past times are honored and guests can sit in the presence of the Presidents who have shaped the nation.

The Hall of Presidents

Overview: The leaders of the United States of America gather together in this patriotic film and stage show which reveals the challenges that U.S. Presidents have had to face. All 42 men who have served as President are portrayed by amazingly life-like Audio-Animatronic figures. The theater seats 700 guests.

Thrill Time: 18 minutes

Be Aware of: This attraction has shorter operating hours than the rest of the Magic Kingdom. Consult your Times Guide for operating hours.

Helpful Hints: This is a great attraction to enjoy later in the day when you want to sit down and rest for a while. The show starts on the hour and half hour. Unless it is a crowded day, you could easily arrive at the attraction a few minutes before show time and avoid a queue line wait.

For the best view of the Audio-Animatronic Presidents, sit towards the front. For the best view of the entire presentation, which includes a 180 degree screen, sit in the center of the theater about half way back from the stage.

Disabled Access: Guests may remain in their wheelchair or motorized scooter. Disney's assistive listening devices interact with this attraction. Reflective captioning is available.

• • • • • • • • • • • • • • • • • • •

⚫ **Look for**: Find a portrait of Theodore Roosevelt, a portrait of Jimmy Carter, Herbert Hoover's fly reel and George Bush's sky diving helmet.

1. The portrait of what U.S. President is on the $10 bill?

2. The portrait of what U.S. President is on the dime?

3. Which two Presidents are featured on both U.S. paper currency and coins?

4. In which month are U.S. Presidential elections always held?
A. October
B. November
C. December

5. U.S. Presidential elections are held how often?
A. Every three years
B. Every four years
C. Every five years

6. Unscramble the following President's names:

YMIJM ETRACR   (Hint: He was a peanut farmer)
DLONRA AEANGR   (Hint: The oldest President ever elected)
RADCIRH OINXN   (Hint: The only President that resigned)
AAAHMRB OINLLNC   (Hint: He served during the Civil War)
RGEEOG GTSHNNIOWA   (Hint: The first U.S. President)

7. Which President once got stuck in the White House bathtub?
A. John Adams
B. Harry Truman
C. William Howard Taft

8. An inaugural parade for which President was hosted at Epcot in 1985?
A. Jimmy Carter
B. George H.W. Bush
C. Ronald Reagan

9. Richard Nixon made his famous "I am not a crook" speech to Associated Press editors at which Walt Disney World® Resort property in 1973?
A. Disney's Contemporary Resort
B. Disney's Polynesian Resort
C. Disney's Fort Wilderness Resort

10. Which of the following Presidents is not featured on Mt. Rushmore?
A. Theodore Roosevelt
B. Franklin D. Roosevelt
C. Thomas Jefferson

The Haunted Mansion

Overview: Hop aboard a Doom Buggy and take an eerily comical ride through a haunted mansion. Each Doom Buggy can hold two adults comfortably or squeeze in two adults and a small child.

Thrill Time: 8 minutes

Be Aware of: Though this ride is a comical look at a haunted house, children (and even some adults) might not enjoy this attraction. Portions of the attraction are dark and there are a variety of ghosts, skeletons, bats, etc. In the graveyard scene, many figures pop up out of the ground unexpectedly which can be frightening.

Guests must pass through turnstiles in the standard queue. Guests walk on a moving walkway to enter and exit the Doom Buggies. At one point in the attraction your Doom Buggy will travel backwards down a hill.

Helpful Hints: There are a couple of ways to jump far ahead in the queue line. First, in the outside queue line just before the entrance of the building most people will form a single line. When a cast member comes out to start loading the attraction they will ask for everyone to move as far up as possible, leaving no "dead" space in the outer areas of the queue. Be sure to move up quickly when the request is made (most guests try to be polite and wait around a while) and you can instantly cut your wait time.

Once you enter the building, there is still a pre-show to enjoy before entering the room where you will actually board the vehicles. Look for an aging portrait (above the fireplace) when you enter the building and pay careful attention to which direction you move from the portrait – either left or right. If you go to the left room, the exit door leading to the loading area (it's hidden) will be the second wall panel on your right as you walk in. If you're shown inside the right room, the exit door will be the second wall panel on your left. If you get confused, just look for the wall panel without trim on the ground. Be aware, though, that the cast member will have everyone move to the "dead" center of the room so that as many people can be accommodated as possible. Because of this, sometimes it pays to be one of the last few people entering the room so that you can stand on the outside of the circle of people and exit quickly.

This queue line becomes very long immediately following the parade. Don't visit this attraction for 30 minutes after the parade has passed the Haunted Mansion area unless you want to stand in a lengthy queue line.

Parent/Guardian Switch option is available.

Disabled Access: Guests must transfer from their wheelchair or motorized scooter to board this attraction. The moving walkway can be stopped for boarding. The disabled queue line is located to the right of the standard queue. Disney's handheld captioning devices interact with this attraction.

• • • • • • • • • • • • • • • • •

👁 **Look For**: In the small graveyard on the left before entering the building, you will find several tombstones with comical epitaphs. The names are all tributes to Disney designers and artists who worked on the attraction. Occasionally, the tomb of Mr. Gracey (named after Disney Imagineer Yale Gracey who is supposedly the owner of the house, although no official Disney storyline has ever been written for the attraction) is freshly dug up to make it look like a recent burial.

Also, be sure to keep an eye out for Madame Leota's tombstone at the far right side of the graveyard just before you enter the building. The bust on the tombstone frequently opens her eyes and looks around. (Madame Leota, whose face appears in the crystal ball inside the attraction, was named after Disney Imagineer Leota Toombs Thomas.)

♀ *Scavenger Hunt*: Find gold bats on top of queue line stanchions, a bat on a weathervane and a bird carved into a tombstone.

1. On which holiday would you be most likely to visit a haunted house?

Guess the answer to the following three ghost jokes:

2. What do ghosts do in theme parks?

3. What kind of ghost lives in a haunted house on the beach?

4. What kind of fruit do ghosts like to put on their cereal?

5. Which famous Paramount Studios cartoon character is nicknamed "The Friendly Ghost"?
A. Felix
B. Casper
C. Matilda

6. What is the name of the creepy, crawly children's book series that is written by R. L. Stine?
A. *Fear Factor*
B. *Goosebumps*
C. *Foster's Home for Imaginary Friends*

7. Find the following words that are associated with haunted houses in the word search below: spider, witch, cobweb, black cat, spirit, bats, cemetery, ghost, spooky, creak, stormy night, boo and ghoul.

```
R T S A I O M A W O R A R I T M
B C R E A K L Q I Z T M B E A J
X Y O L C E M E T E R Y L O L Z
S L T B I B E I C V W M A A O B
S O D Z W Z A R H E Y P C K C G
P G L K C E G T S P O O K Y E H
I N H J M U B C S A A U C G I O
D S T O R M Y N I G H T A P F U
E A P H S P I R I T J F T I D L
R R V W S T G T K A H A F M B L
```

8. When you exit The Haunted Mansion you will pass by a wall of burial sites outside. Each plaque features the name of someone who has passed away. If you say the names quickly, though, you will discover that they are really comical phrases dealing with the afterlife. See if you can decipher the meaning of the following names that are on the plaques. Be sure to stop by the burial site and pet cemetery at the end of the attraction, too.

- C.U. Later
- M.T. Tomb
- I.M. Ready
- Pearl E. Gates
- Rustin Peace
- Hal Lusinashun
- Hap A. Rition
- Claire Voince
- Wee G. Bord
- Paul Tergyst
- Manny Festation

9. Which famous comedian starred in the 2003 Disney film *The Haunted Mansion* which was inspired by this attraction?
A. Eddie Murphy
B. Steve Martin
C. Billy Crystal

10. Which one of the following actors did not appear in the 1984 hit film *Ghost Busters*?
A. Bill Murray
B. Dan Aykroyd
C. Eddie Murphy

11. Which 1999 film features a little boy who sees dead people and a child psychologist who is trying to help him?
A. *Wide Awake*
B. *Signs*
C. *The Sixth Sense*

12. Which famous Stephen King novel was turned into a movie starring Jack Nicholson who played a novelist who stays in a haunted hotel and has a mental breakdown?
A. *The Shining*
B. *Pet Sematary*
C. *The Dark Tower*

13. Which 1963 movie, based on a novel by Shirley Jackson, features a ghost researcher investigating the haunted Hill House and the horrors that soon take place?
A. *The Haunting*
B. *Carrie*
C. *The Exorcist*

14. Which 1982 movie features a family living with ghosts who suddenly become menacing and kidnap their daughter?
A. *Gremlins*
B. *Psycho*
C. *Poltergeist*

Liberty Square Riverboat

Overview: Enjoy a peaceful boat ride on the Rivers of America aboard the 450-passenger Liberty Belle Riverboat as it travels around Tom Sawyer Island.

Thrill Time: 16 ½ minutes

Be Aware of: This attraction has shorter operating hours than the rest of the Magic Kingdom. Consult your Times Guide for operating hours.

This attraction closes during inclement weather such as thunder and lightning.

There is very little seating aboard. The seats are located on the upper level which can only be accessed by climbing stairs. Anyone unable to climb stairs must stay on the lower level.

Helpful Hints: The boat sails on the hour and half hour. Unless it's a crowded day, you could easily arrive at the attraction a few minutes before departure time and avoid a queue line wait.

This is a great attraction for anyone who needs to relax for a while, even though you might not be able to sit down. If you want to secure a seat for the boat ride, arrive early and head towards the upper levels immediately. Though this is an outdoors attraction, there are areas of shade and cover within the boat.

There are some great picture taking opportunities of the Haunted Mansion, Tom Sawyer Island and Big Thunder Mountain Railroad while traveling the Rivers of America.

Stay on the lower level to watch the machinery (and cast member) which propels the Liberty Belle through the water. Head up to the upper level for a peek into the captain's quarters and great views of the paddlewheel. Guests are allowed to walk around during the boat ride so feel free to explore.

Parent/Guardian Switch option is available.

Disabled Access: Guests may remain in their wheelchair or motorized scooter. The disabled queue line is at the attraction exits to the left or right of the standard queue line.

• • • • • • • • • • • • • • • • •

1. What kind of boat uses wind to move?

2. Where else in the Magic Kingdom can you ride aboard a large boat that is somewhat similar to the Liberty Belle?

3. Find the following nautical words in the word search below: aft, starboard, bow, bridge, captain, bulkhead, buoy, cabin, deck, fathom, galley, gangway, helm, keel, overboard and port.

```
O  G  R  D  E  C  K  B  T  S  S  O  P  A  G  U
L  V  B  T  Y  C  A  P  T  A  I  N  G  C  F  B
Y  C  E  O  M  F  D  E  E  R  H  B  N  A  M  T
S  T  A  R  B  O  A  R  D  P  A  U  S  B  I  G
A  E  U  D  B  W  O  T  J  H  O  L  C  I  Z  A
I  J  V  B  U  O  Y  S  H  Y  I  K  T  N  R  L
P  G  A  N  G  W  A  Y  A  O  Z  H  E  L  M  L
O  M  I  H  N  B  C  R  Q  R  M  E  U  H  L  E
R  S  K  E  E  L  O  L  D  P  B  A  M  T  V  Y
T  A  B  Z  I  E  O  W  B  R  I  D  G  E  D  A
```

4. True or False: The Mississippi River is the longest river in North America.

5. In what U.S. state are the headwaters of the Mississippi River?
A. Iowa
B. Minnesota
C. Wisconsin

6. Into which body of water does the Mississippi River empty?
A. Gulf of Mexico
B. Atlantic Ocean
C. Pacific Ocean

7. Which state does the Mississippi River not travel through?
A. Michigan
B. Wisconsin
C. Tennessee

MAIN STREET, U.S.A

Stroll down the main street of an early 20th century small town
where horse and carriages transport shoppers, a barbershop quartet
serenades you and unique stores stock all that your heart desires.

Walt Disney World Railroad

See the Walt Disney World Railroad listing on page 82 in the
Frontierland section for complete information about this attraction.

Be Aware of: Guests must climb a flight of stairs to access
the boarding platform at this station. If you are unable to climb
stairs, use the disabled queue line located to the right of the
standard queue.

MICKEY'S TOONTOWN FAIR

Enter the world of Disney's most famous characters as you
explore the cartoon themed hometown of Mickey Mouse, Minnie
Mouse and many of their friends.

The Barnstormer at Goofy's Wiseacre Farm

Overview: Hop aboard a 1920s crop dusting plane for a crazy
ride above Goofy's cornfields before crashing into his barn full of
chickens. This child-sized roller coaster can accommodate two
guests (or three really small children) per car with eight cars per
plane.

Thrill Time: 1 minute

Restrictions: Passengers must be at least 35 inches (89 cm) tall. Children must be at least three years old to ride. Expectant mothers should not ride.

Be Aware of: This attraction closes during inclement weather such as thunder and lightning.

Though this is a kid-sized roller coaster, it's still rough with lots of sharp turns. The Barnstormer has a shorter height restriction and more kid friendly decorations, but the physical affects of any roller coaster are still the same.

Guests must step down into the vehicles for boarding. The lap bar comes very close to the back of the seat which means there is a narrower opening for guests to maneuver between when sitting down in the vehicle than on most other attractions. The attraction vehicles are small and might not accommodate all body types.

Helpful Hints: Mickey's Toontown Fair usually is the most crowded in the morning and early afternoon because it caters to children. If you can, come back in the late afternoon or evening for reduced wait times.

One of the fun aspects of this queue line is watching the roller coaster race along the track which comes through the barn where the queue line is.

Be sure to secure sunglasses and hats before boarding the roller coaster.

Parent/Guardian Switch option is available.

Disabled Access: Guests must transfer from a motorized scooter to a wheelchair that is provided at the attraction. Guests must transfer from their wheelchair to board this attraction. The disabled entrance is at the attraction's exit located to the left of the standard queue line. Service animals are not permitted on this attraction.

● ● ● ● ● ● ● ● ● ● ● ● ● ● ● ● ● ● ● ●

 Scavenger Hunt: In the queue line, find: a picture of Kitty "Hawk," roosters, a barrel of crop dust, a large paintbrush, a crate of flight plans, planes hanging from the ceiling, bell peppers and ears of popcorn.

1. What kind of animal on a farm produces milk for you to drink?

2. What kind of animal on a farm produces eggs for you to eat?

3. What kind of animal on a farm produces wool used in the sweaters you wear?

4. What are pigs famous for rolling around in on a farm?

5. Did you know that almost all of the food that you eat has to be grown on a farm first? Can you guess which ingredients in your breakfast cereal have to be grown on a farm? How about the ingredients in ice cream? What about french fries?

6. What is Goofy famous for saying?
A. "Oh, Boy!"
B. "Gawrsh!"
C. "Phooey!"

7. Which of the following is not a part of Goofy's traditional clothing?
A. Hat
B. Tie
C. Vest

8. Which of these physical characteristics does Goofy not have?
A. Tiny nose
B. Big feet
C. Long ears

9. What is the best way to describe Goofy's personality?
A. Smart with excellent manners
B. Good hearted but klutzy
C. Mean and self centered

10. Is Goofy a human or an animal?

11. There is a famous children's song about a farm in which you sing "E I E I O" in the chorus. What is the name of the farmer in that song?

12. In the same farm song, several farm animals are mentioned. Which of the following animals is not mentioned in the "E I E I O" song?
A. Cow
B. Pig
C. Duck

13. There is another famous children's song in which you also sing letters of the alphabet. It's about a farmer who has a dog. What was the name of the dog?
A. Boomer
B. Billy
C. Bingo

14. Which of the following is not usually used while working on a typical farm?
A. A tractor
B. A scuba tank
C. A shovel

15. Goofy starred in what 1990s television series?
A. *The Goof Troop*
B. *Bonkers*
C. *Tale Spin*

16. What is Goofy's son's name?
A. Monroe
B. Morris
C. Max

17. In what 1995 film did Goofy and his son star in?
A. *A Goofy Movie*
B. *Goof Troop Goes on Vacation*
C. *Father and Son*

18. What was Goofy's original name?
A. Dippy Dawg
B. Harry Horse
C. Klutzy Klown

Judge's Tent and Toontown Hall of Fame

Overview: Meet Mickey Mouse in the Judge's Tent and many more of your favorite Disney characters in the Toontown Hall of Fame.

Thrill Time: Varies – Allow at least 5-10 minutes.

Be Aware of: These attractions have shorter operating hours than the rest of the Magic Kingdom. Consult your Times Guide for operating hours.

The Judge's Tent, which is located at the back of Mickey's Country House, is in a separate location from the Toontown Hall of Fame.

Helpful Hints: The queue lines to meet Disney characters are lengthy throughout the day, especially in the early morning because Mickey's Toontown Fair is a favorite among small children. Visit later in the evening or ask a character escort when the characters might be at other locations within the theme park.

The Toontown Hall of Fame has three different queue lines leading to three different rooms of characters. Make sure you look up and see which line you are entering, as well as which characters are scheduled to be in each room. Typically the three rooms include Disney Pals (such as Minnie Mouse and Pluto), Friends from the Hundred Acre Woods and the Princess Room.

Disney photographers will take your picture in each character greeting location for you to view later in the day at Town Square Exposition Hall. There is an additional fee for Disney's professional photographs.

The Judge's Tent queue line has a video playing of cartoons starring classic Disney characters such as Mickey Mouse, Goofy and Donald Duck. Toontown Hall of Fame has character puzzles throughout part of the queue.

Disabled Access: Guests may remain in their wheelchair or motorized scooter. Disney's assistive listening devices interact with the Judge's Tent. Disney's guest-activated video captioning devices interact with the Judge's Tent.

● ● ● ● ● ● ● ● ● ● ● ● ● ● ● ● ● ●

1. What color is Mickey Mouse's nose?

2. Which Disney character is a bear who lives in the Hundred Acre Wood and has a friend named Christopher Robin?

3. Unscramble the following Disney animated character names:

NIBOR OODH   (Hint: He steals from the rich)
SMANEIJ   (Hint: She fell in love with Aladdin)
OODQUASMI   (Hint: He looks scary but he's really nice)
MIINYJ CKTECRI   (Hint: He carries an umbrella)
CNHIKEC ETILTL   (Hint: He thinks the sky is falling)

4. Which Disney princess would be the most likely to row a canoe?

5. Which Disney princess has red hair?

6. Mushu is the friend of what Disney princess?

7. What Disney animated character is a gypsy who lives in Paris?
A. Meg
B. Esmeralda
C. Basil

8. Mickey Mouse has an official wardrobe of approximately how many different outfits?
A. 50
B. 138
C. 175

9. Approximately how many chocolate covered Mickey Mouse ice cream bars are sold every year at the WDW Resort?
A. 1 million
B. 2.6 million
C. 5 billion

10. Which one of the following characters was the first to debut: Donald Duck, Goofy or Pluto?

11. What was the first Mickey Mouse cartoon ever made?
A. "Steamboat Willie"
B. "Plane Crazy"
C. "The Band Concert"

12. In "Steamboat Willie," which of the following did the original Mickey Mouse have?
A. Shoes
B. Gloves
C. A long, curly tail

For additional character questions, see the Character Meet and Greets Chapter on page 384.

Walt Disney World Railroad

See the Walt Disney World Railroad listing on page 82 in the Frontierland section for complete information about this attraction.

Helpful Hints: At Mickey's Toontown Fair Station, you might be lucky enough to witness the train engineers fueling the steam-powered trains with water from the water tower located to the right of the station. The trains are refueled every second or third time they come through the station.

TOMORROWLAND

Journey into the future where aliens are your neighbors and space ships rocket you into undiscovered lands as you enjoy the futuristic-themed attractions of Tomorrowland.

Astro Orbiter

Overview: A quick moving (15 mph) outdoor rocket ride through the galaxy, Astro Orbiter is the tall, solar system-like structure that is part of the skyline of Tomorrowland. Guests can maneuver the two passenger vehicles up or down to see a birds-eye view of Tomorrowland, Cinderella Castle and the outlying areas of Walt Disney World® Resort.

Thrill Time: 1 ½ minutes

Be Aware of: To board the vehicle, guests must climb up and over a small wing of the rocket and then step down into the vehicle. Guests must use an elevator to ride to the top of the platform and back down.

The rockets bank steeply to the right while in motion. The speed of the rockets increases throughout the ride and traveling at a high speed in a circular motion might induce feelings of motion sickness and dizziness. Children under seven must be accompanied by an adult.

Helpful Hints: Push the rocket higher for a smoother ride. This attraction has a beautiful view of Tomorrowland at night.

Parent/Guardian Switch option is available.

Disabled Access: Guests must transfer from a motorized scooter to a wheelchair that is provided at the attraction. Guests must transfer from a wheelchair and step up into the ride vehicle.

• • • • • • • • • • • • • • • • • •

1. Can you count how many times a minute Astro Orbiter's rockets are circling the planets?
A. 6
B. 11
C. 17

2. What "color" planet is Mars often called?
A. The blue planet
B. The red planet
C. The green planet

3. Put the following planets of our solar system in order of the distance they are from the sun, beginning with the closest.

SATURN   URANUS   VENUS   NEPTUNE
PLUTO   EARTH   JUPITER   MARS
MERCURY

4. What is the largest planet in our solar system?
A. Earth
B. Saturn
C. Jupiter

5. What is the coldest and smallest planet in our solar system?
A. Mars
B. Neptune
C. Pluto

6. How long would it take to travel to Saturn?
A. Seven days
B. Seven months
C. Seven years

7. When you are on the top platform before boarding your rocket, you will see Disney's Contemporary Resort to your left. What was unique about building this resort?
A. The monorail brought supplies to the building site
B. The rooms were built off property and slid into their positions
C. A-frame designs had never been used before

8. Disney's Contemporary Resort can only be seen from Tomorrowland because it fits in with the land's futuristic theme. What is the only other resort that can be seen from inside the Magic Kingdom?
A. Disney's Grand Floridian Resort & Spa
B. Disney's Polynesian Resort
C. Disney's Wilderness Lodge

9. True or False: Disney's Contemporary Resort is the only Disney Resort that has a monorail running through it.

10. Since it began operation in 1971, the number of miles that the Walt Disney World® Resort monorail has traveled would equal the distance of approximately how many trips to the moon?
A. 10
B. 20
C. 30

11. What is the name of the large promenade from the central plaza in front of Cinderella Castle to Tomorrowland?
A. Avenue of the Planets
B. Space Race Blvd.
C. Time Traveler Way

12. Who was not an inspiration for the redesign of Tomorrowland in 1994?
A. Buck Rogers
B. Orville and Wilbur Wright
C. Jules Verne

13. This attraction originally featured rocket vehicles revolving around a Saturn 5-type rocket. What was special about the Saturn 5 rocket?
A. It was the first rocket ever designed
B. It propelled the United States' Apollo missions to the moon
C. It was Russia's first rocket

14. The first rocket launched from NASA's Cape Canaveral, Florida site was called the Bumper 2 and flew higher in the atmosphere than many Space Shuttles do today. In what year was the Bumper 2 launched?

A. 1947
B. 1950
C. 1958

15. Are rockets still launched from NASA's Kennedy Space Center site at Cape Canaveral, Florida?

16. NASA now calls its rockets ELVs. What does ELV stand for?
A. Expendable Launch Vehicle
B. Extra Long Voyage
C. Emergency Locator Vehicle

Buzz Lightyear's Space Ranger Spin

Overview: Help Buzz Lightyear, from the Disney animated film *Toy Story*, defend Earth's supply of batteries from the Evil Emperor Zurg by using laser guns to blast invaders. Two person, spinning vehicles slowly maneuver through glow in the dark rooms where guests hit as many targets as possible and rack up points which are displayed on a monitor inside your vehicle. This video game-like ride is addictive as you constantly try to beat your previous score.

Thrill Time: 4 ½ minutes

FASTPASS AVAILABLE

Be Aware of: Guests enter and exit vehicles from a moving walkway. The vehicles spin around at the beginning of the ride but can soon be controlled by the driver. There are bright, flashing lights at the end of the attraction.

Helpful Hints: Hold down your laser trigger throughout the entire ride and swing it back and forth to win as many points as possible. In the first room, shoot the back of the orange robot's arm or the back of the buzz saw to get 100,000 points.

Parent/Guardian Switch option is available.

Disabled Access: Guests must transfer from a motorized scooter to a wheelchair that is provided at the attraction. Guests may remain in their wheelchair. Disney's handheld captioning devices interact with this attraction.

• • • • • • • • • • • • • • • • • • •

👁 Look For: Check out the batteries on the wall that are facing you when you enter the inside queue line. They are inscribed "Made in Glendale California" which is the real home of Walt Disney Imagineering which creates Disney attractions.

☆ Hidden Mickey Hunt: In the inside queue line you will see two maps of planets. Look for the planet Pollost Prime, which looks similar to Earth. The largest continent on the planet is actually a Mickey Mouse profile facing right.

⚲ Scavenger Hunt: In the queue line, find: a Magic Eight Ball, a View-Master, the planet Chokmil, a square planet, the Planet Z and Sector 9.

1. How many batteries can you count in the queue line?

2. Which of the following planets cannot be found in the Sector maps displayed throughout the queue line?
A. Hallyhoo
B. Torgar
C. Mykalenz

3. Which toy in *Toy Story* says "There's a snake in my boot!"
A. Buzz Lightyear
B. Woody
C. Mr. Potato Head

4. In *Toy Story*, what does Buzz believe is his spaceship which will return him home?
A. Andy's model rocket
B. A remote control car
C. The display box that he came in

5. How does Andy get the Buzz Lightyear toy in *Toy Story*?
A. It was a Christmas present
B. It was a birthday present
C. He bought it with his allowance money

6. Which toy does Bo Peep have a crush on in *Toy Story*?
A. Buzz
B. Woody
C. Rex

7. How many eyes do the *Toy Story* aliens have?
A. One
B. Two
C. Three

8. What color are the little plastic army men who help out the toys in the *Toy Story* movies?
A. Green
B. Black
C. Grey

9. Who is revealed as Buzz's father at the end of *Toy Story 2*?
A. Emperor Zurg
B. Walt Disney
C. G.I. Joe

10. Name two characters in *Toy Story 2* that were not in *Toy Story*.

11. Find the following *Toy Story* and *Toy Story 2* characters in the word search below: Buzz Lightyear, Woody, Mr. Potato Head, Slinky Dog, Hamm, Bo Peep, Rex, Sid, Andy, Bullseye, Jessie, Stinky Pete, Wheezy and Al.

```
A J B L B N B K E W H E E Z Y S
G L O A P U G A S D F C W H C T
S K P Q B S L I N K Y D O G E I
A T E C J T I L R D Q G O L J N
P F E W H D M D S Y Y L D B E K
M R P O T A T O H E A D Y J S Y
I B K H R K M S F N Y H A D S P
G H M D E L P M C A P E I F I E
N B U Z Z L I G H T Y E A R E T
C W E T F R E X J I B M K C H E
```

12. In *Toy Story 2*, the voice of Tour Guide Barbie is supplied by Jodi Benson who was also the voice of which very popular Disney character?
A. Belle
B. Cinderella
C. Ariel

13. Who was originally offered the voice of Buzz Lightyear in *Toy Story*?
A. Steve Martin
B. Billy Crystal
C. Jim Carrey

14. True or False: *Toy Story* was the first fully computer generated full-length feature film.

15. Which toy that is featured in the *Toy Story* films was the first toy ever advertised on network television?
A. Slinky
B. Mr. Potato Head
C. Barbie

109

16. What was Buzz Lightyear originally going to be called in *Toy Story*?
A. Lunar Larry
B. Rocket Robbie
C. Space Ace

17. Unscramble the following words and phrases seen and heard throughout the indoor queue line:

RTAS NDOMMCA
TCROES
APCSE GERNAR
SERTBAEIT
GACITALC NACEALLI
OT YTINFINI NDA DONYBE

Space Mountain

Overview: A spine tingling ride through the universe, Space Mountain blasts guests off in six-passenger rockets through the galaxies, planets and stars of deep outer space. The vehicles feel like they are traveling at breathtaking speeds through glow in the dark tunnels with sharp turns and sudden drops, but in reality they're only traveling 28 mph. Space Mountain, at a height of 180 feet, is one of the three "mountain" thrill rides of the Magic Kingdom.

Thrill Time: 2 ½ minutes

FASTPASS AVAILABLE

Restrictions: Passengers must be at least 44 inches (112 cm) tall. Guests should be in good health and free from high blood pressure, heart, back or neck problems, motion sickness or other conditions that could be aggravated by the ride. Expectant mothers should not ride.

Be Aware of: Once inside the building, the queue line and the ride are dark to encourage the feeling of space. The indoor queue line has many inclines.

The left side of the indoor queue line has a few stairs. If you cannot climb stairs, consult a cast member as to whether you are entering a queue line with stairs. Guests must be able to step down into the vehicle for boarding. A steep moving walkway leads from the vehicle's exit point to the exit of the building.

Helpful Hints: Be sure to secure your loose items in the rocket's mesh pockets because piles of personal items are recovered on the attraction's floor each night.

Members of your party who choose not to experience Space Mountain can enjoy the Tomorrowland Arcade which is located at the attraction's exit.

Parent/Guardian Switch option is available.

Disabled Access: Guests must transfer from a motorized scooter to a wheelchair. Guests must transfer from a wheelchair and step down into the ride vehicle. The disabled queue line is to the right of the standard queue line. Service animals are not permitted on this attraction.

• • • • • • • • • • • • • • • • • •

◉ Look For: The meteors on the dome above you prior to boarding the vehicles are reportedly chocolate chip cookies.

☆ Hidden Mickey Hunt: Some of the shooting stars seen through the windows and in the sky inside the building pass by in clusters of three which form a Mickey Mouse head shape.

1. On the FX-1 Tracking Network that you see directly in front of you when you enter the building, how many objects have the tracking coordinates of 7584.3?

2. On the FX-1 Tracking Network, find the names Sirius and Real Sirius. Do you think that these are real stars or are they made up?

In the indoor queue line on your left, you will see pictures of several famous space objects. The following three questions relate to those pictures.

3. Take a good look at the Comet Bradfield because you might not ever see it again. Can you guess how long it takes the comet to make its way through the inner solar system?
A. 100 years
B. 500 years
C. 1,000 years

4. Can you guess why the North American Nebula was given its name?
A. Because it resembles the continent of North America
B. Because it was discovered by a North American astronomer
C. Because all sky objects have a North American title

5. Can you find a horse's head in any of the objects on the wall?

6. Is there much oxygen in outer space?

7. How would your life be different if you lived in outer space? What problems would you have with eating? With sleeping? Would you need to exercise?

8. Unscramble the following words of items found in space:

MREEITOET
LLIONCONTESAT
KLMIY YAW
RTAS
MTECO
RLSOA MSYTES

9. All of the signs of the zodiac are named after constellations in the night sky. For instance, the Trifid and Lagoon Nebulas which are shown in the queue line are part of the constellation of Sagittarius which forms the image of a centaur which is half man

and half horse. The sun passes by each constellation once per year, always in the same chronological order, creating 12 segments of time named after the 12 constellations. Find the following zodiac signs in the word puzzle below: Sagittarius, Aries, Leo, Taurus, Virgo, Capricorn, Gemini, Libra, Aquarius, Cancer, Scorpio and Pisces.

```
A V L I B R A S I E M A B E V Q
A W E T G B D K F S C O R P I O
C R O S A G I T T A R I U S J E
A H I N J U P G D L Q C G M U F
N P L E O C R K C A A R E H T S
C J I T S F B U Y J D V M G D M
E C P S E M H Q S N E L I B K E
R M U I C A P R I C O R N R A R
G R U E O E L B R J M R I V G A
H K B D F G S A Q U A R I U S O
```

10. The 1998 Disney film *Armageddon* features a team which is sent into space to do what?
A. Drill into an asteroid and insert a nuclear bomb
B. Rescue a crashed Space Shuttle on the Moon's surface
C. Capture a nuclear reactor that is flying through space

11. Which 1966 television show featured a crew, captained by James Kirk, on a mission to explore new worlds in outer space?
A. *Star Wars*
B. *Star Trek*
C. *Space Rangers*

12. Who was the first American in space?
A. Neil Armstrong
B. Alan Shepard
C. Gus Grissom

13. Who was the first man to walk on the Moon?
A. Neil Armstrong
B. Alan Shepard
C. Buzz Aldrin

14. The famous phrase "Houston, we have a problem" was uttered on which problematic Apollo mission?
A. Apollo 13
B. Apollo 14
C. Apollo 15

15. How many Apollo missions landed on the Moon?
A. One
B. Four
C. Six

16. What was the name of the first U.S. Space Station in 1973?
A. Space Habitat
B. Skylab
C. Freedom Station

17. When was the first Space Shuttle mission?
A. 1980
B. 1981
C. 1982

18. What was the name of the first privately manned vehicle to fly beyond Earth's atmosphere in 2004?
A. SpaceShipOne
B. Voyager
C. Space Transporter

Stitch's Great Escape!

Overview: Guests enter the Galactic Federation Prisoner Teleport Center, which guards alien prisoners, not knowing that an alien will soon be on the loose and widespread panic will ensue. As one of 132 unsuspecting recruits, you will be guided through the policies and procedures of guarding aliens before entering the theater where Experiment 626 (also known as Stitch), from the Disney animated film *Lilo & Stitch*, accidentally escapes and wrecks havoc on everyone inside. This is not a ride, nor is it a stage show…the best way to describe this attraction is an "experience" that you won't likely forget.

Thrill Time: 14 minutes

FASTPASS AVAILABLE

Restrictions: Guests must be 40 inches (102 cm) or taller.

Be Aware of: Though this attraction is based on a semi-cute animated cartoon character, the attraction is not suitable for young children and even adults will be surprised at how frightening this attraction can be.

This attraction uses shoulder harnesses in each seat which bounce up and down throughout the show and can be very uncomfortable. The seats of this attraction are also very uncomfortable. The theater is extremely dark throughout the experience. Expect foul smells, misting water, loud sounds and bright, flashing lights.

Helpful Hints: Before the shoulder harness is lowered in the theater, shrug your shoulders up as high as you can. This should help make your experience more comfortable when the harness begins to bounce during the attraction.

When leaving the first pre-show area with the television monitors, go through the far left door to have a front row view of the next pre-show which features an Audio-Animatronic alien.

Parent/Guardian Switch option is available.

Disabled Access: Guests must transfer from a motorized scooter to a wheelchair that is provided at the attraction. Guests may remain in their wheelchair. Disney's assistive listening devices interact with this attraction. Disney's handheld captioning devices interact with this attraction. Disney's guest-activated video captioning devices interact with this attraction. Guests with service animals should check with a host or hostess at this attraction.

• • • • • • • • • • • • • • • • • • •

♀ **Scavenger Hunt**: Find a poster for the Space Home and Garden Show in the outside queue line.

1. As you're standing in the outside queue line, you will pass the back of the FASTPASS kiosks on your right. There are symbols on the kiosks that are actually an alphabet unique to Stitch's Great Escape! When you figure out which symbols correspond to which letters, you can read all kinds of hidden messages in the attraction. What word do you think the symbols on the kiosks stand for?

2. What color fur does Stitch have?
A. Blue
B. Red
C. Brown

3. In Disney's *Lilo & Stitch*, Stitch is able to change the number of arms and legs he has. Which of the following is not a total number of arms and legs that Stitch has at any point in the movie?
A. Four
B. Six
C. Eight

4. In *Lilo & Stitch*, why is it so important that Stitch behave and not get in trouble?
A. He will be sent back to his home planet if he misbehaves
B. Lilo and her sister are trying to impress the social worker
C. Stitch is trying to win the "Best Manners by an Animal" award

5. In *Lilo & Stitch*, where does Lilo find Stitch?
A. In a dog pound
B. He fell through her roof
C. She put an ad in the classifieds for a pet

6. In which state does *Lilo & Stitch* take place?
A. Alaska
B. Hawaii
C. California

7. How many letters are in the Hawaiian alphabet?
A. 12
B. 18
C. 26

8. Throughout *Lilo & Stitch*, the characters talk about the meaning of the Hawaiian word "ohana." What does "ohana" mean?
A. Family
B. Love
C. Honor

9. Which of the following is not a meaning of the word "aloha"?
A. Love
B. Goodbye
C. See you later

Have you ever wanted to know how to speak the Hawaiian language? The following are Hawaiian words, along with their pronunciation, so you can learn to talk like a native Hawaiian.

English	Hawaiian	Pronunciation
yes	ae	eye
no	aole	ah-oh-lay
thank you	mahalo	mah-hah-low
food	kau kau	cow cow
child	keiki	kay-kee
friend	aikane	eye-kah-nay
house	hale	hah-lay
bathroom	lua	oo-ah

10. In which other Disney/Pixar animated film do aliens make an appearance?
A. *Great Mouse Detective*
B. *Finding Nemo*
C. *Toy Story*

11. Which legendary singer's songs make up a large portion of the *Lilo & Stitch* soundtrack?
A. Frank Sinatra
B. Don Ho
C. Elvis Presley

12. What is the name of the top secret U.S. Government military area which is thought to be conducting research on aliens that crashed to earth?
A. Area 21
B. Area 31
C. Area 51

13. In which U.S. city did aliens supposedly crash in 1947?
A. Fargo, North Dakota
B. Roswell, New Mexico
C. Roswell, Georgia

14. What is the name of the 1938 radio program that created widespread panic when listeners thought they were listening to an actual alien invasion instead of a radio drama?
A. *Monster from Mars*
B. *The Body Snatchers*
C. *War of the Worlds*

15. Which 1997 alien comedy film starred Will Smith and Tommy Lee Jones?
A. *Men in Black*
B. *My Stepmother is an Alien*
C. *Alien Nation*

Tomorrowland Indy Speedway

Overview: Here's your chance to be a race car driver, although at a more leisurely speed of 7 miles per hour. Two drivers per vehicle can race against fellow drivers and maneuver the twists and turns of the course, though you don't have too much control since the cars are locked on tracks. The attraction is patterned after the Indianapolis 500 with the storyline taking a futuristic twist, but the sights, smells and sounds are down to earth Indy.

Thrill Time: 5 minutes

Restrictions: Drivers must be at least 52 inches (132 cm) tall. No one under 12 months old is allowed in the cars. Guests should be in good health and free from high blood pressure, heart, back or neck problems, motion sickness and other conditions that could be aggravated by the ride. Expectant mothers should not ride.

Be Aware of: The entire queue line and attraction are located outdoors. Major portions of this queue are not shaded and the queue line gets extremely hot from the combination of sun reflecting off of the asphalt and engine exhaust. This attraction closes during inclement weather such as thunder and lightning.

While driving, you can be hit by cars from behind, much like bumper cars. There is a flight of stairs in the queue line and exit. If you are unable to climb stairs, contact a cast member for assistance. The volume of this attraction is very loud.

Helpful Hints: During hot Florida days, this attraction should only be visited during the early morning or after the sun goes down because of the intense heat that accumulates.

For those not riding in the race cars who would like to observe or videotape the action, there is a shaded grandstand viewing area with benches and an area track side for standing.

Parent/Guardian Switch option is available.

Disabled Access: Guests must transfer from a wheelchair or motorized scooter and step up and over into the vehicle.

• • • • • • • • • • • • • • • • • •

 Scavenger Hunt: In the queue line, find: a man losing his toupee, the Florida State flag, car #77, a map of the Indianapolis 500 track and an alien driving a race car.

119

Look for the answers to the following five questions in the advertising signs lining the race track and the plaques throughout the queue line.

1. How many aliens can you count?

2. Who was the winner of the Galactic Grand Prix?

3. What is the name of one of Jupiter's moons that is along a race path?

4. What date was the 2002 Brickyard 400 held?

5. Who won the first Indianapolis 500 race in 1911?

6. What's the name of Mattel's tiny die-cast cars that kids love to play with?
A. Hot Wheels
B. Mega Machines
C. Crazy Cars

7. The Walt Disney Company made several movies about an old Volkswagen Beetle nicknamed "The Love Bug" which won car races with the help of its special tricks. What was the name of the car?
A. Harold
B. Humphrey
C. Herbie

8. What number is painted on the front of "The Love Bug"?
A. 47
B. 53
C. 43

9. Disney's *The Love Bug* became the highest grossing film of what year?
A. 1965
B. 1969
C. 1975

10. In 2005, "The Love Bug" entered a NASCAR race for the first time in what Disney film?
A. *Herbie: Gone Wild!*
B. *Herbie: To The Extreme*
C. *Herbie: Fully Loaded*

11. While going through turns, Indy car drivers endure the same G-force as Space Shuttle astronauts during liftoff. The drivers endure a force how many times the weight of gravity?
A. Three
B. Four
C. Five

12. At a race car driver's speed of 220 miles per hour (mph), how long does it take to travel the length of a football field?
A. One second
B. Two seconds
C. Three seconds

13. At speeds of 220 mph, how many times do the front tires of racing cars rotate per second?
A. 15
B. 30
C. 43

14. The Indianapolis 500 is referred to as "The Brickyard" because of the bricks that once lined the racing surface. How many millions of bricks were laid down in 1909 to create the track?
A. 1.7
B. 3.2
C. 4.1

15. Unscramble the following NASCAR drivers' names:

LEHAICM TRLWAIP   (Winner of the 2003 Daytona 500)
FEJF NDGORO   (Winner of the 2005 Daytona 500)
LADE HRATDNRAE RJ   (Winner of the 2004 Daytona 500)
YERTR ENLABTO   (Winner of the 1996 Winston Cup)
EDAL DTEARRNHA   (Nicknamed "The Intimidator")

16. Along the track you will see different colored flags on display. Each of the flag's colors has a specific meaning if it is waved during an Indianapolis race. Match the following flag colors and their meanings:

Checkered flag   Start of the race or a restart

Green flag   Race stops immediately

White flag   Cars must slow immediately

Red flag   Leader has started final lap of the race

Black flag   Leader has been declared a winner

Yellow flag   Driver must proceed to the pits

17. Richard Petty supplies the voice of a character in which 2006 Disney-Pixar animated film about a stock car?
A. *Motors*
B. *Cars*
C. *The Incredibles*

18. Where in the Walt Disney World® Resort can you ride in or drive a stock car at speeds up to 150 mph?

Tomorrowland Transit Authority

Overview: The Tomorrowland Transit Authority (TTA) is a slow moving indoor/outdoor tram ride that brings guests in four person cars (or a combination of six adults and children) through observation points of the Space Mountain and Buzz Lightyear's Space Ranger Spin attractions and provides a leisurely, narrated tour through Disney's idea of a prototypical community of the future. This attraction gives you a good overall orientation of Tomorrowland with a birds-eye view.

Thrill Time: 10 minutes

Be Aware of: A steep moving walkway leads to and from the vehicle entrance and exit. Portions of the attraction are extremely dark.

Helpful Hints: This attraction typically has one of the shortest wait times of all Magic Kingdom attractions. A great orientation to the attractions of Tomorrowland, the TTA is a chance to sit back and relax while developing a game plan for the area's attractions. Even on hot days, the breeze on the ride is refreshing and the attraction is interspersed with moments of air-conditioning.

Parent/Guardian Switch option is available.

Disabled Access: Guests must be able to stand on a steep moving ramp and then enter and exit the vehicle via a moving walkway. The moving walkway cannot be stopped at this attraction. Disney's handheld captioning devices interact with this attraction.

• • • • • • • • • • • • • • • • • • •

1. What "color" line is the TTA advertised as on signs throughout Tomorrowland?

2. How many moving parts do the TTA vehicles have?
A. 0
B. 25
C. 1,000

3. What futuristic-looking transportation device (which guests can try out at Epcot and Disney cast members use regularly) is the first self-balancing, electric powered vehicle that will likely improve transportation in the future?
A. Segway Human Transporter
B. Genesis Roamer
C. Future Scooter

4. Along the ride you will see a mockup of Walt Disney's vision of a working community of tomorrow named the Experimental Prototype Community of Tomorrow. This model was the inspiration for what Walt Disney Company creation?

5. What futuristic Hanna-Barbara cartoon series featured a family with a dog named Astro and a robot maid named Rosie?
A. *The Flintstones*
B. *The Jetsons*
C. *The Spaceleys*

6. There have been many attempts at creating planned communities, sometimes called "Utopias." In fact, Disney's dream of Epcot was dubbed "Waltopia." Which of the following have not been planned communities in the United States?
A. New Harmony
B. Oneida
C. Pleasantville

7. The Walt Disney Company had their hand in the creation of a planned community in Florida that is similar to Walt Disney's dream. What is the name of the town?
A. Celebration
B. Imagination
C. Inspiration

Walt Disney's Carousel of Progress

Overview: Follow an Audio-Animatronic family from the days before electricity to the present as they proudly show off the new inventions that have changed their lives. The 112-seat rotating theater gives guests a glimpse into the family's excitement when electric lights, indoor plumbing and even virtual reality games were introduced and changed their lives.

Thrill Time: 20 minutes

Be Aware of: This attraction sometimes has shorter operating hours than the rest of the Magic Kingdom. Consult your Times Guide for operating hours. There is a brief moment of pitch darkness during the show.

Helpful Hints: This is a wonderful attraction to visit when it's hot outside or you're exhausted from walking all day. The chance to sit down for 20 minutes on upholstered seats in a darkened, air-conditioned theater is a welcome respite from the madness of the theme park.

Be sure to look at the video monitors in the queue line which show how Disney developed their Audio-Animatronic technology in the early days. The queue line tends to move quickly as there are six theaters for this attraction which load every few minutes.

Sit in the front rows for the best views of the Audio-Animatronic figures on the stage, however, every seat is good in this small, elevated theater.

The theater doesn't get very dark during the show so most children won't have a problem with darkness.

Parent/Guardian Switch option is available.

Disabled Access: Guests may remain in their wheelchair or motorized scooter. Disney's assistive listening devices interact with this attraction. Disney's handheld captioning devices interact with this attraction. Disney's guest-activated captioning devices interact with this attraction (pre-show only).

• • • • • • • • • • • • • • • • • •

1. Do you think that during your lifetime people will ever be able to live on the moon? How about living under the ocean? Will you ever be able to drive cars that fly through the air?

2. Which Walt Disney World® Resort attraction allows guests to experience virtual reality and other futuristic fun?
A. Disney Quest
B. Cirque du Soleil
C. Fantasia Gardens

3. Where at the Walt Disney World® Resort can you walk through a pavilion of exhibits featuring the technology of the future?
A. Magic Kingdom
B. Epcot
C. Disney-MGM Studios

4. Match the following technological achievements with the year in which they occurred:

First color television broadcasting begins	1876
Telephone invented	1979
First air conditioner invented	1902
Invention of frozen food technology	1990
Model T car invented	1923
First Sony Walkman sold	1908
Penicillin discovered	1951
World Wide Web invented	1946
First credit card issued	1928
Microwave oven technology invented	1950

5. Which U.S. President challenged America to develop the technology to put a man on the moon?
A. Richard Nixon
B. Jimmy Carter
C. John F. Kennedy

6. Which famous artist also invented a variety of modern day marvels nearly 500 years before they could even be built, including the bicycle and automobile?
A. Claude Monet
B. Leonardo Da Vinci
C. Pablo Picasso

7. Which famous inventor of the phonograph created over 1,000 inventions in his lifetime?
A. Thomas Edison
B. Benjamin Franklin
C. Albert Einstein

EVERYTHING ELSE

Not every entertaining experience in the Magic Kingdom involves a queue line. Many of the following attractions do not require guests to stand in a queue line and most do not typically involve a wait time.

- You can always find your favorite characters at Mickey's Toontown Fair where you can walk-through Mickey and Minnie's homes and Donald's Boat in this fanciful land. All of the homes are kid friendly with lots of fun, oversized details that bring these characters to life. **Minnie's Country House** is geared towards little girls with pink and purple decorations and hearts all over. Inside you'll find an interactive kitchen and Minnie's office where she works as editor of a magazine. **Mickey's Country House** gives guests a peek into the life of this important mouse, from his bedroom and kitchen to a garden, garage and Pluto's doghouse outside. From Mickey's Country House guests may choose to enter the queue line for the Judge's Tent where you can meet Mickey Mouse throughout the day. **Donald's Boat** isn't as much a walk through home as it is a water play area with squirting fountains and spraying water. Guests may remain in their wheelchair or motorized scooter.

- **Pooh's Playful Spot** is a colorfully themed playground area for kids age 2-5. With Winnie the Pooh's tree house, oversized honey pots, playful water elements and a soft surface for kids to play on, every child will want to visit this Fantasyland play area.

- The **Main Street Vehicles** are a fun way to travel down Main Street, U.S.A. simply for the fun of it or as transportation to save your aching feet. A horse drawn trolley or other early 1900s vehicles transport guests from Main Street, U.S.A.'s Town Square and Cinderella Castle.

- At the **Frontierland Shootin' Arcade** you can test your rifle skills by shooting at electronic targets in an Old West town. Each play is 50 cents.

- Adventureland's **Shrunken Ned's Junior Jungle Boats** let guests pilot a miniature remote controlled boat through a tropical jungle. Each play is $1.

- The **Tomorrowland Arcade** offers guests a variety of arcade games from 50 cents to $1.

- The **Flag Retreat** on Main Street, U.S.A. is a patriotic display of lowering the flag before sunset every day.

- The **Share a Dream Come True Parade** features your favorite Disney characters in massive snow globe floats that travel throughout Frontierland, Liberty Square and Main Street, U.S.A. See "Helpful Hints and Tips on Surviving Disney Queue Lines" for more parade viewing information or enjoy the "General Magic Kingdom Trivia" or "Main Street, U.S.A. Scavenger Hunt" sections while you are waiting.

- The **SpectroMagic Parade** is held on specially selected nights, usually during the busiest seasons. This visually stunning parade along a darkened route is comprised of floats that light up the night sky with endless amounts of lighting effects, including 600,000 miniature lights and 100 miles of fiber optic cables. Even the Disney character costumes are illuminated in this uniquely different parade. See "Helpful Hints and Tips on Surviving Disney Queue Lines" for more parade viewing information or enjoy the "General Magic Kingdom Trivia" or "Main Street, U.S.A. Scavenger Hunt" sections while you are waiting.

- **Wishes**, the Magic Kingdom's 12-minute fireworks display, is narrated by Jiminy Cricket and highlights the emotional stories of Disney character's wishes coming true against a backdrop of brilliantly colored pyrotechnics and Cinderella Castle. Note: Wishes can be seen from a variety of locations throughout the Magic Kingdom so

129

don't worry about securing a spot long before the show starts. Some of the most popular viewing spots are anywhere on Main Street, U.S.A. and the bridge leading to Tomorrowland because these spots offer a view of the front of Cinderella Castle against the fireworks. Because of the popularity of the show which often is held at park closing, expect very long lines in exiting the Magic Kingdom afterwards. To save your sanity and prevent being run down by a stampede of strollers and tired guests, plan on sitting down for 10-15 minutes and letting the crowds pass, look through the gift shops (though they will be extremely crowded) or enjoy the "General Magic Kingdom Trivia" or "Main Street, U.S.A. Scavenger Hunt" sections before trying to exit the Magic Kingdom.

MAIN STREET, U.S.A. SCAVENGER HUNT

You might not have noticed, but when you first entered the Magic Kingdom and stepped onto Main Street, U.S.A., you were stepping into a real life movie. Walt Disney imagined guests starting their day as if they were entering a film. That's why the walkways from the main entrance are red, just like walking a red carpet. The train tunnel is considered the curtain and theater lobby, and the first thing you smell in the Magic Kingdom is popcorn.

The windows along Main Street, U.S.A. are arranged as the opening credits of a movie. The names of individuals who influenced the design and operation of the Walt Disney World® Resort are immortalized in the windows, just as directors and producers are immortalized in a film's credits. Look in the windows above the shops and restaurants of Main Street, U.S.A. to find the following items:

1. A rainbow and a pot of gold.

2. A drawing of a cat on a window dedicated to Walt's daughter and her second husband.

3. A sign for a Chinese restaurant.

4. A window honoring Walter E. Disney.

5. A picture of a leaking faucet.

6. A rabbit coming out of a hat, a magic ball and playing cards.

7. A window honoring Walt Disney's father, Elias Disney, born in 1895.

8. A tribute to Frank G. Wells, president of the Walt Disney Company from 1984-1994 who scaled six of the seven highest peaks of the seven continents before he died. (Hint: Wells' name

is the highest on Main Street, U.S.A., even higher than Walt Disney's, in a tribute to his passion of mountain climbing.)

9. Windows with musical notes honoring B. Baker, the musical director for Epcot; B. Jackman, the voice of Goofy; and G. Bruns, the composer who wrote "The Ballad of Davy Crockett."

10. A window promoting the "world's largest collector of keychains" dedicated to the director of merchandising at Disneyland and the Walt Disney World® Resort.

11. According to his window, which famous Disney specializes in the gentlemanly sport of racing at sea?

12. A window promoting the tailors to the President.

13. A window labeled "Voice and Singing Lessons." (Be sure to listen under the window for the sound of students practicing scales and dancing.)

Find the following eight items which can be found in various places along Main Street, U.S.A.:

14. A barber shop pole.

15. A mailbox.

16. A green pole with a carved horse's head.

17. A gold bald eagle.

18. A poster for a horse auction.

19. Lady and the Tramp's paw prints.

20. An Indian statue with a James A. Garfield medallion around his neck.

21. A phone inside a gift shop where you can hear the conversation of two women on a party line complaining about the price of hamburger which is five cents a pound.

22. According to the Magic Kingdom dedication plaque at the base of the flag pole, what did Roy O. Disney hope that Walt Disney World would bring to all who visit?

23. What "number" is the Fire Station? (Hint: It is the year that the Magic Kingdom opened)

GENERAL MAGIC KINGDOM TRIIVA

1. Look at a Magic Kingdom guide map to find the following items: *(Note: Guide maps are subject to change)*

- A boat
- Teepees
- Elephants
- A train
- Race cars

2. What "color" is Tomorrowland on the guide map?

3. Name the seven lands of the Magic Kingdom without looking at a guide map.

4. On what day did the Magic Kingdom open?
A. February 1, 1971
B. October 1, 1971
C. December 25, 1971

5. How many cast members work at the Walt Disney World® Resort, making it the largest single site employer in the United States?
A. Around 30,000
B. Around 57,000
C. Around 100,000

6. On average, how many pairs of sunglasses are turned into the Magic Kingdom Lost and Found each day?
A. 10
B. 50
C. 100

7. How many hamburgers are eaten each year at the Walt Disney World® Resort?
A. 10 million
B. 30 million
C. 50 million

8. The Walt Disney World® Resort is roughly the size of the city of San Francisco, California. Approximately how many square miles is the Walt Disney World® Resort?
A. 47 square miles
B. 56 square miles
C. 64 square miles

9. Of the 30, 500 acres of land at the WDW Resort, approximately how much of that land is currently developed?
A. One fourth
B. One half
C. Almost all of it

10. Complete this famous Walt Disney quote: "I only hope that we never lose sight of one thing - that it was all started by a
_____."

11. When Walt Disney announced his plans on November 11, 1965 to build a theme park in Florida, what was the project then known as?
A. Disneyland II
B. The Florida Project
C. Walt Disney World

12. The Magic Kingdom was not the only attraction to open in 1971 at the Walt Disney World® Resort. Which three Disney resorts also opened that year?

13. Which of the following celebrities was not part of the televised opening of the Magic Kingdom in 1971?
A. Julie Andrews
B. Bob Hope
C. Frank Sinatra

14. Most visitors think that the Walt Disney World® Resort is located in Orlando, FL. The resort is actually located in what town?

A. Lake Buena Vista
B. Kissimmee
C. Disneyanna

15. The original designs for the Magic Kingdom included an apartment for the Disney family located in what structure?

A. Cinderella Castle
B. The Haunted Mansion
C. Main Street, U.S.A. gift shops

16. What was the inspiration for the Magic Kingdom's Main Street, U.S.A.?

A. Walt Disney's hometown of Marceline, Missouri
B. Historic pictures of the downtown area of Philadelphia
C. A town square featured in the Disney film *Dumbo*

17. When the Magic Kingdom first opened, guests had to purchase ticket books and then redeem the tickets to ride the attractions. The ticket books sold were for A,B,C, D or E tickets. Which letter corresponded to the most elaborate, exciting attractions in the park?

A. A
B. C
C. E

18. Approximately how many different costume styles are worn by cast members at the Walt Disney World® Resort?

A. 589
B. 2,650
C. 3,500

19. Approximately how many different items of food can a guest choose from on the Walt Disney World® Resort property?

A. 4,700
B. 6,000
C. 10,000

20. How large is the Magic Kingdom?
A. 83 acres
B. 107 acres
C. 289 acres

21. True or False: Florida passed legislation during the development of the Magic Kingdom to create an additional city to accommodate the development of the Walt Disney World® Resort.

22. How many pieces of pyrotechnics are used in Wishes, the Magic Kingdom's fireworks display?
A. 561
B. 683
C. 2,079

23. What is the Night of Joy, a special event held at the Magic Kingdom?
A. A Christmas concert featuring popular musicians
B. A party for couples who've been married at the WDW Resort
C. A concert featuring contemporary Christian performers

24. The Magic Kingdom, as well as Disney's three other theme parks, closed early for the first time in history in preparation for Hurricane Floyd in September of what year?
A. 1999
B. 2000
C. 2002

MAGIC KINGDOM CHAPTER ANSWERS

<u>Adventureland</u>
The Enchanted Tiki Room Under New Management
1. B **2.** C **3.** Hummingbird - a tiny bird whose wings flap very fast; Cardinal - a red bird often associated with winter; Woodpecker - a bird who likes to peck holes in wood; Bluebird - a bird whose feathers appear blue; Dove - a bird associated with the symbol of peace; Flamingo - a pink bird with long legs; Owl - a bird who likes to come out at night; Peacock - a bird with brightly colored feathers; Penguin - a bird who likes the cold **4.** C **5.** B **6.** B **7.** C **8.** B **9.** C **10.** A

Jungle Cruise
Scavenger Hunt: Sedative is by the loading bay on the right **1.** Herd **2.** B **3.** No **4.** A (*Tale Spin*) **5.** See the end of this chapter **6.** Jane **7.** A **8.** C **9.** *George of the Jungle* **10.** C **11.** A **12.** C **13.** Jane Goodall **14.** Bulls; Cows **15.** Filet of Rock Python

The Magic Carpets of Aladdin
1. There are six Abus and six camels (four spitting water in stone work around the ride and two large ones) **2.** No **3.** A **4.** C **5.** A **6.** B **7.** Agrabah; Cave of Wonders; Jasmine; Abu; Rajah; The Sultan; Iago; Street Rat **8.** B **9.** C (He tricked the Genie to get him out) **10.** B **11.** C **12.** C **13.** B **14.** B

Pirates of the Caribbean
Scavenger Hunt: The people playing chess are down a shaft in the queue line **1.** C **2.** B **3.** Tales **4.** A **5.** B **6.** C **7.** A **8.** A **9.** B (He set fire to hemp weavings in his beard) **10.** Walk the plank; Weigh anchor; Davy Jones locker; Land lubber; Mutiny; Galleon; Treasure chest; Cannon; Scurvy; Doubloon; Galley **11.** C **12.** C

Swiss Family Treehouse
1. B **2.** A **3.** A **4.** B **5.** B **6.** A **7.** C **8.** Apple; Pine; Birch; Walnut; Fir; Elm; Spruce; Poplar

Fantasyland

Ariel's Grotto
1. B **2.** A **3.** B **4.** B **5.** C **6.** A **7.** C **8.** A **9.** A **10.** A (The Living Seas) **11.** Shark Reef at Typhoon Lagoon and The Living Seas at Epcot

Cinderella's Golden Carrousel
Scavenger Hunt: The horses will be on the outermost row **1.** C **2.** C **3.** B **4.** A **5.** B **6.** C **7.** A **8.** B **9.** Left **10.** B **11.** C **12.** C **13.** B (Mary Poppins' horse is in the Great Movie Ride queue) **14.** True (King Stefan's Banquet Hall) **15.** B **16.** A

Cinderellabration
Scavenger Hunt: Gargoyles are on each side of the front entrance of Cinderella Castle by the balcony; the crest is above the main entrance and the lions are in the banners on either side of the castle **1.** 18 **2.** B **3.** A **4.** C **5.** A **6.** A **7.** B **8.** A

Dumbo the Flying Elephant
Scavenger Hunt: Elephants are near the queue line covers and the stork is hanging in a gold frame around the top of the attraction **1.** A **2.** C **3.** B **4.** A **5.** A **6.** Bears **7.** B **8.** C **9.** Acrobat; Big top; Lion; Cotton candy; Juggling; High wire; Peanuts; Ring master; Trapeze **10.** True **11.** A **12.** B **13.** False **14.** A **15.** C **16.** A **17.** B

"it's a small world"
1. B **2.** Laughter; Tears; Fears; Share **3.** C **4.** C (The song is also sung in English, Japanese and Spanish) **5.** French, German, Japanese, Portuguese and Spanish **6.** C **7.** A **8.** Europe **9.** Japan **10.** A **11.** C **12.** B

Mad Tea Party
2. C **3.** C **4.** B **5.** B **6.** A **7.** C **8.** C **9.** B **10.** Spades, diamonds and clubs **11.** B **12.** B **13.** C **14.** A **15.** B **16.** A **17.** B

The Many Adventures of Winnie the Pooh
1. B **2.** B **3.** B **4.** C **5.** Ta Ta For Now **6.** A **7.** A **8.** C **9.** Winnie the Pooh - likes to say "Oh, bother;" Rabbit - his nickname is Long Ears; Piglet - sometimes stammers when talking; Tigger - made out of rubber and springs; Roo - kangaroo who plays with Tigger; Kanga - she is a mother; Eeyore - likes to say "Thanks for

noticing;" Owl - very smart with lots of stories; Christoper Robin - he always sorts things out **10.** C **11.** C **12.** C **13.** C **14.** C **15.** A **16.** B **17.** B **18.** A

Mickey's PhilharMagic
Scavenger Hunt: Artwork is the large mural, umbrellas are in the Willie the Whale poster and the microphone is in the *Hercules* poster **1.** C **2.** B **3.** C **4.** B **5.** B **6.** B **7.** C **8.** A **9.** See the end of this chapter **10.** A **11.** C **12.** A **13.** B

Peter Pan's Flight
1. C **2.** B **3.** A **4.** True **5.** Second; Morning **6.** C **7.** B **8.** C **9.** B **10.** B **11.** B **12.** No **13.** A **14.** Left **15.** A **16.** A **17.** C **18.** C **19.** True **20.** A **21.** C **22.** A **23.** A

Snow White's Scary Adventures
1. Grumpy, Dopey, Sleepy, Sneezy, Bashful, Doc and Happy **2.** C **3.** B **4.** A **5.** A **6.** B **7.** So she won't be killed **8.** Emerald; Pearl; Ruby; Sapphire; Opal; Diamond **9.** C **10.** C **11.** C **12.** Yes - when kissed by Snow White and when she wakes up **13.** C **14.** B **15.** C **16.** True **17.** A **18.** B **19.** C

Storytime with Belle
Scavenger Hunt: The rose is in the iron double doors and the lions are under the benches **1.** Cinderella, Jasmine, Snow White Ariel, Mulan, Sleeping Beauty and Pocahontas **2.** C **3.** A **4.** B **5.** C **6.** A **7.** A **8.** B **9.** B **10.** C **11.** C (*Beauty and the Beast: The Enchanted Christmas*) **12.** A

Frontierland
Big Thunder Mountain Railroad
Scavenger Hunt: On the left, outside of the windows just before the ramp leading to the loading area **1.** See the end of this chapter **2.** A **3.** A **4.** A **5.** C **6.** B **7.** A **8.** A **9.** B **10.** C **11.** C **12.** C **13.** C **14.** B **15.** A **16.** B

Country Bear Jamboree
Scavenger Hunt: Bear with angel wings is carved into a frame **1.** A **2.** A **3.** A **4.** A **5.** B **6.** A **7.** True **8.** A **9.** B **10.** C **11.** C **12.** B **13.** B **14.** B

Splash Mountain
1. A **2.** A **3.** C **4.** *Alice in Wonderland* **5.** C **6.** B **7.** A **8.** B **9.** B **10.** B **11.** *Who Framed Roger Rabbit* **13.** A **14.** Blizzard Beach and Typhoon Lagoon **15.** Jungle Cruise, Pirates of the Caribbean, Tom Sawyer Island, "it's a small world" and Liberty Square Riverboat **16.** A **17.** An old Southern term for brother **18.** B **19.** A **20.** C **21.** B

Tom Sawyer Island
1. A **2.** C **3.** Fort Wilderness Resort and Campground **4.** A (*The Celebrated Jumping Frog of Calaveras County*) **5.** A **6.** A **7.** C **8.** C **9.** *The Adventures of Tom Sawyer* came first in 1876, then *The Adventures of Huckleberry Finn* in 1885

Walt Disney World Railroad
1. Choo choo **2.** Caboose **3.** B **4.** B **5.** A **6.** B **7.** A **8.** See the end of this chapter **9.** A **10.** B **11.** B **12.** C

Liberty Square
The Hall of Presidents
1. Alexander Hamilton **2.** Franklin D. Roosevelt **3.** George Washington (quarter and the $1 bill) and Abraham Lincoln (penny and $5 bill) **4.** B **5.** B **6.** Jimmy Carter; Ronald Reagan; Richard Nixon; Abraham Lincoln; George Washington **7.** C **8.** C **9.** A **10.** B (Abraham Lincoln and George Washington are also featured)

The Haunted Mansion
Scavenger Hunt: The gold bats are in the loading area and the weathervane is on top of the house **1.** Halloween **2.** Ride the roller-ghosters **3.** A sand-witch **4.** Boo-berries **5.** B **6.** B **7.** See the end of this chapter **8.** See you later; Empty tomb; I am ready; Pearly gates; Rest in peace; Hallucination; Apparition; Clairvoyance; Weegee board; Poltergeist; Manifestation **9.** A **10.** C **11.** C **12.** A **13.** A **14.** C

Liberty Square Riverboat
1. Sailboat **2.** The ferry from the Transportation and Ticket Center to the Magic Kingdom **3.** See the end of this chapter **4.** True - 2,552 miles **5.** B **6.** A **7.** A

Mickey's Toontown Fair
The Barnstormer at Goofy's Wiseacre Farm
1. Cow or goat 2. Chicken 3. Sheep 4. Mud 5. Wheat, rice, oats and corn; Milk and eggs; Potatoes 6. B 7. B 8. A 9. B 10. Human, because he walks upright 11. Old MacDonald 12. A 13. C 14. B 15. A 16. C 17. A 18. A

Judge's Tent and Toontown Hall of Fame
1. Black 2. Winnie the Pooh 3. Robin Hood; Jasmine; Quasimodo; Jiminy Cricket; Chicken Little 4. Pocahontas 5. Ariel 6. Mulan 7. B 8. C 9. B 10. Pluto debuted in 1930, then Goofy in 1932 and Donald Duck in 1934 11. B ("Plane Crazy" was the first cartoon made but the third to be released) 12. C

Tomorrowland
Astro Orbiter
1. B 2. B 3. Mercury, Venus, Earth, Mars, Jupiter, Saturn, Uranus, Neptune and Pluto 4. C 5. C 6. C 7. B 8. A (The Victorian-themed resort can be seen from the Victorian-themed train station on Main Street, U.S.A.) 9. True 10. C 11. A 12. B 13. B 14. B 15. Yes, it's NASA's primary ELV launch location 16. A

Buzz Lightyear's Space Ranger Spin
2. A 3. B 4. C 5. B 6. B 7. C 8. A 9. A 10. Bullseye, Jessie, Stinky, Wheezy, Mrs. Potato Head and Al 11. See the end of this chapter 12. C 13. B 14. True 15. B 16. A 17. Star command; Sector; Space ranger; Batteries; Galactic Alliance; To infinity and beyond

Space Mountain
2. Sirius is the real name of a star, Real Sirius is just a joke 3. C 4. A 6. No 8. Meteorite; Constellation; Milky Way; Star; Comet; Solar system 9. See the end of this chapter 10. A 11. B 12. B 13. A 14. A 15. C 16. B 17. B 18. A

Stitch's Great Escape
1. FASTPASS 2. A 3. C 4. B 5. A 6. B 7. A (A,E,I,O,U,H,K,L,M, N,P,W) 8. A 9. C 10. C 11. C 12. C 13. B 14. C 15. A

Tomorrowland Indy Speedway
2. Al Unserbot 3. Io 4. August 4 5. Ray Harroun 6. A 7. C 8. B 9. B 10. C 11. B 12. A 13. C 14. B 15. Michael Waltrip; Jeff Gordon;

Dale Earnhardt Jr.; Terry Labonte; Dale Earnhardt **16.** Checkered
Flag - leader has been declared a winner; Green Flag - start of the
race or a restart; White Flag - leader has started final lap of the
race; Red Flag - race stops immediately; Black Flag - driver must
proceed to the pits; Yellow Flag - cars must slow immediately **17.**
B **18.** Richard Petty Driving Experience

Tomorrowland Transit Authority
1. Blue **2.** A **3.** A **4.** Epcot theme park **5.** B **6.** C **7.** A

Walt Disney's Carousel of Progress
2. A **3.** B (Innoventions) **4.** First color television broadcasting
begins - 1951; Telephone invented - 1876; First air conditioner
invented - 1902; Invention of frozen food technology - 1923;
Model T car invented - 1908; First Sony Walkman sold - 1979;
Penicillin discovered - 1928; World Wide Web invented - 1990;
First credit card issued - 1950; Microwave oven technology
invented - 1946 **5.** C **6.** B **7.** A

Main Street, U.S.A. Scavenger Hunt
1. Rainbow Paint Co. window above Emporium near the Harmony
Barber Shop **2.** William and Sharon Lund Antiques window above
Uptown Jewelers **3.** Above Casey's Corner **4.** A window above the
Plaza Ice Cream Parlor facing Cinderella's Castle **5.** Main Street
Water Works window above the Main Street Athletic Club shop **6.**
Dyer Predictions window in the alley between the Market House
and Uptown Jewelers **7.** In the alley between the Market House
and Uptown Jewelers **8.** Seven Summits Expeditions window
above the Market House **9.** Windows above the Harmony Barber
Shop **10.** In the alley between the Market House and Uptown
Jewelers **11.** Roy E. Disney's window above the Market House **12.**
Liberty Square Tailors window over The Chapeau **13.** Located in
the alley between the Market House and Uptown Jewelers **14.**
Outside of Harmony Barber Shop **15.** In front of Casey's Corner,
Emporium, Market House, Disney Clothiers, Plaza Ice Cream
Parlor, Town Square Exposition Hall and City Hall **16.** In front of
Uptown Jewelers, the train station, Disney Clothiers, Emporium,
City Hall, Market House and the Confectionery **17.** On top of the
flagpole **18.** Near the gate between the Fire Station and Harmony
Barber Shop **19.** In front of Tony's Town Square Restaurant **20.** In

front of the Market House **21.** In the Market House on the wall facing the alley **22.** Joy, inspiration and new knowledge **23.** No. 71

General Magic Kingdom Trivia

1. Teepees are to the right of Big Thunder Mountain Railroad, the elephants are at Dumbo the Flying Elephant, the train is on the outskirts of the park and the race cars are at Tomorrowland Indy Speedway **2.** Purple **3.** Main Street, U.S.A., Adventureland, Frontierland, Liberty Square, Fantasyland, Mickey's Toontown Fair, Tomorrowland **4.** B **5.** B **6.** C **7.** A **8.** A **9.** A **10.** Mouse **11.** B **12.** Disney's Contemporary Resort, Disney's Polynesian Resort and the Fort Wilderness Resort and Campground **13.** C **14.** A **15.** A **16.** A **17.** C **18.** C **19.** B **20.** B **21.** False - two cities were created **22.** B **23.** C **24.** A

Jungle Cruise

```
BNGAPJBLFAIHDCKG
JSIHBWKINGLOUIEJ
RHDERAMGSLUKQNFB
AEFBMTGRKBJTAEGO
ERQJFDYHPWCYIASA
LEKCOLONELHATHIM
HKCHLGAJWEOLCGPI
BHGMOWGLIMRHFJBQ
MAAPFENKDBTAHERD
DNQCKIASCGBALOOF
```

Mickey's PhilharMagic

```
NFLUTEXDHYGDRUMA
MUISVCGLSAITZHDY
NJCLARINETRUMPET
GKLUPXTWIRVPEIZF
BUVFAIOKMOCGCAPY
DAITSVBPGMFYLNFR
RMOTCIOZHBJKMORF
BYLUACELLOKDCBOI
VCITERMPZNNQRTAM
RSNIAPVRTEGEALPL
```

144

Big Thunder Mountain Railroad

```
PLAAGOLDDUSTESV
IPROSPECTORESET
HICROPBDFGNLZDU
DCMESSTVXPURDIA
LKFSHOVELIGEPMI
QGNOOBVCCQGGJER
EUICXAXEAHEKMNR
ALTTGGBRILTOPTI
PCBMFORTUNEUXAU
SHVEXSTREAMUISN
```

Walt Disney World R.R.

```
ABSIGNALQMETCRDE
RSTEAMIDEVSBLMSN
WTRCXYPDIUMFGAEG
BAAPOXXTHBOXCARI
GTCHIAOUQNKLAFIN
MIKSTMLNBREGBKLE
KOHGONONAOOCOIHE
BNDCSFREIGHTOUOR
RMOPAASLHCOMSERH
ALBCONDUCTOREINW
```

The Haunted Mansion

```
RTSAIOMAWORARITM
BCREAKLQIZTMBEAJ
XYOLCEMETARYLOLZ
SLTBIBEICVWMAAOB
SODZWZARHEYPCKCG
PGLKCEGTSPOOKYEH
INHJMUBCSAAUCGIO
DSTORMYNIGHTAPFU
EAPHSPIRITJFTIDL
RRVWSTGTKAHAFMBL
```

Liberty Square Riverboat

```
OGRDECKBTSSOPAGU
LVBTYCAPTAINGCFB
YCEOMFDEERHBNAMT
STARBOARDPAUSBIG
AEUDBWOTJHOLCIZA
IJVBUOYSHYIKTNRL
PGANGWAYAOZHELML
OMIHNBCRQRMEUHLE
RSKEELOLDPBAMTVY
TABZIEOWBRIDGEDA
```

Buzz Lightyear's Space Ranger Spin

```
AJBLBNBKEWHEEZYS
GLOAPUGASDFCWHCT
SKPQBSLINKYDOGEI
ATECJTILRDQGOLJN
PFEWHDMDSYYLDBEK
MRPOTATOHEADYJSY
IBKHRKMSFNYHADSP
GHMDELPMCAPEIFIE
NBUZZLIGHTYEARET
CWETFREXJIBMKCHE
```

Space Mountain

```
AVLIBRASIEMABEVQ
AWETGBDKFSCORPIO
CROSAGITTARIUSJE
AHINJUPGDLQCGMUF
NPHEOCRKCAAREHTS
CJITSFBUWJDVMGDM
ECPSEMHQSNELIBKE
RMUICAPRICORNRAR
GRUEOELBRJMRIVGA
HKBDFGSAQUARIUSO
```

145

Epcot is a theme park of discovery. The park is separated into two lands - Future World, which features entertaining ways to learn about the science of today and the technology of the future, and the World Showcase, which brings the authentic sights, sounds and flavors of far off lands to the Walt Disney World® Resort. Thanks to the magic of Disney, you'll never realize that you're learning about science and world cultures as you zip around on thrill rides, savor foreign foods and enjoy the shows and attractions of Epcot.

Guest Information Board Location: Past Spaceship Earth between the Innoventions buildings in the pin trading kiosk.

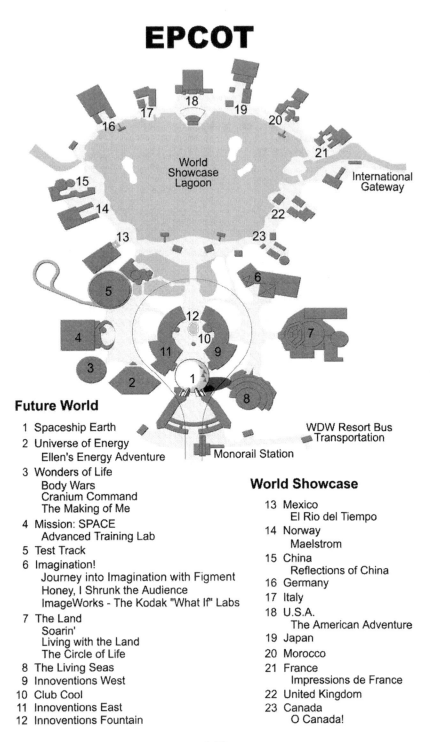

EPCOT

World
Showcase
Lagoon

International
Gateway

Future World

1 Spaceship Earth
2 Universe of Energy
   Ellen's Energy Adventure
3 Wonders of Life
   Body Wars
   Cranium Command
   The Making of Me
4 Mission: SPACE
   Advanced Training Lab
5 Test Track
6 Imagination!
   Journey into Imagination with Figment
   Honey, I Shrunk the Audience
   ImageWorks - The Kodak "What If" Labs
7 The Land
   Soarin'
   Living with the Land
   The Circle of Life
8 The Living Seas
9 Innoventions West
10 Club Cool
11 Innoventions East
12 Innoventions Fountain

WDW Resort Bus
Transportation
Monorail Station

World Showcase

13 Mexico
   El Rio del Tiempo
14 Norway
   Maelstrom
15 China
   Reflections of China
16 Germany
17 Italy
18 U.S.A.
   The American Adventure
19 Japan
20 Morocco
21 France
   Impressions de France
22 United Kingdom
23 Canada
   O Canada!

Epcot Tips

- The World Showcase opens later than Future World, typically at 11 a.m. Future World closes earlier than the World Showcase, except for selected attractions which stay open until park closing. Be sure to pick up a "Times Guide" for current operating hours.

- Epcot has a second theme park entrance called the International Gateway which is often less crowded. Located in the World Showcase between the France and United Kingdom pavilions, it is easily accessible from Disney's Beach Club Resort, Disney's Yacht Club Resort, Disney's Boardwalk Inn, and the Walt Disney World Swan and Dolphin. At this entrance, guests can purchase tickets, rent strollers and wheelchairs and leave Epcot to explore the restaurants and shops of the nearby Disney resorts. Note: Guests who are not staying at one of the above resorts cannot park at the resorts to access this entrance.

- Because Epcot is so large, walking from one location to another can be extremely time consuming. It's especially important in this theme park to think ahead about which attractions you would like to visit and when in order to save valuable time as well as wear and tear on your feet.

- Friendship water taxis are a convenient and easy way to access the central area of World Showcase without having to walk a far distance. You can board a water taxi in the World Showcase landing between Mexico and Canada for a destination of either Germany or Morocco. Taxis stop operating at least an hour before IllumiNations: Reflections of Earth.

- Kidcot Fun Stops, which are fun learning and craft stations for kids, are located at selected Future World attractions and in each country's pavilion in the World Showcase.

FUTURE WORLD

Future World is dedicated to fulfilling Walt Disney's dream of showcasing the technology of tomorrow. Throughout the varied pavilions and attractions of Future World, you will find entertaining ways to learn about science, technology and the environment. Though the concept of learning while at a theme park might seem unusual (and boring), some of the attractions of Future World are among the most popular and exciting of the entire Walt Disney World® Resort.

Body Wars

Overview: This 40-passenger motion simulator ride takes you on an exciting journey through the human body and its major organs as you are miniaturized to the size of a single cell and rush through the body's bloodstream.

Thrill Time: 5 minutes

Restrictions: Passengers must be at least 40 inches (102 cm) tall. Guests should be in good health and free from high blood pressure, heart, back or neck problems, motion sickness and other conditions that could be aggravated by the ride. Expectant mothers should not ride.

Be Aware of: This attraction is open seasonally. Check your Times Guide for operating hours.

This attraction is a very rough simulator ride and can induce motion sickness. If the sight of blood makes you sick, you might not want to experience this attraction.

Helpful Hints: Parent/Guardian Switch option is available.

Disabled Access: Guests must transfer from a motorized scooter to a wheelchair that is provided at the attraction. Guests must transfer from a wheelchair to the vehicle seat. Disney's guest-activated captioning devices interact with this attraction. Service animals are not permitted on this attraction.

• • • • • • • • • • • • • • • • • • • •

1. How many lungs does a human have?
A. 1
B. 2
C. 3

2. Where are your tonsils located?

3. What mineral is important for the development of your bones?

4. How many chambers does your heart have?
A. One
B. Three
C. Four

5. Where is your thyroid?
A. Brain
B. Neck
C. Stomach

6. Does an artery carry blood away from or to the heart?

7. Which of the following is responsible for processing the toxins in your body?
A. Esophagus
B. Bladder
C. Liver

8. Each day, the average heart beats approximately how many times?
A. 100,000
B. 500,000
C. 660,000

9. Each day, the average heart pumps approximately how many gallons of blood?
A. 50
B. 145
C. 2,000

10. The average human lungs process approximately how many liters of air a day?
A. 900-1,000
B. 8,000-9,000
C. 12,000-13,000

The Circle of Life

Overview: Timon and Pumbaa from the Disney animated film *The Lion King* are excited about building a tourist resort until Simba teaches them how overdeveloping the land is hurting the Earth. With compelling footage of Earth's devastation, as well as examples of the positive ways humans are protecting the Earth, the 410 guests who enjoy this film will leave with a desire to protect our environment.

Thrill Time: 12 ½ minutes

Be Aware of: During the movie there will be some images of fire and injured animals from environmental tragedies.

To access most of the seating, you will have to climb steps. If you cannot climb steps, ask a cast member to use the disabled queue line for entrance into the theater, however, the seating in this section is limited.

Depending on where in the theater you sit and choose to exit, you will exit onto either the first or second level of The Land pavilion.

Helpful Hints: The queue line area has limited bench seating and a video presentation with fun facts about the Earth's environment.

The movie is best viewed from the center or back of the theater. After exiting the queue line area, you will walk down a hallway to enter the theater. The first door to your right will lead to the upper portions of the theater and the second door to your right will lead to the front of the theater.

The Land pavilion features Sunshine Seasons food court and The Garden Grill character dining restaurant. It is easy to have a great meal and experience three attractions without leaving the building.

Disabled Access: Guests may remain in their wheelchair or motorized scooter. Disney's assistive listening devices interact with this attraction. Reflective captioning is available.

• • • • • • • • • • • • • • • • • •

1. What kind of animal is the Disney character Pumbaa from *The Lion King*?
A. Warthog
B. Anteater
C. Buffalo

2. What kind of animal is the Disney character Timon from *The Lion King*?
A. Mole
B. Monkey
C. Meerkat

3. What does "Hakuna Matata," Pumbaa and Timon's favorite saying, mean?
A. Eat more bugs
B. No worries
C. Welcome to our jungle

4. There are many ways you can help or hurt the environment while you are vacationing at the Walt Disney World® Resort.

Which of the following ideas will reduce the amount of waste in our environment and which will produce too much waste?

- Requesting that your Disney souvenirs be put in one plastic bag instead of several bags
- Drinking only a little bit of a beverage in a plastic bottle and then throwing it away
- Reusing your towels at your hotel
- Feeding birds french fries and potato chips when you eat an outdoors lunch
- Throwing cigarette butts and trash on the ground instead of putting it in a trash can
- Using only one theme park guide map for everyone instead of each person using their own
- Taking only as many napkins as you need when you order food at a concession stand

5. What is the name of the Walt Disney World® Resort's policy of reducing, reusing and recycling items to help the environment?

6. On average, what percent of trash in a United States landfill is paper?
A. 13%
B. 29%
C. 40%

7. What is the most common trash item found on the world's beaches?
A. Aluminum cans
B. Plastic drink bottles
C. Cigarette filters

8. Americans throw out approximately how many plastic bottles each hour?
A. 250,000
B. 2.5 million
C. 25 million

9. Each American uses the paper equivalent of how many trees each year?
A. One
B. Two
C. Three

10. In 1989, the *Exxon Valdez* spilled more than 11 million gallons of crude oil into the waters of Alaska's coastline, the largest oil spill in the U.S. To understand how much oil this was, imagine having 11 million gallons of milk. If you were to drink one gallon of milk a day, how many years would it take to drink all 11 million gallons?
A. 458 years
B. 2,096 years
C. 30,137 years

11. In 2002, a tanker called the *Prestige* spilled 77,000 tons of oil into the water, 1,000 tons more oil than the *Exxon Valdez* spill. In which country did this oil spill take place?
A. Spain
B. Japan
C. Canada

12. True or False: The trash that a country produces must stay in landfills within that country.

Cranium Command

Overview: Take a comical journey through a 12-year old boy's brain as he gets ready for school and encounters anxiety, love, and the normal trials and tribulations of an adolescent male. Buzzy, a newly recruited Audio-Animatronic pilot, struggles with coordinating all of the functions of the boy's brain during this stage and film show in a 200-seat theater. Well known comedians, such as George Wendt, Dana Carvey and Jon Lovitz, star as major body organs such as the stomach, heart and brain.

Thrill Time: 12 minutes

Be Aware of: This attraction is open seasonally. Check your Times Guide for operating hours.

The four and a half minute pre-show film can become extremely crowded because of the small space it occupies. There are loud noises, smoke and red flashing lights during the show.

Helpful Hints: A digital countdown at the entrance of the attraction alerts you to how much time you will have to wait until the next theater show. On the left side of the queue line, be sure to check out the puzzles on the wall.

In the pre-show area, the doors in the very front of the room lead to the front rows of the theater. The best views of the show are from the center of the middle and back rows. To sit in the center of the theater, allow several guests to enter a row before you because the cast members will instruct everyone to move to the far end of the row before sitting down.

Disabled Access: Guests may remain in their wheelchair or motorized scooter. Disney's assistive listening devices interact with this attraction. Disney's handheld captioning devices interact with this attraction (pre-show only). Reflective captioning is available.

• • • • • • • • • • • • • • • • •

 Scavenger Hunt: In the queue line, find a poster with George Washington and a poster with a baby.

On the right side of the queue line, you will find a plaque depicting what the brains of famous people might have looked like. Find the following people's brains: Walt Disney, Florence Nightingale and Thomas Edison.

1. It's easy to injure your brain if you fall while riding a bike or skating. What should you wear to protect your brain from injury?
A. Knee pads
B. Gloves
C. Helmet

2. Which character in *The Wizard of Oz* didn't have a brain?
A. Tin Man
B. Scarecrow
C. Lion

3. How much does the average human brain weigh?
A. One pound
B. Two pounds
C. Three pounds

4. How much does the average baby's brain weigh?
A. One pound
B. Two pounds
C. Three pounds

5. Which brain weighs more – a human's or a Bottlenose Dolphin's?

6. The human brain is divided into two separate parts – the left side and the right side. Each side controls different mental activities. Which side of your brain controls your math abilities? Which side of your brain helps you recognize other people's faces? Which side of your brain controls your speech?

7. The left side of your brain controls what side of your body?

8. True or False: The Swordfish has a "brain heater" which warms its brain when it swims in cold water.

9. True or False: The larger your brain is, the smarter you are.

10. In the Cranium Command show, Dana Carvey and Kevin Nealon perform their famous *Saturday Night Live* "pump you up" skit which parodies which famous body builder?

Ellen's Energy Adventure

Overview: Join Ellen DeGeneres and Bill Nye the Science Guy as they travel back in time to learn about the importance of energy and discover new ways to create energy. Six 80-passenger, slow moving vehicles transport guests on a journey 220 million years into the past to encounter dinosaurs and other wild creatures, while several films along the attraction route illustrate Earth's history as well as Ellen's comical struggle to be a winning contestant on the game show *Jeapordy!*

Thrill Time: 27 minutes

Be Aware of: Though this attraction is listed in the guide map as being a 45 minute show, the actual attraction is 27 minutes long. Once you leave the queue line, you will be escorted to a pre-show area for a seven minute film. From the pre-show, you will be taken into a loading room with the ride vehicles and it will take several minutes to load all of the guests. Though the entire experience lasts about 45 minutes, the attraction is not nearly that long.

There are bright, flashing lights during the pre-show video. The vehicles slowly rotate on large platforms during brief portions of the ride. This attraction briefly mentions the "Big Bang Theory." Aerial views during one of the films could lead to a touch of motion sickness.

If you sit on the far right side of the vehicles, you might get wet from a spitting dinosaur. Though a majority of the attraction involves watching films, young children might be scared by the Audio-Animatronic growling dinosaurs that surround the vehicles during a brief portion of the attraction.

Helpful Hints: Because the pre-show area has several movie screens in a semi-circular pattern, the best views will be in the back of the room. There is very limited bench seating in the pre-show.

All vehicles provide basically the same view, regardless of what vehicle you board and where in the vehicle that you sit. There will be six vehicles all traveling at the same time in a line. If you want to be in the front vehicle, exit through the far left doors of the pre-show area and board the front row of the far left vehicle in the very front of the room.

Parent/Guardian Switch option is available.

Disabled Access: Guests must transfer from a motorized scooter to a vehicle seat or a wheelchair provided at the attraction. Guests many remain in their wheelchair. Disney's assistive listening devices interact with this attraction. Disney's handheld captioning devices interact with this attraction.

• • • • • • • • • • • • • • • • • •

1. What are some simple things you can do at home to conserve energy?

2. Ellen DeGeneres supplied the voice for which Disney animated character who also calls Epcot home?
A. Crush
B. Dory
C. Figment

3. What was Ellen DeGeneres' profession in the sitcom *Ellen* which aired on ABC (owned by the Walt Disney Company) from 1994-1998?
A. Chef
B. Actress
C. Bookstore owner

4. The Universe of Energy pavilion creates much of the energy for Ellen's Energy Adventure using two acres of what kind of alternative power source?
A. Windmills
B. Hydroelectric power
C. Solar panels

5. Solar power occurs when sunlight is used to create energy. Solar power is becoming so common that many items that you use or see every day might be powered by the sun. Name some common items that use solar power.

6. At the beginning of 2004, the amount of energy being produced in the United States by wind power was enough to supply how many American homes with their annual electricity needs?
A. 520,000
B. 1 million
C. 1.6 million

7. The wind power used worldwide produces the same amount of electricity (enough to power 9 million average American homes or 19 million average European homes) as how many large nuclear power plants?
A. 4
B. 12
C. 25

8. The U.S. Department of Energy estimates that the world's winds could theoretically supply how much of the world's energy needs?
A. Half of the world's energy needs
B. Five times the world's energy needs
C. Fifteen times the world's energy needs

9. What is hydroelectric power?
A. Energy made from hydrogen
B. Energy made from flowing water
C. Energy made from vegetable oils

10. Is the use of hydroelectric power in the U.S. expected to increase or decrease by the year 2020?

11. Which country produces the largest amount of hydroelectric power in the world?
A. Canada
B. United States
C. Japan

12. Approximately how much of the world's electricity is created by water power?
A. 1/8
B. 1/5
C. 1/3

13. The world's first hydroelectric power plant opened in Wisconsin in what year?
A. 1882
B. 1912
C. 1945

14. According to the U.S. Department of Energy, approximately how much of a home's energy is used to power appliances that are turned off but still plugged in, such as televisions, coffee makers and toaster ovens?
A. 10%
B. 20%
C. 25%

15. According to the U.S. Environmental Protection Agency, the average home produces how much more greenhouse gas than the average car?
A. Twice as much
B. Three times as much
C. Four times as much

16. Which electrical appliance uses more energy – a laptop computer or a single sized electric blanket?

17. Which electrical appliance uses more energy – a refrigerator or a 27-inch television?

18. Which electrical appliance uses more energy – a coffee maker or a hairdryer?

19. Which electrical appliance uses more energy – a clothes iron or a clock radio?

Honey, I Shrunk the Audience

Overview: Professor Wayne Szalinski from the Disney film *Honey, I Shrunk the Kids* is being presented the Inventor of the Year Award. When the scatter-brained professor brings his shrinking machine to the awards ceremony, mayhem ensues as the 570-guest audience is accidentally shrunk and soon discovers what life is like when you're the size of an ant.

Thrill Time: 13 ½ minutes

FASTPASS AVAILABLE

Be Aware of: There are many aspects to this show which may be frightening to children and adults. If you are scared of mice or snakes (such as seeing hundreds of mice or an enormously large snake on the screen) you will not want to experience this show. There are bright, flashing lights, a larger-than-life roaring lion, misting water and a seating platform which gently bounces your seat at certain points during the show.

The pre-show area can become very crowded as nearly 600 people are ushered into a small, standing room only space. Guests must wear 3-D glasses for the best experience of the show.

Helpful Hints: Your FASTPASS ticket will only be valid for a ten minute time span. Be sure to look at the time frame that your ticket tells you to return to the show.

When in the pre-show area looking at the wall of doors, the doors to the far left will lead you to the back rows of the theater and the doors to the far right will lead you to the front rows of the theater.

If a member of your party does not want to experience the show, a good place for them to wait for you is in ImageWorks – The Kodak "What If" Labs. Located just outside of the Honey, I Shrunk the Audience attraction, the fun-filled labs have a multitude of computer games and high tech ways to learn about science. There's also a variety of picture taking stations sponsored

162

by Kodak which allow you to play around with digital images or create a personalized Disney portrait or souvenir for purchase.

Children who might be bothered by the 3-D effects can still enjoy the attraction without wearing the 3-D glasses.

Parent/Guardian Switch option is available.

Disabled Access: Guests may remain in their wheelchair or motorized scooter. Disney's assistive listening devices interact with this attraction. Reflective captioning is available. Guests with service animals should check with a host or hostess at this attraction.

• • • • • • • • • • • • • • • • • • • •

Look at the quotes on the right-hand wall in the indoor queue line area to fill in the blanks of the following two quotes.

1. "Imagination is more important than _____."

2. "Imagination is the _____ of life's coming attractions."

3. According to Thomas Edison, "To invent you need a good imagination and a pile of _____."

4. If you could be shrunk to the size of an ant, would you? Why or why not?

5. In the Disney film *Honey, I Shrunk the Kids*, the Szalinski children and their friends are shrunk to what size?
A. One quarter of an inch
B. One inch
C. Three inches

6. In *Honey, I Shrunk the Kids*, the tiny children are trying to escape from which location?
A. A busy city street
B. Their backyard
C. Their basement

7. In the 1997 Disney film *Honey, We Shrunk Ourselves*, who is accidentally shrunk along with Professor Szalinski and his wife?
A. No one else was shrunk
B. Their neighbors
C. Professor Szalinski's brother and his wife

8. In the 1992 Disney film *Honey I Blew Up the Kid*, after being zapped by one of Professor Szalinski's machines, the professor's baby grows larger every time he comes in contact with what?
A. The dog
B. Dairy foods
C. Electricity

9. Which of the following is not the name of one of the Szalinski children in the *Honey* movies?
A. Adam
B. Andrew
C. Amy

10. Which actor portrayed the role of Professor Wayne Szalinski in all three of the *Honey* movies?
A. John Goodman
B. Rick Moranis
C. Matthew Broderick

11. Which actor, famous for his roles in *Bosom Buddies* and *Newhart*, portrayed Professor Wayne Szalinski in the television show *Honey, I Shrunk the Kids*?
A. Bob Newhart
B. Tom Hanks
C. Peter Scolari

12. Rick Moranis supplied the voice of Rutt for which Disney animated feature?
A. *Brother Bear*
B. *Atlantis: The Lost Empire*
C. *Chicken Little*

13. Which of the following films has Rick Moranis not starred in?
A. *Ghost Busters*
B. *The Flinstones*
C. *The Goonies*

14. The photography company Kodak is the sponsor of Honey, I Shrunk the Audience. Kodak estimates that what percentage of the amateur photographs taken in the United States each year are taken at Walt Disney World® Resort or the Disneyland Resort?
A. 2%
B. 4%
C. 10%

15. The man who invented the first simple camera for consumers in 1888 was the founder of Kodak. What was his name?
A. George Eastman
B. Thomas Edison
C. K. Dak

16. Where does the Kodak company name come from?
A. It is the name of a mountain range
B. It is the name of a river
C. Kodak's founder simply made it up

17. What color of packaging is the distinctive trademark of Kodak products?
A. Green
B. Black
C. Yellow

Journey Into Imagination with Figment

Overview: The popular Disney character Figment, a purple dragon which represents the figment of your imagination, leads guests on an exploration of the five senses as they journey in two-row cars (each row can seat three to four adults) through examples of touch, taste, sight, smell and sound.

Thrill Time: 7 minutes

Be Aware of: Portions of this attraction are extremely dark. There will be the smell of skunk, as well as a very bright flash of light and burst of air at the end of the attraction.

Helpful Hints: Figment often makes character appearances outside of the attraction building. Contact a cast member for appearance times.

Parent/Guardian Switch option is available.

Disabled Access: Guests may remain in their wheelchair or motorized scooter. Disney's handheld captioning devices interact with this attraction.

• • • • • • • • • • • • • • • • • • •

1. A person who is blind has lost which one of their five senses?
A. Sound
B. Sight
C. Touch

2. A person who is deaf has lost which one of their five senses?
A. Taste
B. Sound
C. Sight

3. If a person is nearsighted, what does that mean?
A. They can only see things that are close to their eyes
B. They can only see things that are far away from their eyes
C. They have perfect vision

4. If you lost your sense of smell, which one of the other five senses would you probably lose, too?
A. Sound
B. Sight
C. Taste

5. Name a food that tastes sour.

6. Name a food that tastes salty.

7. Did you know that the taste buds on your tongue can only distinguish certain tastes on certain areas of your tongue? If you have a piece of candy or other type of sweet, try this experiment: carefully put the candy on the tip of your tongue and then on the side of your tongue. On which area of your tongue can you distinguish the sweet taste? If you have something salty, do this experiment again and see if you can figure out where your salty taste buds are.

8. Which famous woman lost both her sense of sight and sound?

9. True or False: In decibel levels, a car horn is louder than a baby's cry.

10. Which of the following is not one of the most sensitive parts of your body?
A. Lips
B. Feet
C. Fingers

11. Approximately how many taste buds are we born with?
A. 500
B. 6,700
C. 10,000

12. How often does the average person blink their eyes each day?
A. 680
B. 11,500
C. 21,000

13. How many working parts do the eyes have?
A. 700
B. 10,000
C. 2 million

14. Approximately how often are the taste buds on your tongue regenerated?
A. Your body can't grow new taste buds
B. Once a day
C. Every 10 days

15. Does color blindness affect more men or women?

16. When is your sense of smell at its best?
A. In the morning
B. Around noon
C. Late at night

17. The average human can recognize how many different types of odors?
A. 10,000
B. 250,000
C. One million

18. Dogs have how many more smell receptors than humans?
A. Ten times more
B. Twenty times more
C. Fifty times more

The Living Seas

(Note: Portions of The Living Seas were closed for refurbishment at the time of publication. The following information is based on the original attraction and is subject to change.)

Overview: The Living Seas is an entire pavilion dedicated to exploring our underwater world, very similar to an aquarium. The pavilion houses the largest saltwater aquarium on earth, with plenty of viewing locations to spot a dolphin, shark, stingray or any one of the 70 species of fish in the coral reef. The stars of the Disney-Pixar animated film *Finding Nemo* are showcased here, too, with the comical interactive show Turtle Talk With Crush (where an animated Crush actually talks with the 150-member audience – no two shows will ever be alike!) and Bruce's Sub House (a walk through exhibit space with fun facts about sharks and opportunities to take pictures with replicas of Bruce, Chum and Anchor). Also in The Living Seas is a manatee tank caring for injured or orphaned animals, fish tanks housing clown fish (Nemo from *Finding Nemo* is a clown fish), and presentations of scuba diving, fish feeding and dolphin encounters.

Thrill Time: Turtle Talk With Crush is 14 ½ minutes long. Allow at least 15 minutes to quickly look around the pavilion. Plan on spending much more time if you want to explore the exhibits or watch an animal encounter.

Be Aware of: There is very limited bench seating throughout The Living Seas. Turtle Talk With Crush has bench seating without back rests.

Helpful Hints: The Living Seas has restroom facilities, telephones, water fountains and a gift shop inside the pavilion, as well as an escalator and elevator for access to the second floor.

In the Turtle Talk With Crush theater, there are benches for the adults while kids are encouraged to sit on the floor in the front of the theater so that Crush can "talk" with them. Tell your kids not to be shy about sitting on the floor - once the show starts everyone tries to get a spot up front so that they can talk to Crush (parents can sit with their children, but only in the back sections of the floor). If your child wants to have the unique experience of talking with an animated character which will call him or her by name, be sure to think of a question about the underwater world, turtles, fishes, etc. before the show starts. When Crush asks if the humans have any questions for him, if your child is one of the first with their hand in the air they have a very good chance of talking with Crush. Be sure to stick around after the show is over, too. Crush comes back out to watch the humans leave and continues his antics as guests are exiting the theater. While waiting in the queue line, children can have fun in Bruce's Sub House which is nearby and within view of adults standing in portions of the queue line.

Fish feedings, dolphin presentations and scuba diving are held throughout the day, typically starting around 10 a.m. with the last show around 4 p.m. If you would like to schedule your visit to The Living Seas to watch one of these shows, stop by Guest Relations and have them contact The Living Seas for the show schedule (cast members at the Tip Board might be able to contact The Living Seas, as well), or talk to the cast member outside of The Living Seas pavilion. Show times are also posted on the second floor of The Living Seas as you enter the aquarium corridor.

Disabled Access: Guests may remain in their wheelchair or motorized scooter. Disney's assistive listening devices interact with this attraction. Reflective captioning is available. Disney's guest-activated captioning devices interact with this attraction.

• • • • • • • • • • • • • • • • • • •

1. What word does Crush from Disney's animated film *Finding Nemo* like to say a lot?
A. Cool
B. Dude
C. Sweet

2. What type of animal are Crush and Squirt in *Finding Nemo*?
A. Sea turtles
B. Sharks
C. Stingrays

3. In *Finding Nemo*, Dory is known for which trait?
A. Short term memory
B. Laziness
C. Rudeness

4. In *Finding Nemo*, where was Nemo brought after he was captured?
A. A restaurant
B. An eye doctor's office
C. A dentist's office

5. What is the name of the starfish in *Finding Nemo*?
A. Sunshine
B. Peach
C. Apple

6. *Finding Nemo* takes place in the waters of which tropical location?
A. The Florida Keys
B. Australia's Great Barrier Reef
C. The Big Island of Hawaii

7. If all of the water from The Living Seas was put into one gallon milk jugs and then laid side by side, how many miles would the milk jugs stretch?
A. 26
B. 347
C. 540

8. The Living Seas is the largest saltwater aquarium on Earth. Can you guess how many millions of gallons of water are in The Living Seas aquarium?
A. 5.7
B. 10.4
C. 100.9

9. Would Spaceship Earth fit inside The Living Seas aquarium?

10. Approximately how fast can a sea turtle swim?
A. Up to 5 miles per hour
B. Up to 10 miles per hour
C. Up to 20 miles per hour

11. Approximately how many species of starfish are there?
A. 1
B. 890
C. 2,000

12. Approximately how many different types of sharks are there?
A. 53
B. 189
C. 350

13. Oceans cover approximately how much of the Earth's surface?
A. 50%
B. 70%
C. 90%

14. Guess how many gallons of water are estimated to be on Earth.

15. According to NASA research, if all of the ice in Earth's glaciers and ice sheets melted, the sea level would rise approximately how many stories?
A. 2
B. 14
C. 26

16. Find the following names of fish in the word search below: flounder, minnow, tuna, halibut, tilapia, swordfish, catfish, cod, salmon and bass.

```
S N C E W A L D P T O G B M A F
K W P M I N N O W V I N C S C J
H Y O A F S G C T B U L R D O R
A B M R C I T U N A A L A S D N
L S T J D O K E G U B H R P W E
I R A U H F L O U N D E R P I L
B H N L A R I Y D S C M B I E A
U C I F M D P S O K W B A S S D
T J A L G O V E H U A H T F C J
B E T D P B N C A T F I S H B A
```

172

17. A character from Disney's *20,000 Leagues Under the Sea* shares the name with a character from *Finding Nemo*. Which character name is used in both films?
A. Nemo
B. Dory
C. Marlin

Living with the Land

Overview: Take a relaxing boat ride through working farming areas that grow the food used in many Walt Disney World® Resort restaurants. After a journey through examples of the world's varied landscapes, your guide will explain the unique crops that are grown by scientists from the Walt Disney World® Resort, NASA, the United States Department of Agriculture and Nestle in The Land's varied greenhouses, including nine pound lemons, Mickey-shaped cucumbers and plants that grow without soil. Each boat has nine rows which can each accommodate four adults or a combination of five adults and children.

Thrill Time: 15 minutes

FASTPASS AVAILABLE

Be Aware of: Portions of this attraction have thunder and lightning elements. A brief portion of this attraction has a heavy, smoke-like water mist. Because these are working greenhouses in the Florida sun, the portion of the ride that floats through the covered greenhouses can be very hot and humid.

Helpful Hints: The Land pavilion features Sunshine Seasons food court and The Garden Grill character dining restaurant. It is easy to have a great meal and experience three attractions without leaving the building.

Because these are working greenhouses, it is best to visit this attraction during the day.

Parent/Guardian Switch option is available.

Disabled Access: Guests must transfer from a motorized
scooter to a wheelchair that is provided at the attraction. Guests
may remain in their wheelchair. Because wheelchairs will not fit
in the standard queue line, you must see a cast member who will
give you a Return Line Ticket that will be dated and stamped with
a time to return to the FASTPASS line for entry into the attraction.
The time that is put on the ticket is generally the time that you
would have boarded the attraction if you stayed in the normal
queue line (for instance, if it's 2 p.m. when you arrive at the
attraction and it's a 30-minute wait, the cast member will give you
a Return Line ticket for 2:30 p.m.). Disney's handheld captioning
devices interact with this attraction.

• • • • • • • • • • • • • • • • • • • •

☆ **Hidden Mickey Hunt**: In the mural behind the boat
landing area, find bubbles near the bottom of the mural which
form a hidden Mickey.

Find the answers to the following three fill in the blank questions
in the quotes that decorate the queue line wall.

1. "Our environment is like a patchwork _____."

2. Francis Bacon said that "Nature is not governed except by
_____ her."

3. "I may be only one person, but I can be one person who makes
a _____."

4. Florida is well known for growing what type of fruit?
A. Oranges
B. Apples
C. Pineapples

174

5. What U.S. state is famous for growing potatoes?
A. Colorado
B. Georgia
C. Idaho

6. How many tons of fruits and vegetables are grown at The Land pavilion and then served in Walt Disney World® Resort restaurants?
A. 11
B. 15
C. 30

7. Which of the following crops grow in the soil underground and which grow on trees or plants above ground?

- Peanuts
- Almonds
- Bananas
- Carrots
- Garlic
- Corn

8. The Land uses special Mickey-shaped plastic forms to grow certain vegetables and fruits to resemble a Mickey Mouse head. Which of the following crops has The Land not yet been able to grow to resemble Mickey Mouse?
A. Watermelons
B. Pumpkins
C. Oranges

9. Approximately how many pounds of watermelon are served every year at the Walt Disney World® Resort?
A. 500,000
B. 750,000
C. One million

10. Approximately how many miles of grass are mowed at the Walt Disney World® Resort each year?
A. 300,000
B. 450,000
C. 700,000

11. Approximately how many bedding plants and annuals are planted each year at the Walt Disney World® Resort?
A. 1 million
B. 2 million
C. 3 million

12. From 2002-2003, how much of the United State's citrus came from Florida?
A. Nearly 55%
B. Nearly 68%
C. Nearly 75%

13. Approximately 95% of Florida's oranges go where?
A. Overseas food markets
B. Orange juice processing plants
C. Supermarkets across the United States

14. Florida is called America's "Winter Salad Bowl" because it produces approximately how much of the nation's fresh vegetables in January, February and March of each year?
A. 60%
B. 80%
C. 97%

15. Florida grows approximately how much of the world's grapefruit?
A. 25%
B. 45%
C. 75%

16. True or False: Tomatoes are a member of the vegetable family.

17. Which Florida city grows over 75% of the United States' winter strawberries?
A. Plant City
B. Sarasota
C. Miami

18. Unscramble the following types of fruits and vegetables that are grown on farms throughout Florida:

OCRART
TECULET
OOCAAVD
MNRELOTEAW
RINTANEEG
MMOOSHRU
AEPRG
TTOOMA
SHDRAI
BBRREELUY

The Making of Me

Overview: This film about human reproduction and birth manages to educate younger guests about a sometimes taboo subject without giving too many detailed specifics that would embarrass the 86 members of the theater audience. Martin Short stars in the humorous yet enlightening film which includes images of fetal development and live footage of the birth process.

Thrill Time: 14 minutes

Be Aware of: This attraction is open seasonally. Check your Times Guide for operating hours.

A steep ramp leads to the front of the theater. Guests can avoid the ramp and sit in the back rows. The theater has bench seating without back rests.

Helpful Hints: While waiting outside the theater for the next show to begin, there are nearby interactive exhibits for children to play with and still be in full view of their parents.

Disabled Access: Guests may remain in their wheelchair or motorized scooter. Disney's assistive listening devices interact with this attraction. Reflective captioning is available.

• • • • • • • • • • • • • • • • • •

1. What is the average amount of time that it takes for a baby to develop inside their mom before they are born?
A. Three months
B. Six months
C. Nine months

2. If a baby is born before it has spent nine months inside its mother, what is it called?
A. Premature
B. Early riser
C. Impatient

3. According to a popular myth, what type of bird brings new babies to their moms and dads?
A. An eagle
B. A stork
C. A dove

4. What is the color that is normally associated with baby girls? What color is normally associated with baby boys?

5. What are two babies born at the same time to the same mother called?

6. What are three babies born at the same time to the same mother called?

7. What are four babies born at the same time to the same mother called?

8. What are five babies born at the same time to the same mother called?

9. By what age can most babies laugh?
A. At birth
B. One month
C. Three months

10. Unscramble the following words of items that babies often need:

TTOELB   (Hint: It is what a baby drinks from)
EARPID   (Hint: Babies wear them on their bottoms)
RPACEIFI   (Hint: This often prevents a baby from crying)
BRIC   (Hint: It is where a baby sleeps)
REALTT   (Hint: It is a baby toy that makes noise)
GHHI AHCIR   (Hint: It is where a baby eats from)
BBI   (Hint: It is what protects a baby's clothes from food)
RLLTEOSR   (Hint: It is what a parent pushes their baby in)
IEKBLAN   (Hint: It is a nickname for a blanket)
OOSBEIT   (Hint: It is what babies wear on their feet)

11. When a baby has been growing for three months inside its mother's womb, how big is it?
A. The size of an acorn
B. The size of a lime
C. The size of a watermelon

Mission: SPACE

Overview: If you've ever wondered what it's like to be an astronaut, hop aboard an X-2 rocket capsule in Mission: SPACE for an authentic astronaut experience guided by Gary Sinise. As part of the crew of the International Space Training Center in the year 2036, you'll feel the pull of G-forces as your rocket lifts off, the wonder of weightlessness and the exhilaration of landing on the planet Mars as you perform simple crew duties during your mission. Each rocket capsule has a team of four people, with 10 capsules on each trainer and a total of four trainers that can be operating at once. There's no denying that Mission: SPACE is as close as most people will get to being out of this world.

Thrill Time: 4 minutes

FASTPASS AVAILABLE

Restrictions: Passengers must be at least 44 inches (112 cm) tall. Guests should be in good health and free from high blood pressure, heart, back or neck problems, motion sickness and other conditions that could be aggravated by the ride. The maneuvers in this ride can result in nausea and disorientation even if you have never experienced motion sickness before. Expectant mothers should not ride. Anyone who cannot tolerate enclosed spaces, simulators or spinning should not experience this attraction. Disney advisories warn that motion sickness is more prevalent in anyone who is experiencing a headache or inner ear problems, as well as anyone who has a history of migraines, vertigo or anxiety.

Be Aware of: This attraction is INTENSE. There's no way to ignore the medical warnings routinely broadcast throughout the inside queue line which is a good thing since many people could potentially have an adverse reaction to experiencing the simulation. If you are concerned about a medical condition that could be aggravated by the simulator, it would be wise not to experience Mission: SPACE. Even guests who typically do not have adverse reactions to thrill rides have come away feeling a little woozy from this one.

Note: At press time, Disney had decided to eliminate the centrifuge (the spinning action which has caused so many negative physical effects for guests) on two of its Mission: SPACE trainer simulators. Guests are now asked whether or not they want to experience the attraction with or without the centrifuge. Though it is expected that Disney will keep a non-spinning simulator available at all times, be sure to ask a cast member about your options before entering the queue line.

Large bags and backpacks cannot be accommodated in the simulator vehicles. During Mission: SPACE, your shoulder harness will press down against your body. The individual seats on this attraction are narrow and cannot accommodate all body types.

Helpful Hints: It should go without saying, but do not eat a heavy meal before experiencing this attraction! However, you do want to make sure you have something light in your stomach as low blood sugar levels can contribute to the feeling of motion sickness during the attraction. Be sure you are well hydrated and well rested before experiencing Mission: SPACE to reduce the chances of an adverse physical reaction.

If you are concerned about motion sickness, save this attraction for later in the day. Though many people will tell you to experience Mission: SPACE first thing in the morning while the queue lines are shorter, if you do get sick, the remainder of your day in Epcot might not be pleasant.

Water fountains are located at the beginning of the inside queue line. There are small compartments for your personal belongings in the simulator. Air sickness bags are also available within the simulator.

Before boarding the simulators, each guest will be given a crew assignment which will require you to perform certain tasks during the simulation (the task is just pressing a button). When you are directed to the 10 queue lines of four numbers each in the pre-show area, you will unknowingly be given your crew assignment. The first person in each line will be the Engineer, the next guest will be the Commander, the third guest in line will be the Pilot and the last guest will be the Navigator. After this pre-show, you will then move into the hallway outside of the simulator for another mission briefing where you can still change positions. The guest standing to the far right will be the Engineer and the guest to the far left will be the Navigator.

Because so many guests are unable to experience Mission: SPACE with the rest of their party, there is a wonderfully designed entertainment section, Advanced Training Lab, at the exit of the attraction where you can wait for members of your party. In this complex you will find Space Base, where young children can climb in a playground setting; Postcards from Space, where you can email a digital image of yourself against a space background; Expedition Mars, a computer game in which you explore Mars; and Mission: SPACE Race computer games where you can play individually or against a group of other guests. This area can be accessed from the ramp to the left of the attraction entrance.

Parent/Guardian Switch option is available.

Disabled Access: Guests must transfer from their wheelchair or motorized scooter to board this attraction. Disney's guest-activated video captioning devices interact with this attraction (pre-show only). Service animals are not permitted on this attraction.

• • • • • • • • • • • • • • • • • • •

👁 **Look For**: On the hub of the large rotating gravity wheel, look for the Horizons logo that represents the attraction that was previously located in the Mission: SPACE site.

In the indoor queue line, find the answers to the following four questions.

1. In what number bay of the International Space Training Center is the indoor queue line?

2. What was the top speed of the Lunar Roving Vehicle that was used in Apollo missions 15, 16 and 17?

3. Who was the first woman in space?

4. In what year did the first family travel into space?

5. Have you ever dreamed about being an astronaut? If you became an astronaut, would you rather live and work on the Moon, on Mars or in the International Space Station?

6. Is the temperature on Mars usually warm or cold?

7. Is there water on Mars?

8. Do you think that anything is living in outer space other than the life on planet Earth?

9. Which month of the year has a name that is derived from Mars?

10. How many moons does Mars have?
A. None
B. One
C. Two

11. How long is a year on Mars (the amount of time it takes to make a full revolution around the sun)?
A. 485 Earth days
B. 687 Earth days
C. 1,253 Earth days

12. When was the first successful exploration of the biology of the planet Mars?
A. 1976
B. 1989
C. 1994

13. Is Mars smaller or larger than Earth in diameter?

14. Which of the following does Mars not have?
A. The solar system's tallest known volcano
B. The solar system's deepest known sea
C. The solar system's largest known canyon system

15. When Mars is at its closest position to Earth, approximately how many days does it take to travel between the planets at a speed of approximately 7,300 miles per hour?
A. 58
B. 200
C. 1,267

16. From 1959 to 1976, the United States and the Soviet Union sent a total of how many rockets to the Moon?
A. 15
B. 29
C. 37

17. Why does Mars look red?
A. Large amounts of oxidized iron (rust) in the soil
B. Atmospheric conditions make it look red
C. It reflects the red rays of the sun

18. Has anyone ever walked on Mars?

19. How many men worldwide have walked on the surface of the Moon?
A. 6
B. 12
C. 18

20. How long does it take the Space Shuttle to make one orbit around Earth? (Hint: Astronauts aboard the Space Shuttle see 16 sunrises and sunsets each day.)
A. 30 minutes
B. 90 minutes
C. 130 minutes

21. NASA estimates that the first trip to bring people to the Moon to stay for an extended period of time will occur when?
A. Between 2010 and 2015
B. Between 2015 and 2020
C. There are no current plans to have people live on the Moon

22. How long is a day on Mars?
A. 22 hours and 18 minutes
B. 24 hours
C. 24 hours and 40 minutes

23. Mars is home to Mount Olympus, the tallest known volcano in the solar system. With a summit height of 17 miles above the planet's baseline surface elevation, how much taller is Mount Olympus compared to Mount Everest, Earth's tallest mountain?
A. Three times as high
B. Four times as high
C. Six times as high

24. With a diameter of 370 miles, Mount Olympus is roughly the same size as which U.S. state?
A. New Mexico
B. Delaware
C. Alaska

25. Many people wonder why we spend so much money to go into space. One of the benefits of space travel is improved technology that can then be used on Earth. Match the following products that are used on Earth with the space program applications that they were originally developed for:

Joystick	Space suit
Invisible braces	Detect toxic vapors in space station
Ski boots with folds	Detect the birth of stars
Cordless tools	Correct errors in spacecraft signals
Smoke detector	Advanced ceramic research
Ear thermometer	Produce clear images from spacecraft
Bar coding	Apollo lunar rover
Medical imaging	Track millions of space craft parts
TV satellite dish	Used for drilling on the moon

26. NASA is planning on retiring the Space Shuttle in what year and replacing it with a more modern space flight vehicle?
A. 2010
B. 2020
C. NASA has no plans to retire the Space Shuttle

Soarin'

Overview: Take a breathtaking flight over famous California landscapes such as Yosemite National Park, Napa Valley, Disneyland and Los Angeles. This unique attraction suspends you 40 feet in the air while you are surrounded by an 80-foot diameter dome projecting IMAX images. You'll experience the sensation of flying as your feet dangle from one of 87 seats, the wind rushes past you and the scents of California linger in the air.

Thrill Time: 5 minutes

FASTPASS AVAILABLE

Restrictions: Passengers must be at least 40 inches (102 cm) tall.

Be Aware of: Anyone with a fear of heights might want to think twice about experiencing the Soarin' attraction. You will be suspended 40 feet in the air, but you will actually feel like you are flying much, much higher. Guests who are highly susceptible to motion sickness might also want to reconsider experiencing this attraction.

Because of the nature of this attraction, if you are wearing sandals, flip flops, or any type of shoe that could easily fall off, you will be asked to remove your shoes and place them in the storage container under your seat. Large bags and backpacks will not fit in the under seat storage area and will need to be stored elsewhere before riding the attraction.

The individual seats on this attraction are narrow and might not accommodate all body types.

The smells of orange blossoms, pine forests and ocean spray are piped in during the attraction.

Helpful Hints: If you want to reduce your wait time and don't have a FASTPASS time, utilize the singles line. The singles line takes individual guests from the queue line to fill empty single seats. You must be willing to split from your party and possibly ride the attraction at different times (though this is not always the case), but you will save a lot of time waiting in line.

Stay on the right side of the queue line to have an unobstructed view of the television screens with changing trivia questions that are featured in a portion of the queue. Once you enter the corridor with blue lights, your wait time is approximately 20 minutes.

The Land pavilion features Sunshine Seasons food court and The Garden Grill character dining restaurant. It is easy to have a great meal and experience three attractions without leaving the building.

Disabled Access: Guests must transfer from their wheelchair or motorized scooter to board this attraction. Disney's guest-activated video captioning devices interact with this attraction (pre-show only). Service animals are not permitted on this attraction.

• • • • • • • • • • • • • • • • • • • •

1. Name three Disney characters that can fly.

2. What other attractions at the Walt Disney World® Resort also make you feel like you are flying?

3. Where did the Wright brothers make their historic flight?
A. Kitty Hawk, NC
B. Dayton, OH
C. Cocoa Beach, FL

4. Which of the following was not the name of one of the Wright brothers who made the historic first flight?
A. Orville
B. Maxwell
C. Wilbur

5. On December 17 of what year did the Wright brothers make the historic first powered flight?
A. 1892
B. 1903
C. 1915

6. How long did the first powered flight last?
A. 2 seconds
B. 12 seconds
C. 1 minute

7. Charles Lindbergh is famous for being the first person to accomplish which historic achievement in the *Spirit of St. Louis* plane in 1927?
A. First person to fly non-stop from California to New York
B. First person to fly from California to Hawaii
C. First person to cross the Atlantic Ocean

8. What is the name of the Air France airplane which was the world's only supersonic passenger jetliner (it flew at twice the speed of sound) before it was retired in 2003?

9. What is the name of the hot air balloon in the shape of Mickey Mouse's head that is sometimes used by the Walt Disney Company?
A. *Mickey Mania*
B. *Magic Express*
C. *Ear Force One*

10. Match the following cities with the three letter code of their airport:

Orlando, FL	LAX
Baltimore, MD	LAS
Tokyo, Japan	MEX
Atlanta, GA	PHX
Cincinnati, OH	RSW
Fort Myers, FL	SYD
Honolulu, HI	TYS
Knoxville, TN	BWI
Las Vegas, NV	EWR
Los Angeles, CA	MAN
Newark, NJ	CVG
Phoenix, AZ	MCO
San Francisco, CA	HNL
Sydney, Australia	ATL
Manchester, U.K.	SFO
Mexico City, Mexico	NRT

11. According to the Airports Council International, which airport had the most passengers pass through it in 2005?
A. Atlanta, Georgia
B. Los Angeles, California
C. Las Vegas, Nevada

12. According to the Airports Council International, the Orlando International Airport is the 12th busiest in the U.S. and the 21st busiest in the world, based on the number of passengers in 2005. Approximately how many passengers passed through the Orlando International Airport in 2005?
A. Nearly 20 million
B. Nearly 34 million
C. Nearly 50 million

13. At the end of 2005, the highest percentage of U.S. passengers flying into Orlando International Airport came from what U.S. area?
A. Newark, New Jersey
B. Washington, D.C.
C. Chicago, Illinois

14. Amelia Earhart was the first woman to fly non-stop across the United States in what year?
A. 1928
B. 1932
C. 1935

15. An ancient Greek myth told the story of a boy and his father who were trying to escape from captivity and created wings so that they could fly. The wings worked, but the boy flew too close to the sun which melted the wax which held his wings together and he died. What was the boy's name in this myth?
A. Icarus
B. Amadeus
C. Pegasus

Spaceship Earth

Overview: Spaceship Earth, the icon of Epcot, houses a ride through the evolution of communication. Your two-row time machine (each row seats two adults or a combination of three adults and children) will take you back to the dawn of recorded history as you witness Audio-Animatronic scenes of some of the most important communication inventions of our time, including cavemen's communication, the development of the printing press and the popularity of radio dramas. Guests are able to witness the future of communication, too, with simulations of what technology might be like in the not-so-distant future.

Thrill Time: 13 ½ minutes

Be Aware of: Guests enter and exit the time machines from a moving walkway. Utilize the disabled queue line if you have trouble walking on a moving platform.

The vehicles travel through Spaceship Earth with bumpy, sometimes jarring movements. While traveling throughout the sphere, there will be moments when your vehicle travels backward. The seats in your time machine are hard plastic and can be very uncomfortable.

In one scene, there is a heavy odor of smoke. There are bright, flashing fiber optic lights during a portion of the attraction.

Helpful Hints: The best time to visit this attraction is in the afternoon. As guests first enter Epcot in the morning, everyone wants to visit the icon of the park, which is also the very first attraction that they encounter, thus creating unbearable queue lines for the first part of the day. Plan to visit this attraction later in the day when the crowds are in World Showcase and you want an extended opportunity to sit down in a cool, enclosed environment.

Parent/Guardian Switch option is available.

Disabled Access: The disabled queue line is located past the standard queue on the right side of Spaceship Earth. Guests must transfer from their wheelchair to board this attraction. The moving walkway can be stopped for boarding. Disney's handheld captioning devices interact with this attraction. Guests with service animals should check with a host or hostess at this attraction.

• • • • • • • • • • • • • • • • • •

⚲ Scavenger Hunt: In the mural to the right of the building's entrance, find a person sitting cross-legged and a space station.

1. How many legs does Spaceship Earth sit upon?

2. What is the difference between an area code and a zip code in the United States?

3. What is a blog?
A. A computer virus which steals personal information
B. A type of journal published on the internet
C. A type of cell phone

4. The ancient Egyptians did not have an alphabet. What is the name of the pictures that they used to represent ideas and sounds in written communication?

5. Who invented the telephone in 1876?

6. How many triangles are on the outside of Spaceship Earth?
A. 5,897
B. 9,456
C. 11,324

7. How much rainwater falls off of the Spaceship Earth sphere during Florida's rainstorms each year?
A. None
B. 2 tons
C. 16 tons

8. How much does the Spaceship Earth sphere weigh?
A. 1 million pounds
B. 9 million pounds
C. 16 million pounds

9. Spaceship Earth, with its giant Sorcerer Mickey wand, is the tallest attraction on Walt Disney World® Resort property. How tall is it at the highest point?
A. 214 feet
B. 239 feet
C. 256 feet

10. Spaceship Earth was inspired by the geodesic dome designs of architect Buckminster Fuller. For what reason did Fuller design the geodesic dome?
A. To accommodate astronauts on the Moon
B. To reduce greenhouse gases from escaping into the ozone
C. To put an end to poverty with quickly constructed housing

11. Vista Florida Telephone System on the Walt Disney World® Resort property installed the nation's first commercial fiber optic phone cable in which year?
A. 1978
B. 1982
C. 1983

12. How many letters are in the modern day English alphabet?

13. How many letters are in the Greek alphabet?

14. How many letters are in the Hawaiian alphabet?

15. UPS (the shipping company) was founded in 1907 to help customers communicate globally by sending letters and packages quickly. In 2005, how many packages and documents did UPS deliver worldwide?
A. 1.8 billion
B. 3.75 billion
C. 15 billion

16. The United States Postal Service delivers more mail to more addresses than any other postal system in the world.
Approximately how much of the world's cards and letters does the United States Postal Service deliver?
A. 25%
B. 32%
C. 44%

17. In 1860, the Pony Express began as a private enterprise to deliver mail more quickly across the United States. At that time, cross-country mail used to take months to deliver. The fastest delivery time of the Pony Express was President Lincoln's inaugural address which took how long to travel to California from Washington, D.C.?
A. 4 days and 23 hours
B. 7 days and 17 hours
C. 10 days and 1 hour

18. Though Johann Gutenberg is given the credit for inventing the printing press, a printing press with moveable type was actually invented in which country over 400 years before Gutenberg's invention in the 1400s?
A. Egypt
B. Japan
C. China

19. In what year was the first pager designed for consumer use introduced?
A. 1974
B. 1983
C. 1985

20. Which country's government developed the earliest beginnings of the internet in 1969?
A. Japan
B. United States
C. United Kingdom

21. The first public cell phones were tested in Chicago in what year?
A. 1977
B. 1980
C. 1983

Test Track

Overview: The fastest attraction on Walt Disney World® Resort property takes you on an exhilarating ride through a recreation of the proving grounds used for General Motors (GM) vehicles. In your six-passenger test vehicle (two rows of three passengers each), you will experience extreme heat and cold, brake and impact testing and suspension testing on a variety of road surfaces before accelerating to speeds of up to 65 miles per hour as you bank around the Test Track facility.

Thrill Time: 4 ½ minutes

FASTPASS AVAILABLE

Restrictions: Passengers must be at least 40 inches (102 cm) tall. Guests should be in good health and free from high blood pressure, heart, back or neck problems, motion sickness and other conditions that could be aggravated by the ride. Expectant mothers should not ride.

Be Aware of: This attraction closes during inclement weather such as thunder and lightning. The queue line can be extremely loud due to the nature of the demonstrations.

Guests must take a large step down into the vehicle for boarding. The vehicle seats are molded plastic, narrow, and close to the ground and might not accommodate all body types.

Due to the compact nature of the cars, there is no storage area to stow personal belongings. Be sure to secure hats, sunglasses and other items that could fly off as you speed around the open track at 65 mph.

Helpful Hints: If you want to reduce your wait time and don't have a FASTPASS ticket, utilize the singles line. The singles line takes individual guests from the queue line to fill empty single seats in each car. You must be willing to split from your party and possibly ride the attraction at different times (though this is not always the case), but you will save a lot of time by not waiting in the standard queue line.

In the queue line, after you pass the wall across from section 5b that is covered with a variety of street signs, the pre-show boarding area is just around the corner.

The far left and right seats in the front row of the vehicles have a little less leg room because of the wheels.

At the exit of the Test Track attraction you will enter a fun showroom called the Inside Track Discovery Center. This is a great place for members of your party who are not experiencing Test Track to have some fun while waiting for the rest of the party. To access the Inside Track Discovery Center and gift shop from outside of the attraction, take the right-hand path through the FASTPASS kiosks. Inside you will find the newest models of GM vehicles that you are welcome to sit in and take pictures of. There is also the Dreamchasers attraction which is a tour through the creative processes used by GM designers as they create new products. The Dreamchasers attraction does not have a height requirement and can therefore be enjoyed by children who are not able to ride Test Track.

Parent/Guardian Switch option is available.

Disabled Access: Guests must transfer from their wheelchair or motorized scooter to board this attraction and step down into the vehicle. For guests concerned about their ability to board the Test Track vehicles, a Test Track car is located in a private area where guests can practice boarding and unloading. Disney's assistive listening devices interact with this attraction (pre-show and demonstration area). Disney's guest-activated video captioning devices interact with this attraction (pre-show and Dreamchaser). Disney's handheld captioning devices interact with this attraction (pre-show only). Service animals are not permitted on this attraction.

• • • • • • • • • • • • • • • • • • •

👁 **Look for**: In the queue line, look at the white crash test vehicle in section 5b. On the passenger door behind the driver's door, there is an inspection sticker which is signed "Mickey."

☆ **Hidden Mickey Hunt**: Across from section 10a there is a toolbox on your left hand side. The washers on top of the toolbox form a hidden Mickey head.

♀ **Scavenger Hunt**: Find the following items in the indoor queue line:
- A red tool chest
- A wrench
- A calendar dated June 1927
- A "Danger High Voltage" sign
- A car radio
- An X-ray of a wheel
- A baby in a car seat
- A yellow sign with a mama duck and baby ducks
- Crash dummies
- A cracked windshield
- An airbag

Answer the following five questions based on the informational plaques found in the standard queue line.

1. In which section will you find the "Seat Jounce and Squirm" test?

2. The world's first automotive proving ground was created in 1924 in which U.S. city and state?

3. In section 5a, what is the test item number of the V-6 Engine being tested?

4. In which Colorado location does General Motors do some of its brake testing?

5. In section 10a, what type of tire is being tested in the Suspension Test?

6. Approximately how many parts in a car must all work together for the car to run properly?
A. 5,000
B. 15,000
C. 80,000

7. True or False: Each of Test Track's test vehicles have a combined computer processing power that exceeds the computer processing power of the Space Shuttle.

8. The General Motors Corporation and Walt Disney World® Resort have been working together since 1977. General Motors gave away a car every day during what Walt Disney World® Resort celebration?
A. Disney's Tencennial Celebration
B. Disney's 15th Birthday Party Celebration
C. Disney's 25th Anniversary Celebration

9. What was the original name of the division of General Motors Corporation which would go on to be named GMC Truck and then GMC?
A. Rapid Motor Vehicle Company
B. Oakland Motor Car Company
C. Durant-Dort Carriage Company

10. What was the original name of the division of General Motors Corporation which would go on to be named Pontiac?
A. Rapid Motor Vehicle Company
B. Oakland Motor Car Company
C. Old Motor Works

11. When was General Motors Corporation founded?
A. 1897
B. 1908
C. 1931

12. When did the Ford Motor Company produce the Model T Ford, the first car that was affordable for many Americans and revolutionized the way Americans traveled?
A. 1907
B. 1908
C. 1912

13. Find the following General Motors Corporation brands of cars in the word search below: Saturn, Saab, Pontiac, Oldsmobile, Hummer, GMC, Chevrolet, Cadillac and Buick.

```
K A N D V R S T G O F C P S R A
C P B J S U A I H U M M E R C L
W H H E A O T A W P T O B M A F
M L E S A M U L C G O K E H D J
A G B V B L R S D B S N U C I B
U I C J R T N C Y A N W T M L O
O L D S M O B I L E J D R I L A
C S H D P F L W K R G G P N A D
R B U I C K A E T E C M M Y C C
E A A N B O T N T B S C H F I L
```

14. Unscramble the following General Motors Corporation models of vehicles:

TUENRCY   (Hint: It's a Buick)
SCEEALDA   (Hint: It's a Cadillac)
HAEOT   (Hint: It's a Chevrolet)
VYEON   (Hint: It's a GMC)
LHOUTTEESI   (Hint: It's an Oldsmobile)
SNFUEIR   (Hint: It's a Pontiac)
EUV   (Hint: It's a Saturn)

WORLD SHOWCASE

The World Showcase celebrates the culture of 11 countries around the world. The pavilions do not represent one part of a country, but rather a combination of the places and traditions that each country is famous for. All of the pavilions offer the traditional food, merchandise and entertainment that is native to their land, and many of the cast members in each pavilion are natives of that country.

The six country's pavilions with attractions that have queue lines are listed in this portion of the guidebook. The attractions are listed alphabetically by country name.

Canada

O Canada!

Overview: This 360-degree film in a 300-guest theater takes you on a breathtaking journey to famous locations throughout Canada, including Quebec, the Canadian Rockies, Vancouver, Toronto and the Calgary Stampede.

Thrill Time: 17 ½ minutes

Be Aware of: There is absolutely no seating in this theater. Guests are able to lean against rows of metal rails, but you cannot sit on top of the rails or on the floor. Portions of this film might induce feelings of motion sickness in highly susceptible individuals.

Helpful Hints: A digital countdown in the queue area lets you know exactly when the next show will begin. There is very limited bench seating in the queue line of this attraction. Kids will enjoy sitting next to the large picture windows in the queue which overlook the waterfall area.

Standing in the middle of the theater allows you to see all nine screens easily by turning around.

Disabled Access: Guests may remain in their wheelchair or motorized scooter. The disabled queue line is located past Le Cellier restaurant. Disney's assistive listening devices interact with this attraction. Reflective captioning is available.

• • • • • • • • • • • • • • • • • • •

Scavenger Hunt: In the indoor queue line, find: a person wearing a red and black plaid shirt, a lantern, a shovel, a barrel, a pick and a pulley mechanism.

1. Where is Canada located in relation to the United States?
A. To the north of the United States
B. To the south of the United States
C. To the east of the United States

2. In Disney's 2003 animated film *Brother Bear*, which of the following was not the name of a moose who spoke with a Canadian accent?
A. Rutt
B. Koda
C. Tuke

3. Which of the following U.S. states does not share a border with Canada?
A. Minnesota
B. Montana
C. Nebraska

4. How many provinces does Canada have?
A. Four
B. Eight
C. Ten

5. How many territories does Canada have?
A. None
B. Three
C. Four

6. Which of the following Canadian cities has not hosted an Olympic Games?
A. Montreal
B. Calgary
C. Toronto

7. What type of tree leaf is featured on the Canadian flag?
A. Oak
B. Maple
C. Chestnut

8. What is Canada's capital city?
A. Ottawa
B. Quebec City
C. Winnipeg

9. Which Canadian province voted in 1995 on whether or not to break away from Canada (they voted no)?
A. Prince Edward Island
B. Nova Scotia
C. Quebec

10. True or False: Canada is larger than the United States in land size.

11. True or False: The entire population of Canada is less than the population of California.

12. The CN Tower in Canada, used for telecommunications, is the world's tallest tower. In which city is the CN Tower located?
A. Toronto
B. Calgary
C. Vancouver

13. In Canada, what is a Mountie?

A. A type of pastry

B. A member of the Royal Canadian Mounted Police

C. A type of shoe worn in cold climates

14. Find the following Canadian provinces and territories in the word search below: Nova Scotia, New Brunswick, PEI (abbreviated for Prince Edward Island), Newfoundland and Labrador (these will be found as two separate words), Quebec, Ontario, Manitoba, Saskatchewan, Alberta, British Columbia, Yukon, NW Territories and Nunavut.

```
N E W B R U N S W I C K L S C R
B Q M A N I T O B A I L A N O V
M U D Y C Y F O V L K Q B M N A
N E W F O U N D L A N D R Y T L
K B P V W K B N L O S S A M A B
O E T E I O R W Q M Y C D W R E
D C C L I N U N A V U T O B I R
S A S K A T C H E W A N R T O T
Q B R I T I S H C O L U M B I A
N K N W T E R R I T O R I E S A
```

China

Reflections of China

Overview: This 360-degree film in a 300-guest theater that is a replica of China's The Hall of Prayer for Good Harvests takes you on a breathtaking journey to famous locations throughout China, including Beijing, the Great Wall of China, Inner Mongolia, Tiananmen Square, the Yangtze River and Hong Kong.

Thrill Time: 12 ½ minutes

Be Aware of: There is absolutely no seating in this theater. Guests are able to lean against rows of metal rails, but you cannot sit on top of the rails or on the floor. Aerial portions of this film might induce feelings of motion sickness in highly susceptible individuals.

Helpful Hints: A digital countdown in the queue area lets you know exactly when the next show will begin. There is plenty of seating in the queue area. Standing in the middle of the theater allows you to see all nine screens easily by turning around.

Disabled Access: Guests may remain in their wheelchair or motorized scooter. Disney's assistive listening devices interact with this attraction. Reflective captioning is available.

• • • • • • • • • • • • • • • • • • • •

👁 **Look for**: After you pass through the turnstiles of the building, stand in the center of the dome. If you lift your head to the ceiling and talk loudly, you can feel the echo of your words coming back down. Your whispers will also be amplified in this area.

When you are standing in the center of the dome, look at the floor. You will notice a center stone surrounded by many more rows of stones. Each row contains a number of stones that is a multiple of three, a lucky number in China. If you look around the dome you will notice four major red columns which represent the four seasons. Looking upward you will see 12 smaller columns representing the 12 months. The three rows of squares surrounding the dome represent the Earth because the Earth was originally believed to be square. The circular area in the very center of the dome represents Heaven.

🎍 **Scavenger Hunt**: Find a poster of artwork from Disney's *Mulan* and a painting with a waterfall.

Have you ever wanted to talk like someone who lives in China? Here are some simple Mandarin (China's official national language) words to learn so that you can talk like many of the Chinese.

English	Mandarin	Pronunciation
hello	ni hao	nee how
goodbye	zaijian	dsai-jian
my name is ___	wo jiao	waw jyaow
thank you	xiexie	shie-shie
one	yi	ee
two	er	are
three	san	sahn
four	si	suh
five	wu	woo

1. In Disney's 1998 animated film *Mulan*, what is the name of Mulan's dragon sidekick?
A. Eggroll
B. Mushu
C. Khan

2. Which comedian supplied the voice for Mushu in *Mulan*?
A. Eddie Murphy
B. Chris Rock
C. Will Smith

3. When Mulan enters the army to fight the Huns, what masculine name does she change her name to?
A. Ping
B. Manchu
C. Robert

4. When did Hong Kong Disneyland open?
A. November 14, 2004
B. February 20, 2005
C. September 12, 2005

5. How long is the Great Wall of China?
A. 589 miles
B. 3,946 miles
C. 11,678 miles

6. Why was the Great Wall of China built?
A. To protect China from raids by nomadic tribes
B. To keep the Chinese within their own country
C. It was intended to be a symbol of Chinese architecture

7. There are many different languages spoken in China. How many major dialect groups are there in China?
A. 8
B. 12
C. 200

8. The 2008 Olympics will be held in which city in China?
A. Beijing
B. Macau
C. Xi'an

9. What type of fiber is China well known for producing?
A. Wool
B. Cotton
C. Silk

10. What Chinese form of medicine involves tiny needles inserted into strategic points on the skin?

11. What is the name of the Chinese art of arranging your environment in order to change the quality of your life?

12. China is home to the world's third largest river. What is the name of the river?

France

Impressions de France

Overview: This five-screen film transports you to the beautiful vistas and classical images of France, including Paris, the

Riviera, Notre Dame, Versailles and the country's snow capped mountains. The theater has a capacity of 350 guests.

Thrill Time: 18 minutes

Be Aware of: Guests must enter and exit the theater using steep ramps. Aerial portions of this film might induce feelings of motion sickness in highly susceptible individuals.

Helpful Hints: This is a wonderful attraction to visit when it's hot outside or you're exhausted from walking all day. The upholstered seats, mellow music and cool air-conditioning are a welcome respite from the madness of the theme park. Sit towards the back of the theater so that you can easily see all five screens.

Disabled Access: Guests may remain in their wheelchair or motorized scooter. Disney's assistive listening devices interact with this attraction. Reflective captioning is available.

• • • • • • • • • • • • • • • • • • •

℗ Scavenger Hunt: In the indoor queue line, find: a painting of water lilies, candles, a picture of Quasimodo and the gargoyles, a picture of the Notre Dame and a "Spitting Gargoyle."

Have you ever wanted to talk like someone who lives in France? Here are some simple words to learn so that you can speak French.

English	French	Pronunciation
hello	bonjour	bohn-jhoor
goodbye	au revoir	o ruh-vwahr
my name is ___	je m'appelle	jhuh ma-pell
thank you	merci	mair-see
one	un	oon
two	deux	duh
three	trois	twah
four	quatre	kaht-ruh
five	cinq	sank

1. In Disney's 1996 animated film *The Hunchback of Notre Dame*, what is Quasimodo's job in the Notre Dame?
A. He cleans the floors
B. He is the bell ringer
C. He is the minister

2. In *The Hunchback of Notre Dame*, what is the name of the beautiful gypsy girl that Quasimodo meets at the Festival of Fools?
A. Meg
B. Aurora
C. Esmeralda

3. In *The Hunchback of Notre Dame*, why does Quasimodo never leave the Notre Dame?
A. He is embarrassed because of the way he looks
B. He doesn't like people
C. He is under a curse that prevents him from leaving

4. Name two of the talking gargoyles in Disney's film *The Hunchback of Notre Dame* who were named after the author of the classic French novel.

5. In which city is Notre Dame, the beautiful cathedral where Napoleon crowned himself emperor, located?
A. Limoges
B. Paris
C. Marseilles

6. France is very famous for the sweet pastries that can be found throughout the country. Which of the following food items is France not famous for, as well?
A. Cheese
B. Apples
C. Wine

7. What is the name of the river that cuts through the city of Paris?
A. Seine
B. Thames
C. Rhine

8. The Eiffel Tower in the France pavilion was built using Gustave Eiffel's original blueprints of the famous Paris landmark. This tower was built using a forced perspective, which makes it appear farther away than it actually is. To which scale is Epcot's Eiffel Tower compared to Paris' Eiffel Tower?
A. One tenth of scale
B. One twentieth of scale
C. One hundredth of scale

9. Gustave Eiffel designed the structure of what famous American icon that was a gift from the country of France?
A. The Statue of Liberty
B. The Golden Gate Bridge
C. The Washington Monument

10. The celebrity-studded International Film Festival is held in what French city each year?
A. Nice
B. Cannes
C. Lyon

11. France's Disneyland Resort Paris was originally called Euro Disney when it opened. When was the name changed to Disneyland Resort Paris?
A. October 1994
B. June 1996
C. November 1998

12. What was the opening day of Disneyland Resort Paris?
A. October 8, 1990
B. January 1, 1991
C. April 12, 1992

Mexico

El Rio del Tiempo

Overview: Take a relaxing water ride through the history and culture of Mexico as you sail past a Mayan temple under a midnight sky, listen to persistent vendors at an outdoor market, catch an underwater glimpse of Mexico's coastal wonders and watch Audio-Animatronic children dressed in colorful outfits dance and sing under a sky bursting with fireworks. Each of the boat's five rows seats a maximum of three adults.

Thrill Time: 6 ½ minutes

Be Aware of: There is a smoky mist at the beginning of the ride. At the end of the attraction, there are fireworks sounds and the boats sometimes bump together as you are waiting to exit.

Helpful Hints: This attraction is located within the Mexico pavilion which looks like an ancient temple on the outside and contains a festive night time market on the inside. This attraction typically has a short queue line.

Parent/Guardian Switch option is available.

Disabled Access: Guests must transfer from a motorized scooter to a wheelchair that is provided at the attraction. Guests may remain in their wheelchair. The disabled queue line is located at the attraction exit to the left. Disney's handheld captioning devices interact with this attraction.

• • • • • • • • • • • • • • • • • • •

Have you ever wanted to talk like someone who lives in Mexico? Here are some simple words to learn so that you can talk like a Mexico native.

English	Spanish	Pronunciation
hello	hola	oh-lah
goodbye	adios	ah-dyohss
my name is ___	me llamo	may yah-mo
thank you	gracias	grah-see-ahss
one	uno	ooh-noh
two	dos	dohs
three	tres	trayss
four	cuatro	kwah-troh
five	cinco	seen-koh

1. Which of the following is not considered a Mexican food?
A. Guacamole
B. Taco
C. Egg roll

2. Where is Mexico in relation to the United States?
A. To the north of the United States
B. To the south of the United States
C. To the west of the United States

3. What is the name of the famous large hat worn in Mexico that has a very wide brim and is used in the Mexican Hat Dance?

4. Which of the following U.S. states does not share a border with Mexico?
A. New Mexico
B. Texas
C. Louisiana

5. Which Disney animated film had its world premiere in Mexico City in 1944?
A. *The Three Caballeros*
B. *Dumbo*
C. *The Fox and the Hound*

6. What is the translation of the name of this attraction, El Rio del Tiempo?
A. River of Time
B. Wet Ride
C. Mexican Waters

7. What is Mexico's capital city?
A. Mexico City
B. Cozumel
C. Tijuana

8. Which of the following cities in Mexico is not a port that you could sail to on a cruise ship?
A. Guadalajara
B. Cabo San Lucas
C. Ensenada

9. What do the following attractions in Mexico have in common: Tulum, Chichen Itza, and Uxmal?
A. They are all deluxe resort towns
B. They are all cruise ship ports of call
C. They are all famous ruins

10. Mexico is well known for its two ancient civilizations – the Mayans and the Aztecs. Which civilization came first?

11. How many states does Mexico have?
A. None
B. 31
C. 56

Norway

Maelstrom

Overview: Enjoy a seafaring adventure onboard a Viking boat (four rows each seat three adults or a combination of four adults and children) as you journey through the lure and legend of this Scandinavian country.

Thrill Time: 3 ½ minutes

FASTPASS AVAILABLE

Be Aware of: There are portions of the ride when your boat plunges down short drops (you will be facing forwards or backwards for these drops). The attraction is dark and one portion has a bright, strobing light. Trolls and growling polar bears rising up on their hind legs are found in the attraction. You might get splashed with water at some points in the attraction. The boat ride can sometimes be a little rough.

Helpful Hints: For a great view of the Norway pavilion, sit in the back row of the boat. At one point, the boat will travel backwards and guests in the back row will be at the edge of the pavilion's waterfall and can enjoy a unique view of the pavilion.

At the end of the attraction, guests gather in a seaside village area and must wait until the theater doors open before they can exit the attraction. You are permitted to walk through the theater to exit the attraction quickly, however, the five minute film is quite interesting if you have ever wanted to know a little bit more about this seafaring country.

The Viking ship next to the pastry shop is a great place for kids to play while you are waiting on other members of your party who are riding the Maelstrom.

Parent/Guardian Switch option is available.

Disabled Access: Guests should transfer from a motorized scooter before entering the queue line. Guests must transfer from their wheelchair to board this attraction and climb two steps to board the boat. Disney's assistive listening devices interact with this attraction (theater only). Reflective captioning is available (theater only). Disney's handheld captioning devices interact with this attraction (ride only).

• • • • • • • • • • • • • • • • • •

☆ **Hidden Mickey Hunt**: In the mural above the boat loading area, a Viking in the ship with a red and white striped sail on the left side of the mural is wearing Mickey Mouse ears.

⚲ _Scavenger Hunt_: On the "Milestones in Norwegian Exploration" map on the right wall of the queue line, find: a Viking ship, the Northwest Passage, the Atlantic Ocean, the Great Pacific Ocean, Viking routes and a red crest with a lion.

On the mural above the loading area, find: a cruise ship, a lighthouse, polar bears, boys climbing on rocks, a sea monster rising from the water and a green monster rising from the landscape.

Have you ever wanted to talk like someone who lives in Norway? Here are some simple words to learn so that you can talk like a Norwegian.

English	Norwegian	Pronunciation
hello	god dag	goo dagh
goodbye	ha det	hah deh
my name is ___	jeg heter	jai heh-tehr
thank you	takk	takk
one	en	ehn
two	to	too
three	tre	treh
four	fire	fee-reh
five	fem	fehmm

1. What kind of food is Norway famous for?
A. Strawberries
B. Chicken
C. Seafood

2. What is the name of the famous Norwegian folktale in which three goats try to cross a bridge that a mean troll lives under?

3. In Norway's city of Copenhagen there is a famous statue of which character from a Hans Christian Andersen story that inspired one of Disney's animated films?
A. Peter Pan
B. Sleeping Beauty
C. The Little Mermaid

213

4. Where is Norway located?
A. To the south of the United Kingdom
B. To the north of Finland
C. To the west of Sweden

5. What is the capital of Norway?
A. Bergen
B. Oslo
C. Lillehammer

6. Norway is famous for its fjords. What is a fjord?
A. A long, narrow sea inlet bordered by steep cliffs
B. An ancient cave with Viking carvings
C. Large glaciers which average five stories tall

7. Which of the following cities in Norway has not hosted an Olympics?
A. Oslo
B. Bergen
C. Lillehammer

8. Norway is one of five nations where polar bears can primarily be found. Which of the following countries does not have a population of polar bears, as well?
A. United States
B. Poland
C. Greenland

9. Norway is famous for its Viking heritage. Vikings were predominantly farmers and craftsmen that came from Norway and two other northern countries. Which of the following was not a country that Vikings came from?
A. Denmark
B. Sweden
C. Russia

10. What is a Viking boat called?
A. A longship
B. A clippership
C. A schooner

11. When was the Viking age?
A. 3rd century to the 6th century
B. 8th century to the 11th century
C. 17th century to the 19th century

12. When the famous Viking Leif Eriksson discovered North America (he was the first European to land on the continent), what did he call it?
A. Norseland
B. Vinland
C. Vikingland

13. Leif's father, the famous Viking called Erik the Red, was the first European to explore and colonize what other country?
A. Greenland
B. Sweden
C. Iceland

14. Norway has approximately how much of the oil and gas reserves remaining in Europe?
A. 25%
B. 50%
C. 80%

U.S.A.

The American Adventure

Overview: This film and stage show located in an elegant 1,024-seat theater is a trip down memory lane that pays tribute to the people and events that have shaped America since its earliest beginnings. Audio-Animatronic hosts Ben Franklin and Mark Twain narrate recreations of historical moments such as the landing of the Mayflower, women's suffrage, the creation of the National Park System, the Boston Tea Party and the Civil War. Politicians, entertainers, athletes and news makers are all portrayed by a large cast of Audio-Animatronics figures in a stirring tribute to Americana.

Thrill Time: 30 minutes

Be Aware of: Guests must climb stairs or use escalators to enter The American Adventure theater in which there are steep ramps that slope upward and downward to access the seating area. If the ramps or escalators will pose a problem for you, ask a cast member to bring you to the second floor by elevator.

Helpful Hints: Be sure to visit The American Adventure during a time when the Voices of Liberty will be performing in the theater's rotunda. The Voices of Liberty, a much loved tradition in Disney entertainment, is an a cappella group dressed in Colonial costumes who sing patriotic and folk music. Show times are listed in Epcot's "Times Guide." The audience will be asked to move into the center of the rotunda for the best acoustics, and seating will be on the marble floor unless you've secured a bench around the center floor.

This is one of the few attractions where waiting can be a pleasure. Because of the large capacity of the theater, you don't need to hold your place in line unless it's a very crowded day so feel free to wander around or even leave the pavilion and come back just before the next show. An art gallery on the right hand side of the building hosts rotating exhibits and is easily accessible while you are waiting for the next show. There's also seating throughout the spacious, air-conditioned building with plenty of interesting items to look at.

This is a wonderful attraction to visit when it's hot outside or you're exhausted from walking all day. The chance to sit down for half an hour on upholstered seats in a darkened, air-conditioned theater is a welcome respite from the madness of the theme park. Sit closer to the front of the theater to have the best view of the many Audio-Animatronics in the show.

Disabled Access: Guests may remain in their wheelchair or motorized scooter. See a cast member to utilize the elevator to

the theater entrance. Disney's assistive listening devices interact
with this attraction. Reflective captioning is available.

• • • • • • • • • • • • • • • • • • •

👁 **Look For**: Find the painting with a plane that is to your
left as you enter the building. Notice where the nose of the plane is
pointing as you stand on the left side of the painting. Now, walk to
the right of the painting and notice where the plane's nose is
pointed. No matter where you go, the nose of the plane will seem
to be pointing at you in this optical illusion.

In the Ellis Island painting on the wall to the left of the building
entrance, find the little girl with the #3 tag located in the lower
right corner. Keep your eyes on the little girl's eyes and walk back
and forth in front of the painting. Her eyes will seem to follow you
in this optical illusion.

☆ **Hidden Mickey Hunt**: On the first and second floors,
there are large gold carved panels in the alcoves next to the theater
entrance and the alcoves with the escalators. Look in the corners
of each panel to find a Mickey head made of three circles formed
by the gold braiding.

In the Industrial Age painting on the far-right of the wall across
from the building entrance, the rivet holes on top of the column
beam to the left of the man form a hidden Mickey.

In the Frontier painting, second from the right on the wall across
from the building entrance, the black spots behind the cow's front
leg form a hidden Mickey.

In the painting that features school children, on the far right of the
wall to the left of the building entrance, find the little girl with a
red bow in her hair sitting next to the teacher. In the white shadow
of the bow is a hidden Mickey.

In the painting located on the far left of the left wall from the
building entrance, find the woman in the bottom center of the

painting wearing a hat with pink flowers. The flowers form a Hidden Mickey.

In the Space Shuttle painting on the wall across from the building entrance, find the men holding the Space Shuttle plans. The wings of the shuttle on those plans form Mickey ears.

⚲ Scavenger Hunt: On the first floor of The American Adventure, find: golden eagles, the Texas State Flag, a quote by Walter Elias Disney, a copy of the Declaration of Independence, Native Americans burying fish in holes in the ground, a Columbia Shuttle Mission patch and a woman reading a book.

On the second floor of The American Adventure, find: golden eagles, a painting of a lady carrying pink flowers in her dress and "The World's 100 Best Short Stories" collection.

1. The United States of America has how many states?
A. 35
B. 49
C. 50

2. Complete the following phrase: "American as _____ pie."

3. Which figure in The American Adventure is Disney's only Audio-Animatronic figure to walk up stairs?
A. Benjamin Franklin
B. Mark Twain
C. George Washington

4. Approximately how many clay bricks were used in the Colonial mansion which houses The American Adventure?
A. 50,000
B. 110,000
C. 540,000

5. According to Walt Disney, what is America's most important export?
A. Beef
B. Medical supplies
C. Laughter

6. What is the United States' national anthem?
A. "The Star-Spangled Banner"
B. "America the Beautiful"
C. "God Bless America"

7. What is the United States of America's capital city?
A. New York City
B. Philadelphia
C. Washington, D.C.

8. Unscramble the following U.S. states:

INGYOMW   (Hint: Location of Yellowstone National Park)
OIARAZN   (Hint: You can find the Grand Canyon here)
CHIIANGM   (Hint: It's famous for producing automobiles)
SSIIOURM   (Hint: St. Louis is a city in this state)
EDROH NDLIAS   (Hint: It's the smallest state)
AAIICLFORN   (Hint: Location of Yosemite National Park)
GGEOIAR   (Hint: Savannah is a city in this state)

9. Which of the following is not a territory of the United States?
A. Puerto Rico
B. Guam
C. Bermuda

EVERYTHING ELSE

Not every entertaining experience at Epcot involves a queue line. The following attractions and entertainment do not require guests to stand in a queue line and typically do not involve a wait time.

- **Innoventions East** and **Innoventions West** are pavilions housing fun, interactive exhibits about the cutting edge technology of tomorrow. Innoventions provides hours of entertaining experiences, from learning more about a Segway Human Transporter to playing a game of electronic bowling. The exhibits are geared towards all ages, with child friendly exhibits such as the Pizza Game and How to Escape a Burning House to adult friendly exhibits such as the Ultimate Home Theater. With plenty of video games and a boisterous atmosphere inside, Innoventions is not a stuffy learning center but a fun-filled attraction not to be missed at Epcot. Some of the more popular exhibits in Innoventions might have a short wait time.

- **IllumiNations: Reflections of Earth** is the nighttime spectacle at Epcot incorporating fireworks, lasers, fire and fountains. It would be unfair to simply call this a fireworks show as IllumiNations: Reflections of Earth encompasses the entire World Showcase, from the massive Earth globe in the World Showcase Lagoon which displays video images to the country's pavilions outlined in lights against the night sky. The highly popular 13-minute show, with its stirring music and breathtaking pyrotechnics, is a wonderful way to end your day at Epcot. Note: Though guests reserve seating for IllumiNations: Reflections of Earth about an hour before the show, it is not necessary to waste time by reserving seating. The best views will come from the waterfront locations and raised viewing areas, but because the show incorporates so many different elements, guests will still be able to enjoy a majority of the show from any location within the World Showcase that is nearby the lagoon. (Views of the Earth globe and water effects might be blocked by guests standing in front of you, but the fireworks, lasers, lights and fire will still be visible.) Because of the popularity of the show, expect very long lines in exiting the World Showcase afterwards. The quickest exit will be near the Mexico and Canada pavilions, which are also the most crowded viewing areas because everyone else has the same idea. To save your sanity and prevent being run down by a stampede of strollers and tired guests, plan on sitting down for 10-15 minutes and letting the crowds pass or try your hand at the "International Scavenger Hunt" section before trying to exit Epcot.

- Six of the eleven countries in the World Showcase have attractions and are listed in the attractions section. However, the remaining five countries are not to be missed. **Germany** is a quaint pavilion with Bavarian charm and plenty of beer steins; **Italy** displays the refined elegance of the nation with tinkling fountains and stately buildings; **Japan's** beautifully landscaped gardens and unique architecture create plenty of photo opportunities; **Morocco** is a welcoming pavilion with mosaic-laden buildings and small paths leading to rug and basket shops; and the **United Kingdom's** merchandise shops are located in a variety of traditional English buildings along with a hedge garden and small outdoor park.

- **Kidcot Fun Stops** are a fun way for children to learn while exploring the attractions of Epcot. Located in each pavilion of the World Showcase and in several of the major attractions of Future World, these child friendly stations are staffed by cast members who help the child create a craft that represents the attraction or pavilion that they are visiting.

- The **Innoventions Fountain**, the large fountain behind Spaceship Earth, presents a "water ballet" every 15 minutes with synchronized shooting waters against a backdrop of ever changing music.

- **Club Cool** lets guests enjoy free samples of Coca-Cola products from around the world.

- **ImageWorks – The Kodak "What If" Labs** are fun-filled labs that have plenty of computer games and high tech ways to learn about science. There's also a variety of picture taking stations sponsored by Kodak which allow you to play around with digital images or create a personalized Disney portrait or souvenir for purchase. It's a great place for children to be loud and jump around without fear of being reprimanded. Some of the more popular experiences in ImageWorks might have a short wait time.

- The **Mission: SPACE Advanced Training Lab** is a space-themed complex with Space Base, where young children can climb in a playground setting; Postcards from Space, where you can email a digital image of yourself against a space background; Expedition Mars, a computer game in which you explore Mars; and Mission: SPACE Race computer games where you can play individually or against a group of other guests. Some of the more popular games in this Lab might have a short wait time.

INTERNATIONAL SCAVENGER HUNT

Find the following items located in each country's pavilion as you explore the World Showcase or while you are waiting for IllumiNations: Reflections of Earth. All of the items are in open view as you walk through the pavilion and will not be found within the restaurants, shops, or attractions of the pavilion unless otherwise noted. Be sure to check out the bonus items at the end of the list so that you can search for these more challenging items, as well.

Mexico *(Note: This pavilion is located inside the temple building)*
An erupting volcano
A piñata
A fountain
Rugs hanging off of a balcony
A birdcage with a parrot

Norway
A waterfall
A statue of a marathoner
A roof covered in grass
A fireplace
A wooden puffin
A pretzel and crown

China
Fuzzy birds on strings
A sign for the Street of Good Fortune
Carved dragon heads
A large, white carved elephant
A birdcage
A picture of a lotus blossom
Tiny carvings of a Chinese girl and animals

Germany
A knight slaying a dragon
A miniature train

A cluster of grapes
A crest with the symbol of a bear

Italy
A man holding a conch shell
Wine barrels
A golden angel
A soldier standing on top of a beast
A winged lion statue

U.S.A.
A weather vane
A golden eagle
An American flag
An image of Martin Luther King, Jr.

Japan
A waterfall
Large paper lanterns
Gold bells
Fish in a pond
Japanese warriors on horseback
A sign that says "Konnichiwa"

Morocco
Baskets
Mosaic patterns
Rugs
A working water wheel
Plates hung on the side of a building forming a Mickey head
Clay jugs on top of a building

France
Old posters
A heart in scrollwork
A golden book
A court jester in a stone carving
A "4 La Maison du Vin 4" sign
A woman with a paint palette and brushes

United Kingdom

A red telephone booth
A cottage with a thatched roof
A hedge maze
A painted picture of a tea cup and teapot
Toy soldiers
Smoke stacks covered in soot
A "Tudor Lane" sign

Canada

A totem pole
A waterfall
Snow shoes
An axe
Maple leaf cutouts
A red telephone booth
A sign for Canadian National Hotels

Bonus Items

(These items can be found throughout the World Showcase)
Bikes near a canal
A Fleur de Lis created out of plants
A replica of Doges Palace
A replica of a 14th century fortress named Akershus
A replica of a Torii gate like the one found in Hiroshima Bay
A copy of a letter from George Washington to His Majesty
Mohammed III *(This item is found in the lobby of a restaurant that serves couscous)*

GENERAL EPCOT TRIVIA

1. Look at an Epcot guide map to find the following items: *(Note: Guide maps are subject to change)*

- The monorail
- A boat
- The Eiffel Tower
- A fountain
- Planets
- A large strand of DNA
- A Japanese pagoda

What color is in every World Showcase country's flag?

What shape is on Japan's flag?

2. When was the grand opening of Epcot?
A. November 1, 1981
B. October 1, 1982
C. May 5, 1985

3. Who dedicated Epcot on October 24, 1982?
A. Michael Eisner
B. Roy O. Disney
C. E. Cardon Walker

4. On Epcot's opening day, there were only nine country's pavilions located in the World Showcase. Which of the following was an opening day pavilion?
A. Norway
B. Morocco
C. Germany

5. If you walked the entire promenade around the World Showcase Lagoon today, how far did you walk?
A. 1 mile
B. 1.3 miles
C. 1.8 miles

6. During IllumiNations: Reflections of Earth, a 28-foot diameter Earth globe is prominently featured in the show. If you were to fill this globe with Ping-Pong balls, how many do you think it would take?
A. 150,000
B. 1 million
C. 20 million

7. IllumiNations: Reflections of Earth requires how many computers to produce the show?
A. 1
B. 23
C. 67

8. During IllumiNations: Reflections of Earth, the buildings around the World Showcase light up. The amount of lighting that it takes to light up the outlines of these buildings is comparable to stretching the lights approximately how many times across San Francisco's Golden Gate Bridge?
A. 2
B. 6
C. 10

9. Where in Epcot can you find an ale warmer that will heat your beer to 55 degrees?
A. United Kingdom's Rose & Crown Pub & Dining Room
B. Restaurant Marrakesh in Morocco
C. Biergarten in Germany

10. Approximately how many miles of bratwurst are served every day at the Germany pavilion's Biergarten restaurant?
A. 2 miles
B. 10 miles
C. 26 miles

11. Approximately how many hours a year are spent removing dead blooms from the rose gardens in Epcot?
A. 50
B. 400
C. 1,000

12. How large is Epcot?
A. 100 acres
B. 175 acres
C. 300 acres

13. Which one of the following Future World pavilions was not open on Epcot's opening day in 1982?
A. The Living Seas
B. The Land
C. Universe of Energy

14. Which country's pavilion in the World Showcase is the only government sponsored pavilion?
A. Norway
B. Morocco
C. Canada

15. What was the original name of Epcot when it opened in 1982?
A. Epcot Center
B. Innoventions
C. Ep Cot

16. What do the initials in Epcot stand for?

17. On a typical day, approximately how many Walt Disney World® Resort guests use the Monorail system?
A. 25,000
B. 95,000
C. 150,000

18. Approximately how many Cokes are consumed each year at the Walt Disney World® Resort?
A. 20 million
B. 50 million
C. 100 million

19. The Walt Disney World Dolphin Resort, which is located near the International Gateway entrance of Epcot, was designed by which famous architect?
A. Michael Graves
B. Frank Lloyd Wright
C. I.M. Pei

20. The fastest attraction on Walt Disney World® Resort property is located in Epcot. Which attraction is it?

21. Which of the following events is not held at Epcot?
A. International Flower and Garden Festival
B. Grad Nite
C. International Food and Wine Festival

22. How many resorts were open on the Walt Disney World® Resort property when Epcot opened in 1982?
A. 6
B. 8
C. 15

23. What was the estimated cost of Epcot when it opened in 1982?
A. 560 million dollars
B. 1 billion dollars
C. 2 billion dollars

24. True or False: When Epcot first opened, there was no Disney character merchandise for sale within the park.

EPCOT CHAPTER ANSWERS

<u>Future World</u>
Body Wars
1. B **2.** Throat **3.** Calcium **4.** C **5.** B **6.** Away **7.** C **8.** A **9.** C **10.** B

The Circle of Life
1. A **2.** C **3.** B **4.** Reduce; Produce; Reduce; Produce; Produce; Reduce; Reduce **5.** Environmentality **6.** C **7.** C (Over 6 million found from 1996-2000) **8.** B **9.** B **10.** C **11.** A **12.** False – Many countries, including the U.S., ship their trash to other countries or accept other country's trash to put in their landfills

Cranium Command
1. C **2.** B **3.** C **4.** A **5.** Dolphin's - it weighs five pounds **6.** Left; Right; Left **7.** Right **8.** True **9.** False - If this were true, elephants would be smarter than humans because their brain weighs 11 lbs. **10.** Arnold Schwarzenegger

Ellen's Energy Adventure
1. Unplug appliances; turn your DVD player off after watching a movie; limit opening the refrigerator door; turn off your computer at night; turn off lights when you leave a room; wear a sweater when it is cold; recycle; reduce car trips **2.** B **3.** C **4.** C **5.** Calculators, watches, roadside emergency phones, roadside construction barriers with flashing lights, outdoor lighting, nightlights **6.** C **7.** B **8.** C **9.** B **10.** Decline because of environmental issues and relicensing **11.** A **12.** B **13.** A **14.** B **15.** A **16.** Blanket **17.** Refrigerator **18.** Hairdryer **19.** Iron

Honey, I Shrunk the Audience
1. Knowledge **2.** Preview **3.** Junk **5.** A **6.** B **7.** C **8.** C **9.** B **10.** B **11.** C **12.** A **13.** C **14.** B **15.** A **16.** C **17.** C

Journey Into Imagination with Figment
1. B **2.** B **3.** A **4.** C **5.** Lemon, lime, sour candy **7.** Sweet tastebuds are on the tip of your tongue, bitter is on the back, sour is on the

sides and salty are all over **8.** Helen Keller **9.** False **10.** B **11.** C **12.** B **13.** C **14.** C **15.** Men **16.** C **17.** A **18.** B

The Living Seas
1. B **2.** A **3.** A **4.** C **5.** B **6.** B **7.** C **8.** A **9.** Yes **10.** C **11.** C **12.** C **13.** B **14.** Over 326 million trillion gallons **15.** C **16.** See the end of this chapter **17.** A (Captain Nemo and Nemo the fish)

Living with the Land
1. Quilt **2.** Obeying **3.** Difference **4.** A **5.** C **6.** C **7.** Under ground; above ground; above ground; under ground; under ground; above ground **8.** C **9.** C **10.** B **11.** C **12.** C **13.** B **14.** B **15.** B **16.** False - They are technically a fruit **17.** A **18.** Carrot; Lettuce; Avocado; Watermelon; Tangerine; Mushroom; Grape; Tomato; Radish; Blueberry

The Making of Me
1. C **2.** A **3.** B **4.** Pink; Blue **5.** Twins **6.** Triplets **7.** Quadruplets **8.** Quintuplets **9.** Bottle; Diaper; Pacifier; Crib; Rattle; High Chair; Bib; Stroller; Blankie; Booties **10.** B **11.** C

Mission: SPACE
1. 12 **2.** 8.7 mph **3.** Valentina Tereshkova **4.** 2030 **6.** Cold - An average temperature of -85 degrees Fahrenheit **7.** There is no liquid surface water, but there are polar ice caps **9.** March **10.** C **11.** B **12.** A **13.** Smaller - Earth is 7,926 miles in diameter and Mars is 4,222 miles **14.** B **15.** B **16.** B **17.** A **18.** No **19.** B **20.** B **21.** B **22.** C **23.** A **24.** A **25.** Joystick controller - Apollo lunar rover; Invisible braces - Advanced ceramic research; Ski boots with folds - Space suit; Cordless tools - Used for drilling on the moon; Smoke detector - Detect toxic vapors in space station; Ear thermometer - Detect the birth of stars; Bar coding - Track millions of space craft parts; Medical imaging - Produce clear images from spacecraft; TV satellite dish - Correct errors in spacecraft signals **26.** A

Soarin'
1. Peter Pan, Tinkerbell, Buzz Lightyear, Dumbo, Flora, Fauna and Merryweather, the Blue Fairy, Iago, Zazu **2.** Mission: SPACE, The Magic Carpets of Aladdin, Dumbo the Flying Elephant, Peter Pan's Flight, Astro Orbiter, TriceraTop Spin **3.** A **4.** B **5.** B **6.** B **7.**

C **8.** Concorde **9.** C **10.** Orlando, FL - MCO; Baltimore, MD - BWI; Tokyo, Japan - NRT; Atlanta, GA - ATL; Cincinnati, OH - CVG; Fort Myers, FL - RSW; Honolulu, HI - HNL; Knoxville, TN - TYS; Las Vegas, NV - LAS; Los Angeles, CA - LAX; Newark, NJ - EWR; Phoenix, AZ - PHX; San Francisco, CA - SFO; Sydney, Australia - SYD; Manchester, U.K. - MAN; Mexico City, Mexico - MEX **11.** A **12.** B **13.** A **14.** B **15.** A

Spaceship Earth
1. Six **2.** Both represent geographical areas - area code used in phone numbers and zip code used in addresses **3.** B **4.** Hieroglyphics **5.** Alexander Graham Bell **6.** C **7.** A (A specially designed gutter system absorbs and funnels the rain away) **8.** C **9.** C **10.** C **11.** A **12.** 26 **13.** 24 **14.** 12 **15.** B **16.** C **17.** B **18.** C **19.** A **20.** B **21.** A

Test Track
Scavenger Hunt: Calendar is in section 3a; Danger High Voltage sign in 4a; Car radio in blue room; X-ray in 7a; Baby in 3b; Duck sign across from 5b; Windshield on left across from 2b; Airbag in 2b **1.** 11a **2.** Milford, Michigan **3.** #V6-389 **4.** Pike's Peak **5.** Uniroyal Tiger Paw **6.** B **7.** True **8.** B **9.** A **10.** B **11.** B **12.** B **13.** See the end of this chapter. **14.** Century; Escalade; Tahoe; Envoy; Silhouette; Sunfire; Vue

World Showcase
Canada - O Canada!
1. A **2.** B **3.** C **4.** C **5.** B **6.** C **7.** B **8.** A **9.** C **10.** True **11.** True **12.** A **13.** B **14.** See the end of this chapter

China - Reflections of China
1. B **2.** A **3.** A **4.** C **5.** B **6.** A **7.** A **8.** A **9.** C **10.** Acupuncture **11.** Feng Shui **12.** Yangtze

France - Impressions de France
1. B **2.** C **3.** A **4.** Victor and Hugo (The author's name is Victor Hugo) **5.** B **6.** B **7.** A **8.** A **9.** A **10.** B **11.** A **12.** C

Mexico - El Rio del Tiempo
1. C **2.** B **3.** Sombrero **4.** C **5.** A **6.** A **7.** A **8.** A **9.** C **10.** Mayans came first from 300-900 A.D., the Aztecs were from 900-1524. **11.** B

Norway - Maelstrom
Scavenger Hunt: Green monster is in the left side of the mural. **1.** C **2.** *Three Billy Goats Gruff* **3.** C **4.** C **5.** B **6.** A **7.** B **8.** B **9.** C **10.** A **11.** B **12.** B **13.** A **14.** B

U.S.A. - The American Adventure
Scavenger Hunt: Eagles in alcoves by theater entrance; Texas state flag by escalators; Native Americans burying fish in painting immediately to right of entrance; Mission patch in space painting on back wall; Woman reading a book in far right painting on left wall **1.** C **2.** Apple **3.** A **4.** B **5.** C **6.** A **7.** C **8.** Wyoming; Arizona; Michigan; Missouri; Rhode Island; California; Georgia **9.** C

International Scavenger Hunt

Mexico: Birdcage is on the balcony to your right as you enter the pavilion.

Norway: Statue is between bakery and Viking ship; Grass covered roof is on left side of pavilion; Fireplace outside of bakery by Stave Church; Wooden puffin in Puffin's Roost shop sign; Pretzel and crown in bakery sign

China: Street of Good Fortune sign on right wall in courtyard leading to gift shop; White elephant in courtyard leading to gift shop; Birdcage is in the rafters on the right across from the gift shop; Lotus blossom is in café signs; Tiny carvings are on top of some buildings on the corner edge of the roof

Germany: Knight is on top of the statue in the fountain; Train is to the right of the pavilion; Grapes are above the Weinkeller wine store sign; Crest with bear is above the Sommerfest sign

Italy: Man is in the fountain in the back of the pavilion; Golden angel is on top of the large tower; Soldier is on top of the right pillar; Lion statue is on top of the left pillar

U.S.A.: The eagle and Martin Luther King, Jr. images are on The American Adventure attraction signs

Japan: Gold bells are hanging from the pagoda; Japanese warriors along bridge leading to gift shop; Sign on left of bridge

Morocco: Water wheel is near the lagoon; Plates and clay jugs are on the building next to the lagoon

France: Posters are on the circular towers in the pavilion; Heart is above the restaurant; Golden book is in the Librairie sign on the corner of the building; Court jester is above Bistro de Paris upper level near the patisserie; 4 La Maison du Vin 4 is across from the patisserie; Woman with paint palette is in the Plume et Palette sign on the building across from the restaurant

United Kingdom: Cottage is across from the Rose & Crown Pub; Hedge Maze is in the back of the pavilion near the stage; Tea cup is in The Queen's Table sign above the tea shop; Toy soldiers are in the Toy Soldier shop; Tudor Lane sign is near the stage area in back of the pavilion

Canada: Waterfall is on the second level behind the shops; snow shoes and axe are on the Northwest Mercantile shop; Maple leaves on fence; Telephone booth on second level; Canadian National Hotels sign on outside of building on second level

Bonus Items: Bikes on bridge leading from U.K. to France; Fleur de Lis near the bridge from U.K. to France; Doges Palace is the large building on the left side of the Italy pavilion; Akershus is the Norway restaurant; Torii gate is by the lagoon in Japan; Washington letter in lobby of Restaurant Marrakesh in Morocco

General Epcot Trivia
1. Monorail is in Future World area; Boat is in World Showcase Lagoon; Fountain is behind Spaceship Earth; Planets are outside Mission: SPACE; DNA is outside the Wonders of Life pavilion; Red; Circle **2.** B **3.** C **4.** C **5.** B **6.** C **7.** C **8.** B **9.** A **10.** C **11.** B **12.** C **13.** A **14.** B **15.** A **16.** Experimental Prototype Community of Tomorrow **17.** C **18.** B **19.** A **20.** Test Track **21.** B **22.** A **23.** B **24.** True

The Living Seas

```
SNCEWALDPTOGBMAF
KWPMINNOWVINCSCJ
HYOAFSGCTBULRDOR
ABMRCITUNAALASDN
LSTJDOKEGUBHRPWE
IRAUHFLOUNDERPIL
BHNLARIYDSCMBIEA
UCIFMDPSOKWBASSD
TJALGOVEHUAHTFCJ
BETDPBNCATFISHBA
```

Test Track

```
KANDVRSTGOFCPSRA
CPBJSUAIHUMMERCL
WHHEAOTAWPTOBMAF
MLESAMULCGOKEHDJ
AGBVBLRSDBSNUCIB
UICJRTNCYANWTMLO
OLDSMOBILEJDRILA
CSHDPFLWKRGGPNAD
RBUICKAETECMMYCC
EAANBOTNTBSCHFIL
```

O Canada!

```
NEWBRUNSWICKLSCR
BQMANITOBAILANOV
MUDYCYFOVLKQBMNA
NEWFOUNDLANDRYTL
KBPVWKBNLOSSAMAB
OETEIORWQMYCDWRE
DCCLINUNAVUTOBIR
SASKATCHEWANRTOT
QBRITISHCOLUMBIA
NKNWTERRITORIESA
```

235

The Disney-MGM Studios celebrates the excitement and intrigue of show business, from the early days of Hollywood to the popular hits of today. Film, television and the music industry inspired every attraction in the theme park. Whether you watch a Broadway style stage show, get an insider's look at movie making or experience a Hollywood inspired thrill ride, the Disney-MGM Studios will have you feeling like a star!

Guest Information Board Location: The intersection of Hollywood Blvd. (the street that you enter the theme park on) and Sunset Blvd. (the first road on your right which leads to Tower of Terror). A Guests Relations booth is also located here for dining reservations.

Disney-MGM Studios

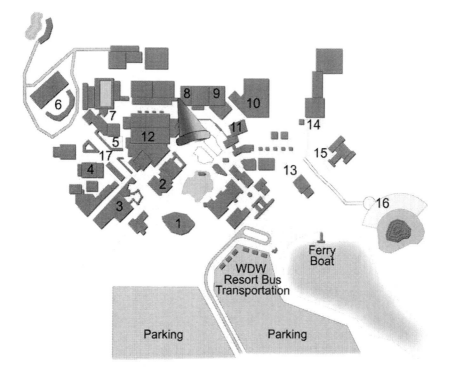

1 Indiana Jones Epic Stunt Spectacular!
2 Sounds Dangerous-Starring Drew Carey
3 Star Tours
4 Muppet *Vision 3-D
5 Honey, I Shrunk the Kids Movie Set Adventure
6 Lights, Motors, Action! Extreme Stunt Show
7 The Disney-MGM Studios Backlot Tour
8 Walt Disney: One Man's Dream
9 Voyage of The Little Mermaid
10 The Magic of Disney Animation
11 Playhouse Disney-Live on Stage!
12 The Great Movie Ride
13 Beauty and the Beast - Live on Stage
14 Rock 'n' Rollercoaster Starring Aerosmith
15 The Twilight Zone Tower of Terror
16 Fantasmic!
17 The Streets of Amercia

Disney-MGM Studios Tips

- Many of the shows at the Disney-MGM Studios are performed at specific times during the day. Look at the Disney-MGM Studios' Times Guide as soon as you enter the park and plan the remainder of your day carefully in order to be able to see all of the shows that you would like.

- Since many of the attractions and shows at the Disney-MGM Studios are located indoors, this theme park is ideal to visit during inclement weather.

- Though at first glance it might not seem that there are as many attractions at the Disney-MGM Studios, the attractions and shows are quite lengthy compared to the attractions in the other theme parks. You won't have to wait in line as often to experience the same amount of thrilling activities as you would at the other Disney theme parks.

ATTRACTIONS

<u>The Disney-MGM Studios Backlot Tour</u>

Overview: Take a 160-passenger tram ride (four adults or a combination of five adults and children in each row) through the backstage areas of Disney-MGM Studios to see props from Disney films as well as experience a fiery mudslide in Catastrophe Canyon. Your Backlot Tour is preceded by a Special Effects Water Tank Show which reveals the secrets of water effects in movie making.

Thrill Time: The Special Effects Water Tank Show is 10 minutes. The Backlot Tour is 16 minutes.

Be Aware of: This attraction closes during inclement weather such as thunder and lightning.

Though this attraction is listed in the guide map as being a 35 minute tour, the actual tour is 16 minutes. After exiting the queue line, you will watch a live 10 minute special effects show before continuing towards the vehicle loading area. You will then likely wait in a smaller queue line before boarding your vehicle. Though the entire experience lasts about 35 minutes, the attraction is not nearly that long.

The Special Effects Water Tank show has loud explosions, gun shots, fire and underwater explosions which can get guests in the front row wet. The Backlot Tour's Catastrophe Canyon segment will shake your vehicle during a simulated flood with explosions and fire.

Steep ramps sloping downward lead from the Special Effects Water Tank show to the queue line for the tram vehicles.

Helpful Hints: Strollers are allowed in the queue line (however, Disney's double strollers are not).

When entering the queue line, there are four rows to choose from. The far left row will lead you to the top row of the viewing area of the Special Effects Water Tank Show. The far right row will lead you to the front row of the viewing area. Guests in the front row might get wet from the special effects, are more exposed to the heat from the fire effects and will have a hard time seeing the television monitors that replay some of the action throughout the show. The far left and far right lanes will give you a better vantage point to see props in the queue line from Disney action films such as *Pearl Harbor*, *The Rock* and *Con Air*. A six minute video on the making of *Pearl Harbor* is shown in the queue line.

The Special Effects Water Tank Show uses volunteers from the queue line. Four volunteers will be chosen, usually from the very front of the queue line unless you talk to a cast member and express interest in being a volunteer. Volunteers will get wet and will be exposed to the water tank effects such as raging waters, gun shots and fiery explosions.

If you're at the front of the queue line when leaving the queue area and entering the Special Effects Water Tank Show, you might be able to skip the show and proceed straight to the tram loading area if you would like. Sometimes guests are allowed to enter the Special Effects Water Tank Show area while the previous guests are still exiting, so it's easy to join the crowd and exit. However, this isn't always possible and the crowd capacity is staggered for a reason. You might be able to skip the show, but you could find yourself simply waiting in line for 10 minutes to board the tram.

In between the Special Effects Water Tank Show and the boarding area for the tram vehicles, there are restrooms and a water fountain. The queue line for boarding the tram is located within a props warehouse with lots of fun things to look at and a video about the making of a Disney film.

When boarding the tram vehicles for the Backlot Tour, it is very important to sit in one of the front two cars of the six-car tram. The tour guide sitting in the front vehicle describes the objects that you are passing when he or she sees it, and if you're in the back of the vehicle it's very frustrating to hear about an object and then see it 30 seconds later.

When entering your row on the tram vehicle, the passengers on the left side of the tram have a good chance of getting wet during the Catastrophe Canyon experience, but they also have better views of the entire tour. Passengers on the right side of the tram will most likely not get wet.

This attraction exits in the American Film Institute Showcase. This intriguing walk through exhibit and gift shop has rotating movie props and costumes from some of your favorite films. It's a great place to meet up with members of your party who choose not to experience this attraction. If you enjoy movie memorabilia, be sure to allow 10-15 minutes to explore the exhibits.

Parent/Guardian Switch option is available.

Disabled Access: Guests using a wheelchair or motorized scooter must stay in the far right lane of the queue line. Guests may remain in their wheelchair. Guests transferring from a wheelchair or motorized scooter must climb three small steps. Disney's handheld captioning devices interact with this attraction. Disney's guest-activated video captioning devices interact with this attraction (Prop Warehouse queue line only).

● ● ● ● ● ● ● ● ● ● ● ● ● ● ● ● ● ● ●

1. Which animated film starred two dogs who share a plate of spaghetti?
A. *All Dogs Go To Heaven*
B. *Fox and the Hound*
C. *Lady and the Tramp*

2. What film featured a set of twins who changed places in order to reunite their parents?
A. *Double Trouble*
B. *The Parent Trap*
C. *Spy Kids*

3. What animated film stars an ogre, a donkey and a princess?
A. *Monsters, Inc.*
B. *Madagascar*
C. *Shrek*

4. In which film does a family have a hilarious adventure on their way to Wally World?
A. *Are We There Yet?*
B. *Rat Race*
C. *National Lampoon's Vacation*

5. What film features five children who win the chance to tour a chocolate factory where strange things start to happen?
A. *Willy Wonka & the Chocolate Factory*
B. *Chocolat*
C. *The Sweet Life*

6. What film stars a Navy S.E.A.L. whose job is to protect five children and a duck?
A. *The Pacifier*
B. *The Million Dollar Duck*
C. *Mr. Nanny*

7. In what film does Nicholas Cage steal the Declaration of Independence to find hidden treasure?
A. *Independence Day*
B. *National Treasure*
C. *Treasure Island*

8. What film stars a teenager who suddenly finds out that she's a princess?
A. *Confessions of a Teenage Drama Queen*
B. *The Princess Diaries*
C. *13 Going On 30*

9. Which movie won the 2005 Academy Award for Best Picture?
A. *The Aviator*
B. *Million Dollar Baby*
C. *Ray*

10. Who has the most Academy Award acting nominations?
A. Meryl Streep
B. Katharine Hepburn
C. Clint Eastwood

11. Which of the following films won at least one of the Academy Award categories that it was nominated for?
A. *Seabiscuit*
B. *The Color Purple*
C. *Dances with Wolves*

12. Who was the youngest actress ever to win an Academy Award for Actress in a leading role?
A. Marlee Matlin
B. Shirley Temple
C. Tatum O'Neal

13. Which of the following films received 14 Academy Award nominations, the highest number a film has ever received?
A. *Titanic*
B. *Gone with the Wind*
C. *Mary Poppins*

14. The following films have all won Academy Awards for Best Picture. Put them in chronological order, from the earliest release to the most recent release date.

- *The English Patient*
- *Shakespeare in Love*
- *Chicago*
- *Forrest Gump*
- *A Beautiful Mind*
- *Gladiator*
- *Titanic*
- *American Beauty*
- *Braveheart*

15. Cross out every other letter of the following words, starting with the second letter of each word, to uncover the names of films

which you might not have realized that the Walt Disney Company helped produce.

GJOWOSD MNOYRANWIQNPG, VDIKELTXNCABM
TBHVE SAIKXPTCH SKEANZSLE
COOPCEKFTJALIQL
PSRGEVTCTZY WAOQMYAKN
SOIPGSNFS
RJAKNFSCOMM
EZVCITTUA
GW.IR. JHAYNSE
CBOYYKOWTPE UAGDLFY
RIEGMJEKMCBVESR TGHKE TSIVTNAMNOS

The Great Movie Ride

Overview: Enjoy a 65-passenger tram ride (12 rows each seat up to five adults) through the evolution of film history as you travel through recreated scenes of movies such as *Mary Poppins*, *Casablanca*, *The Wizard of Oz* and *Raiders of the Lost Ark*. Audio-Animatronics reproduce beloved scenes of a variety of older movies as a real-life tour guide narrates your journey which concludes with a film montage of memorable big screen moments. The attraction is housed in a full scale reproduction of the famous Grauman's Chinese Theatre in Los Angeles.

Thrill Time: 20 ½ minutes

Be Aware of: Many portions of this attraction can be frightening to young children and adults. Gun shots, real fire elements, slithering snakes, and bad guys who hijack your tram for a short period of time can be upsetting. The intense *Alien* scene with its scary noises and heavy smoke effects, as well as the very real looking witch that appears in *The Wizard of Oz* scene, can also be frightening to youngsters.

Helpful Hints: This attraction experiences a heavy increase in guests immediately after the afternoon parade because of its proximity to the parade route.

The best seat location is in the front three rows of the tram vehicle. You won't want to sit anywhere other than the first six rows of the tram vehicle (there are two cars making up the tram vehicle and each has six rows; be sure to only sit in the front car). If the cast member loading the ride tells you to enter lines seven through twelve, politely ask to wait for the next vehicle and request the front rows. You might have to wait another couple of minutes before boarding your vehicle, but the wait will be worth it. Guests sitting in the back rows hear the narration of scenes before actually seeing them and might have trouble seeing the tour guides as they perform.

When you choose a queue line within the Chinese Theater, you're actually choosing which type of show that you will experience. Though the premise of the attraction is the same regardless of which show you see, if you choose the left line you will have a gangster character who will hijack your vehicle after a shoot out in the gangster scene. If you choose the right line, a bandit will hijack your vehicle in the Western scene. If you choose the left line, be especially sure to sit in the front rows of your vehicle. This vehicle will be trailing the bandit vehicle throughout the attraction and guests in the back rows will enter scenes long after they have already started, as well as having a limited view of the witch in *The Wizard of Oz* scene.

Old film trailers are shown in one portion of the queue line.

Parent/Guardian Switch option is available.

Disabled Access: Guests must transfer from a motorized scooter to a wheelchair that is provided at the attraction. Guests may remain in their wheelchair. If you are traveling with a wheelchair you must enter the left hand queue line once inside the Grauman's Chinese Theater building in order to access the disabled ramp. If you transfer from your wheelchair, it will be folded up and put in the front row with you (a tight space for over

20 minutes) unless you request that it be left behind. Disney's assistive listening devices interact with this attraction (pre-show only). Disney's handheld captioning devices interact with this attraction. Guests with service animals should check with a host or hostess at this attraction.

● ● ● ● ● ● ● ● ● ● ● ● ● ● ● ● ● ● ●

☆ *Hidden Mickey Hunt*: Though not a hidden Mickey, there is a hidden Minnie Mouse profile located in the large Hollywood Hills mural behind the vehicle loading area on the far right side above the roof of the gazebo.

♀ *Scavenger Hunt*: If you are in the outside queue line for The Great Movie Ride, some members of your party can go to the courtyard area outside of the entrance of the Chinese Theater to find the following handprints:
- Mickey Mouse
- Donald Duck
- A handprint with a hat and a tie
- C-3PO and R2-D2
- Harrison Ford
- A handprint that says "Happy Birthday Mickey"
- Michael Jackson
- John Travolta

1. What color is the tail of the carousel horse that Julie Andrews rode on in *Mary Poppins*? (The horse is on display in the inside queue line)

Find the answers to the following seven questions in the pre-show film trailers that are shown just before boarding the attraction.

2. In *Alien*, "No one can hear you scream" where?

3. Which actor starred as Ethan Edwards in *The Searchers*?

4. In which film does a character say "Talking pictures are a fad"?

5. "Willing to shoot Captain Rhino" is uttered in which film?

6. Who are the two lead actors in *Mary Poppins*?

7. A transmitter is a "radio for speaking to God" in which film?

8. The song "Ave Maria" is in which Disney animated film?

9. According to a famous song in the Disney film *Mary Poppins*, what helps the medicine go down?
A. A spoonful of sugar
B. A magical word
C. Lollipops and licorice sticks

10. Julie Andrews is the grandmother to Mia in which Disney film series?
A. *Spy Kids*
B. *Harry Potter*
C. *Princess Diaries*

11. What color are Dorothy's famous shoes in *The Wizard of Oz*?
A. Blue
B. Red
C. Yellow

12. What was the name of Dorothy's dog in *The Wizard of Oz*?
A. Toto
B. Tutu
C. Topher

13. In which state is Dorothy's home in *The Wizard of Oz*?
A. Nebraska
B. Kansas
C. Idaho

14. Complete the following famous quote from *Casablanca*: "Here's _____ at you, _____."

15. Which Disney film premiered at Grauman's Chinese Theater, which the façade of The Great Movie Ride is modeled after?
A. *Mary Poppins*
B. *Cinderella*
C. *Snow White and the Seven Dwarves*

16. Which actress starred in the *Alien* movies?
A. Sigourney Weaver
B. Jamie Lee Curtis
C. Andie MacDowell

17. Which famous actor had the starring role in *Singin' in the Rain*?
A. Fred Astaire
B. James Cagney
C. Gene Kelly

18. Who were the lead actor and actress in *Casablanca*?
A. Humphrey Bogart and Ingrid Bergman
B. Fred Astaire and Ginger Rogers
C. Cary Grant and Mary Pickford

19. Who portrayed Dorothy in *The Wizard of Oz*?
A. Debbie Reynolds
B. Elizabeth Taylor
C. Judy Garland

20. During which war did *Casablanca* take place?
A. World War I
B. World War II
C. Spanish-American War

21. True or False: *Casablanca* won the 1943 Academy Award for Best Picture.

Honey, I Shrunk the Kids Movie Set Adventure

Overview: Inspired by the Disney film *Honey, I Shrunk the Kids*, children can experience the world from an ant's perspective in this larger-than-life playground. Towering blades of grass, oversized children's toys and a huge dog nose that snorts will make children feel as if they've been shrunk to the size of an insect.

Thrill Time: Allow an average of 15 minutes.

Be Aware of: This attraction closes during inclement weather. Portions of this attraction are wet because of water effects.

Helpful Hints: This attraction typically doesn't have a queue line. The playground is best experienced by children age 4-10 years old.

Disabled Access: Many portions of this attraction are not accessible to guests with disabilities. Guests should transfer from a motorized scooter to a wheelchair.

● ● ● ● ● ● ● ● ● ● ● ● ● ● ● ● ● ●

Imagine you were the size of an ant. What would be the scariest thing that you see? How could you get from where you are standing to the Studio Catering Company eating area without getting stepped on?

1. Where do ants live?
A. Ant hills
B. Ant towers
C. Ant islands

2. What kind of meal are ants famous for liking?
A. Soup and salad
B. Sushi dinner
C. A picnic

3. Which movie features a worker ant named Z who falls in love with a princess ant named Bala?
A. *A Bug's Life*
B. *Ant Farm*
C. *Antz*

4. Unscramble the following words of items that you might find in a playground:

WGNIS   (Hint: You'll feel like you're flying in the air)
DILSE   (Hint: You'll be headed towards the ground on this)
SSEEWA   (Hint: You need two people to make it work)
NADS XOB   (Hint: You'll need a shovel and pail)
POER DDRELA   (Hint: You can climb up or down)
OUSELYAPH   (Hint: Pretend you have your own home)
RRMYE – OG- NUDRO   (Hint: It spins around in a circle)
NKYOME RASB   (Hint: They're named after an animal)

The Magic of Disney Animation

Overview: The Magic of Disney Animation is a combination of film, animation creation stations and exhibits on past and future Disney animated films. Your journey begins with a film about the basics of Disney animation before you enter a complex with several animation creation stations, including The Sound Stage (where you record your own voice to play with a Disney animated film); Digital Ink and Paint (where you paint animated characters); and You're a Character (where a personality test tells you which Disney animated character you're most like). There is also a meet and greet area with Disney animated characters, as well as the Animation Academy, where guests are instructed how to draw Disney animated characters and then get to keep their artwork afterwards.

251

Thrill Time: Varies. The introductory film is 8 ½ minutes. Allow at least 10 minutes to look around the animation center, much more time if you want to use the animation stations or meet the characters. The Animation Academy is 10 minutes long.

Be Aware of: Though the film has 150 seats, afterwards you must walk through the animation stations where there is limited bench seating.

This attraction typically closes a little earlier than the rest of the park (usually a half an hour or so) and the character meet and greet area closes much earlier than the rest of the theme park (typically around 5 p.m.). Be sure to check your Times Guide for operating hours.

Helpful Hints: If you are not interested in seeing the introductory film, you can skip the queue lines and still enjoy the animation stations. Enter the Animation Gallery gift shop which is to the right of The Magic of Disney Animation attraction entrance and proceed through the open doorway in the back of the shop.

If you choose to view the character animation film, try to sit near the front of the theater so that you can see all of the unique objects that have been placed around the animator's desk.

If you attend the Animation Academy, it's best to be near the front of the queue line so that you are guaranteed an illuminated desk while you are drawing your character. Because there is not enough desk seating for everyone (there are 38 desks but approximately 50 people are allowed in each session), some guests might be given lapboards on which to draw. Though you have the same animation experience either way, it's a lot more fun to draw the characters the way real animators do at an illuminated desk.

Disabled Access: Guests may remain in their wheelchair or motorized scooter. Disney's assistive listening devices interact with this attraction. Reflective captioning is available.

• • • • • • • • • • • • • • • • • • •

♀ **Scavenger Hunt**: In the outside queue line, find concept art (original drawings for a movie) for *Peter Pan*, *The Lion King*, *Hercules*, *Toy Story*, *Bambi* and *101 Dalmatians*.

1. According to the "Character Development" plaque located on the wall in the outdoor queue line, what color was Belle's hair originally going to be in the Disney animated film *Beauty and the Beast*?

2. If you could choose to be one Disney animated character for a day, who would you choose and why?

3. What Disney animated character is a boy made out of wood?
A. Jafar
B. Mushu
C. Pinocchio

4. What Disney animated character has big ears and likes to thump his foot on the ground?
A. Thumper
B. Hopper
C. The Mad Hatter

5. Unscramble the following Disney animated character names:

KNRITE ELBL   (Hint: She can fly through the air)
RCESULHE   (Hint: He's really strong)
MBIAB   (Hint: He's a deer)
WGOMIL   (Hint: He lives in the jungle)
HIPC NAD LAED   (Hint: They always get into trouble)
OOYDW   (Hint: He has a pull string)

6. What are the only words that Pluto has ever spoken in a cartoon?
A. "Feed Me"
B. "Where's Mickey?"
C. "Kiss Me"

7. Which of the following is not true of the Mickey Mouse cartoon "Steamboat Willie" which was released on November 18, 1928?
A. It was the first cartoon with a synchronized soundtrack
B. It was the first Mickey Mouse cartoon released to the public
C. It was the first appearance of Donald Duck

8. Approximately how many individual drawings does it take to make one second of animation in an animated film?
A. 1
B. 8
C. 24

9. What was Daisy Duck's original name when she premiered in the 1937 cartoon "Don Donald"?
A. Donna Duck
B. Daphne Duck
C. Doris Duck

Rock 'n' Roller Coaster Starring Aerosmith

Overview: While touring G-Force Records, you're suddenly invited to a concert by rock legend Aerosmith. The only problem is your private limousine has to navigate Los Angeles traffic to get to the concert on time. What ensues is a thrilling black light effect, night time ride through busy city streets as your 24-seat limo (each car has two rows of two guests each) goes from 0 to 60 miles per hour in 2.8 seconds before whipping you around two loops and a corkscrew on this indoor roller coaster. The vehicles of this gravity defying attraction (you'll experience about four times the force of gravity at takeoff) have five speakers per seat which blast one of five specially recorded Aerosmith songs.

Thrill Time: 1 minute, 15 seconds

FASTPASS AVAILABLE

254

Restrictions: Passengers must be at least 48 inches (122 cm) tall. Guests should be in good health and free from high blood pressure, heart, back or neck problems, motion sickness and other conditions that could be aggravated by the ride. Expectant mothers should not ride.

Be Aware of: There is no place to store loose items within the ride vehicles. The safety restraints of this attraction may not fit all body shapes or sizes. This attraction is very dark and very loud.

Helpful Hints: The outside covered queue area has ceiling fans to help cool guests off.

When you approach the turnstiles in the indoor queue line, the line splits into two queue lines. The right queue line will lead you to the front row of the 1 ½ minute pre-show with Aerosmith.

The front row of the two row vehicles has slightly more leg room.

Parent/Guardian Switch option is available.

Disabled Access: Guests must transfer from a motorized scooter to a wheelchair that is provided at the attraction. Guests must transfer from their wheelchair to board this attraction. Service animals are not permitted on this attraction.

• • • • • • • • • • • • • • • • • • •

Scavenger Hunt: In the indoor queue line, find: a Grateful Dead poster, an eight track player and a Steve Miller Band poster.

1. How tall is the electric guitar in the courtyard of the attraction entrance?
A. 40 feet
B. 50 feet
C. 100 feet

2. Which one of the following performers did not get their start in *The Mickey Mouse Club*?
A. Britney Spears
B. JC Chasez
C. Jessica Simpson

3. Who is the lead singer of Aerosmith?
A. Joe Perry
B. Joey Kramer
C. Steven Tyler

4. In which city was Aerosmith formed in the 1970s?
A. Boston
B. San Francisco
C. Detroit

5. Where is the Rock and Roll Hall of Fame located?
A. Cleveland, OH
B. New York City, NY
C. Los Angeles, CA

6. When was Aerosmith inducted into the Rock and Roll Hall of Fame?
A. They haven't been inducted
B. 1995
C. 2001

7. Unscramble the titles of the following Aerosmith songs:

ZYARC
DDJAE
VIINL' NO ETH DGEE
LKAW SITH YWA
ETWSE ETIOMON
MEADR NO
EDDU (OOSLK KIEL A DYAL)
NGALE

8. Aerosmith didn't have a number one song on the Billboard Hot 100 chart until 1998. With which song for a Disney movie soundtrack did Aerosmith finally have their first number one hit?
A. "I Don't Want to Miss A Thing"
B. "There You'll Be"
C. "True to Your Heart"

9. Match the following songs that reached the number one spot on the Billboard Hot 100 chart with their artist:

"Walk Like an Egyptian"	Guns N' Roses
"Blame It On the Rain"	Tiffany
"What's Love Got to Do With It"	Barry Manilow
"I Will Survive"	Los Del Rio
"Jive Talkin'"	Nelly
"Let Me Love You"	ABBA
"Gettin' Jiggy Wit' It"	OutKast
"Emotions"	Vanilla Ice
"Jessie's Girl"	Mario
"I Think We're Alone Now"	Survivor
"Hey Ya!"	Will Smith
"Macarena"	Milli Vanilli
"Ice Ice Baby"	Rick Springfield
"I Write the Songs"	Christina Aguilera
"Eye of the Tiger"	Gloria Gaynor
"Genie in a Bottle"	Mariah Carey
"Dancing Queen"	Bee Gees
"Hot in Herre"	Tina Turner
"Sweet Child O' Mine"	Bangles

10. Which former *American Idol* finalist got their start as a performer onboard the Disney Cruise Line?
A. Jennifer Hudson
B. Clay Aiken
C. Kimberley Locke

11. Which of the following recording labels is not owned by Disney?
A. Hollywood Records
B. Lyric Street Records
C. Columbia Records

12. Who performed the song "I Love Rock 'n Roll" which topped the Billboard Hot 100 chart in 1982?
A. The Police
B. Joan Jett and The Blackhearts
C. Van Halen

13. What was the first music video ever played on MTV?
A. "Video Killed the Radio Star"
B. "You Better Run"
C. "Thriller"

14. Which male recording artist has had the most number one hits on the Billboard Hot 100 chart since its creation in 1958?
A. Usher
B. Elvis Presley
C. Michael Jackson

15. Which female recording artist has had the most number one hits on the Billboard Hot 100 chart?
A. Mariah Carey
B. Madonna
C. Whitney Houston

16. Which group has had the most number one hits on the Billboard Hot 100 chart?
A. The Supremes
B. The Beatles
C. Boyz II Men

Star Tours

Overview: Journey into the world of *Star Wars* as you board a Starspeeder for a leisurely flight to the moon of Endor, but soon find yourself on a heart pounding adventure through space. Six rooms of flight simulators each bring 40 guests on an exciting *Star Wars Episode IV: A New Hope*-themed flight (five rows each seat eight guests).

Thrill Time: 4 ½ minutes

FASTPASS AVAILABLE

Restrictions: Passengers must be at least 40 inches (102 cm) tall. Guests should be in good health and free from high blood pressure, heart, back or neck problems, motion sickness and other conditions that could be aggravated by the ride. Expectant mothers should not ride.

Be Aware of: This attraction is a very rough simulator ride and can induce motion sickness. There are many bright flashing lights and loud noises during the attraction.

The queue line is an upward inclined ramp. Guests must pass through turnstiles in the standard queue line. Guests must wear a seatbelt during the simulator ride.

Helpful Hints: Star Tours experiences lengthy queue lines immediately after the parade and after the Indiana Jones Epic Stunt Spectacular! and Lights, Motors, Action! Extreme Stunt Show end.

If you would like to experience Star Tours but are concerned about the rough motion simulator ride, it is possible to experience the attraction without simulation. When the attraction has a short wait time, such as towards the end of the night, cast members can turn off the simulator aspect of the attraction in one room so that your party can enjoy the film without the motion. Ask the cast member at the queue line entrance if this option is available.

The roughest ride is in the back of the simulators while the smoothest ride is in the front or middle rows.

Parent/Guardian Switch option is available.

Disabled Access: Guests must transfer from a motorized scooter to a wheelchair that is provided at the attraction. Guests must transfer from their wheelchair to a vehicle seat. Disney's guest-activated video captioning devices interact with this attraction (boarding area only). Service animals are not permitted on this attraction.

• • • • • • • • • • • • • • • • • • •

👁 🎧 **Look and Listen for**: Look upwards to find moving baskets suspended from above. The writing on the side of each basket is the initials and birthdates of Disney Imagineers who created Star Tours. In one of the baskets, you will find a Ken doll dressed like a *Star Wars* character.

There are several announcements broadcast throughout the queue line that have hidden meanings. Listen for Mr. Tom Morrow to be paged. His name was often featured in the attractions of the Magic Kingdom's Tomorrowland as a reference to the future of "Tomorrow."

Listen for Mr. Egroeg Sacul to be paged. The name is George Lucas spelled backwards.

Listen for the page mentioning a vehicle with license plate THX-1138. *THX 1138* was one of George Lucas' earliest films.

⭐ **Hidden Mickey Hunt**: On the moving conveyor belt with the suspended baskets, a metal gear is hanging from the assembly line which looks like an upside down hidden Mickey.

1. Put the following *Star Wars* films in chronological order based on the *Star Wars* storyline: *The Empire Strikes Back, Attack of the Clones, A New Hope, Revenge of the Sith, Return of the Jedi* and *The Phantom Menace.*

2. What was the first *Star Wars* film to be released in theaters?
A. *The Phantom Menace*
B. *A New Hope*
C. *Revenge of the Sith*

3. Which actor portrayed Luke Skywalker in *Star Wars*?
A. Mark Hamill
B. Harrison Ford
C. Dean Stockwell

4. Who is Han Solo's co-pilot?

5. In *Star Wars*, what is the name of the Jedi master?
A. Yoda
B. Jar Jar
C. Tatooine

6. What color is the blade of Darth Vader's light saber?
A. Black
B. Silver
C. Red

7. In the *Star Wars* movies, what is the Death Star?
A. A star which is about to explode
B. A space station
C. An evil cosmic force

8. Find the following *Star Wars* characters and locations in the word search below: Count Dooku, Lando, Dagobah, Coruscant, Watto, Gragra, Mos Espa, sand people and storm troopers.

```
S T O R M T R O O P E R S N C L
L A P C Z M H K F W B N G A O F
W J N V E D A G O B A H I C U D
K A H D R C P W T S W V E B N I
L U T X P N X M O S E S P A T G
A D B T W E G U K E P J M K D N
N C F K O C O R U S C A N T O E
D H A I R O T P L D F S G R O H
O G R A G R A M L H B Y A C K J
W G E L F S D J T E A U I W U D
```

9. What is the name of Han Solo's starship?
A. *Millennium Falcon*
B. *Bespin*
C. *Tantive IV*

10. What is Jabba the Hutt's profession?
A. Crime lord
B. Jedi trainer
C. Moisture farmer

11. Which actress portrayed the role of Padme Amidala in the *Star Wars* films?
A. Carrie Fisher
B. Scarlett Johansson
C. Natalie Portman

12. Which actor supplies the voice of Darth Vader?

13. What is the name of the forest dwellers that live on the moon of Endor?

14. What is the name of the secret ice world Rebel Alliance base in *Star Wars V: The Empire Strikes Back*?
A. Hoth
B. Naboo
C. Felucia

15. Which droid was given the mission of finding Obi-Wan Kenobi in *Star Wars IV: A New Hope*?

16. What was the home planet of Princess Leia Organa in *Star Wars IV: A New Hope*?

17. True or False: Luke Skywalker is Princess Leia's cousin.

18. In which *Star Wars* film did Luke Skywalker learn that Darth Vader was his father?
A. *A New Hope*
B. *The Empire Strikes Back*
C. *Return of the Jedi*

19. Frank Oz, who supplies the voice of Yoda in the *Star Wars* films, supplied the voice of Fungus in which Disney animated film?

20. What was the first feature film produced by Lucasfilm Ltd., George Lucas' production company?

A. *Raiders of the Lost Ark*

B. *Star Wars IV: A New Hope*

C. *American Graffiti*

21. George Lucas, the creator of *Star Wars*, has been collaborating with the Walt Disney Company for many years. What was the name of the 3-D film starring Michael Jackson which ran at Epcot from 1986-1994 for which Lucas was Executive Producer?

A. Magic Journeys

B. Captain Eo

C. Space Voyage

The Twilight Zone Tower of Terror

Overview: According to legend, five guests of the Hollywood Tower Hotel mysteriously vanished in an elevator in 1939 when the hotel was struck by a bolt of lightning. It seems that the old service elevators in the hotel still haven't been fixed, so the 21 guests (three rows of four people each and three rows of three people each) that board the two elevators should brace themselves for a 13 story, gravity-defying drop. Guests never know how many times they will be dropped toward the ground, either, thanks to a random drop sequence.

Thrill Time: 3 minutes

FASTPASS AVAILABLE

Restrictions: Passengers must be at least 40 inches (102 cm) tall. Guests should be in good health and free from high blood pressure, heart, back or neck problems, motion sickness and other conditions that could be aggravated by the ride. Expectant mothers should not ride.

Be Aware of: Portions of this attraction are very dark. Needless to say, anyone with a fear of heights should not experience this attraction. Unless you are seated in the first row, you will have to climb up to three stairs to reach your seat. There is no place to stash loose items within the ride vehicles.

Helpful Hints: The queue line of this attraction has some ledges to sit on while you wait.

Once you've reached the covered patio area of the hotel building, you just need to turn the corner before you've entered the indoor queue and the pre-show area.

There are two rooms for the 1 ½ minute pre-show film featuring Rod Serling, the host of *The Twilight Zone*. If you are shown into the far right room, the room's exit will be in the far left corner as you enter. If you are shown into the far left room, the room's exit will be in the far right corner as you enter. By being one of the first to exit the room, you will shorten the amount of time you must stand in line before boarding an elevator.

Be sure to secure all loose items that you are carrying before entering the elevator, including baseball caps, tickets that you are carrying in your shirt pocket, etc. Because of the nature of the ride, loose items will be suspended in air before you know it.

If you want to prepare yourself before the first drop, notice when you feel a temperature change. For instance, after your elevator moves through the room with the visual special effects, it will come to a stop and you will see a bright green light. At this point, you will probably feel a temperature change (such as the air being suddenly warmer) because your elevator is in the dropping position on the outside of the hotel and you're no longer in a temperature controlled environment. Expect a drop within a few seconds after you notice the temperature difference.

Parent/Guardian Switch option available.

Disabled Access: Guests must transfer from a motorized scooter to a wheelchair that is provided at the attraction. Guests must transfer from their wheelchair to a vehicle seat. Disney's guest-activated video captioning devices interact with this attraction (pre-show only). Service animals are not permitted on this attraction.

• • • • • • • • • • • • • • • • • • •

👁 *Look For*: After passing through the turnstiles, there will be a directory board on the wall in front of you to your left. At the bottom of the case, fallen letters spell out "Evil Tower U R Doomed."

If you are shown into the pre-show room to the left, look at the shelves on the wall across from the entrance. Laying flat on a shelf is a piece of sheet music with the word Mickey in the title.

☆ *Hidden Mickey Hunt*: In the queue line between the pre-show and boarding area, gears on the brick wall to your right before the queue line splits form a hidden Mickey directly under the fire.

⚲ *Scavenger Hunt*: Find an HTH monogram in the queue line. In the indoor queue line, find an old hat covered in dust and wire rimmed glasses on a desk.

1. According to plaques on the hotel building, when was the Hollywood Tower Hotel established?

2. What is a lightning bug?
A. A bug which only comes out after a lightning storm
B. A bug which lights up
C. A sensor which can detect where lightning will strike

3. How many hotels on Disney property can you name?

4. Which Disney hotel has a geyser which erupts?

5. The Hollywood Tower Hotel isn't the only hotel on Disney property that was inspired by California. Which Walt Disney World® Resort property was based, in part, on the famous Hotel Del Coronado in California?
A. The Grand Floridian Resort and Spa
B. Coronado Springs
C. The Beach Club

6. If you had the time to spend one night in each room of all of the hotels and resorts located on Walt Disney World® Resort property, how long would it take you?
A. Approximately 27 years
B. Approximately 50 years
C. Approximately 72 years

7. Which group recorded the famous song "Love in an Elevator"?
A. Kiss
B. The Beatles
C. Aerosmith

8. Who is credited for discovering the law of gravity as he sat under an apple tree and watched an apple fall to the ground?
A. Galileo
B. Sir Isaac Newton
C. Benjamin Franklin

9. Who did experiments with electricity in 1752 using lightning, a kite and a metal key?
A. Thomas Edison
B. Benjamin Franklin
C. Jonas Salk

10. What part of the world is famous for people mysteriously disappearing when they enter it?
A. Jamaica Flats
B. Bermuda Triangle
C. Bahamas Circle

11. In what year was the first safety elevator (an elevator that wouldn't fall back down the shaft) invented?
A. 1852
B. 1896
C. 1921

12. What is the average chance of being struck by lightning in any given year?
A. 1 in 240,000
B. 1 in 700,000
C. 1 in 1,000,000

13. Approximately how many thunderstorms occur worldwide at any given moment?
A. 12
B. 567
C. 1,800

14. The average lightning flash would light a 100 watt light bulb for how many months?
A. 1
B. 3
C. 12

15. Did you know that you are now standing in an area that receives the most lightning in the United States? What nickname has been given to central Florida because it leads the nation in lightning deaths and injuries each year?
A. Electric Row
B. Lightning Alley
C. Lightning Central

16. In which year did The Eagles' famous song "Hotel California" debut?
A. 1965
B. 1971
C. 1977

17. Fill in the blank of this famous quote from the opening sequence of *The Twilight Zone*: "You open this door with the key of _____. Beyond it is another dimension…a dimension

of sound...a dimension of _____...a dimension of
mind...you're moving into a land of both shadow and
_____...of things and _____...you've just crossed over
into the Twilight Zone."

18. When did *The Twilight Zone* first air?
A. 1959
B. 1964
C. 1969

Walt Disney: One Man's Dream

Overview: This walk through exhibit is an intriguing look
into the life of Walt Disney and how he created the Disney empire.
A collection of Walt's personal items (brought out from the Walt
Disney Company Archives for the first time), along with theme
park concept models and video and sound clips, illustrate the
struggles and triumphs the Disney family shared while starting
their animation businesses, creating Mickey Mouse and designing
Disney's theme parks. At the end of the exhibit is a 400-seat
theater which shows an inspiring film, narrated by Walt Disney
himself, detailing the struggles that he encountered in his career.

Thrill Time: Allow at least 10-15 minutes to quickly walk
through the attraction, much more time if you want to read the
various displays. The movie is 16 minutes long.

Be Aware of: There is no seating throughout the exhibit
area.

Helpful Hints: There is typically not a queue line at this
attraction. This attraction exits by the Magic of Disney Animation
attraction.

You do not have to watch the video at the end of the exhibit hall.
If you choose to skip the film, re-enter the exhibit area and exit
through the double pink doors that are in the 1950s timeline area.

Disabled Access: Guests may remain in their wheelchair or motorized scooter. Reflective captioning is available. Disney's handheld captioning devices interact with this attraction.

● ● ● ● ● ● ● ● ● ● ● ● ● ● ● ● ● ●

1. Did Walt Disney have a mustache?

2. What was Walt Disney's favorite meal?
A. Hot dogs and french fries
B. Spaghetti and marinara sauce
C. Chili and beans

3. When was Walt Disney born?
A. January 12, 1900
B. December 5, 1901
C. April 16, 1903

4. In which city was Walt Disney born?
A. Chicago, IL
B. Marceline, MO
C. Hollywood, CA

5. How did Walt Disney and his wife, Lillian, meet?
A. On a blind date
B. They attended school together in Marceline
C. She worked for him in the ink and paint department

6. Where did Walt Disney come up with the idea of Mickey Mouse?
A. In his animation studios
B. On a train ride from New York City
C. One of his fans sent him the idea

7. Where did Walt graduate from college?
A. He didn't attend college
B. Notre Dame University
C. University of California, Berkeley

8. Why did Walt Disney want to build Disneyland?
A. He thought it would be the best way to make a fortune
B. He had a contract with a movie studio to create a theme park
C. To create a clean entertainment place for the whole family

9. How did Walt Disney finance most of his early ventures in animation?
A. His wealthy family loaned him the money
B. He constantly mortgaged everything he owned
C. The federal government gave him a loan to develop cartoons

10. When Walt Disney died on December 15, 1966, which Disney family member took over the design and creation of the Walt Disney World® Resort?
A. His brother, Roy O. Disney
B. His wife, Lillian Disney
C. His daughter, Sharon Disney

SHOWS

<u>Beauty and the Beast - Live on Stage</u>

Overview: The Disney animated classic film _Beauty and the Beast_ comes to life in the 1,900-seat Theater of the Stars. Memorable moments from the film are reenacted in colorful scenes with human and costumed characters. The musical spectacular culminates in the extravagant ballroom scene where Belle, dressed in her shimmering gold dress, dances with the newly transformed Beast.

Thrill Time: 24 minutes

Be Aware of: Though this theater is covered, it is not air-conditioned. Guests must walk up ramps to enter the theater.

Seating for this show is on long metal benches with back rests. To access most of the seating, you will have to climb steps. If you cannot climb steps, ask a cast member to be seated in the disabled section, but you must arrive early because seating in this section is very limited.

During the Beast attack scenes, there are a few loud noises and young children could be scared by the violence of the Beast being attacked.

Helpful Hints: Consult your Times Guide for performance times. The theater opens 30 minutes before show time. If you arrive before the theater opens, you will probably see a line forming along the sidewalk. You do not necessarily have to be in line to enter the theater - crowds of people can file in the large entry area from either side of the street. Another entrance which is sometimes used is in the alleyway on the right side of the theater next to the Carthay Circle Shop and stroller parking. You will have to climb steps at this entrance.

For a quicker and easier exit after the show, sit in the back of the theater. The views are still good, and you won't waste time by waiting for nearly 2,000 people to climb up the stairs and exit.

Musical entertainment starts about 10 minutes before the show. After the show ends, many guests will exit the theater and immediately get in line for Tower of Terror or Rock 'n' Roller Coaster, creating much longer queue lines for these attractions. It's better to have a FASTPASS time scheduled to enjoy these attractions after the show.

Disabled Access: Guests may remain in their wheelchair or motorized scooter. (Helpful Hint: Disabled seating is located in the very front and very back of the theater. Though you may be tempted to utilize the ramps to get to the front of the theater for front row views, the walk back up the steep ramps is tiring. The seating in the back of the theater allows a good view of the show and a much easier and quicker exit.) Disney's assistive listening devices interact with this attraction. Disney's handheld captioning devices interact with this attraction.

• • • • • • • • • • • • • • • • • •

♀ **Scavenger Hunt**: Outside the entrance of the top of the theater, you will find a variety of handprints cast in cement which were created when celebrities visited the Disney-MGM Studios. Find the following handprints:

- One of the stars of *Wheel of Fortune*
- Gilligan
- Two of the stars of *Cheers*
- Tim Conway
- Florence Henderson
- Meshack Taylor
- The host of *Let's Make a Deal*
- The host of *Jeopardy*

1. How many blocks can you count in the arches on the stage?

2. According to the song "Gaston" in the Disney animated film *Beauty and the Beast*, Gaston eats how many dozen eggs a day to be roughly the size of a barge?
A. Three
B. Four
C. Five

3. Why is the small teacup character in *Beauty and the Beast* named Chip?
A. Because there is a tiny chip in the teacup
B. Because it was the mother teapot's favorite name
C. Because the teacup was used to store potato chips

4. What type of kitchen object is Mrs. Potts?

5. What type of household object is Lumiere?

6. What type of household object is Cogsworth?

7. Which former cast member of the television series *M*A*S*H* provided the voice of Cogsworth in *Beauty and the Beast*?
A. David Ogden Stiers
B. Alan Alda
C. McLean Stevenson

8. What *Law & Order* cast member provided the voice of Lumiere in *Beauty and the Beast*?
A. Sam Waterston
B. Jerry Orbach
C. Kelsey Grammer

9. In the *Beauty and the Beast* song "Belle," Belle sings of a little town, full of little people, waking up to say what?
A. Bonjour
B. Hello
C. Good Morning

10. Which two famous singers provided the voice for the pop version of the song "Beauty and the Beast"?
A. Celine Dion and Phil Collins
B. Bette Midler and Peabo Bryson
C. Celine Dion and Peabo Bryson

11. Which popular television and stage actress who also starred in Disney's *Bedknobs and Broomsticks* supplied the voice of Mrs. Potts?
A. Angela Lansbury
B. Betty White
C. Sandy Duncan

12. In Disney's *Beauty and the Beast*, why was the prince transformed into a beast?
A. It was a test to see if people would still like him
B. He wouldn't give an old woman shelter from the cold
C. A family curse caused every male to turn into an animal

13. *Beauty and the Beast* was the first animated feature nominated for an Academy Award for Best Picture in 1991. Did it win?

14. Which song from *Beauty and the Beast* won an Academy Award for Best Song?
A. "Be Our Guest"
B. "Beauty and the Beast"
C. "Something There"

15. In *Beauty and the Beast*, the Beast can't turn back into a human again unless he learns to love and be loved. He must learn this, though, before the last petal drops off of what type of flower that is kept under a glass dome?
A. Daisy
B. Orchid
C. Rose

16. Approximately how many roses can guests see on Walt Disney World® Resort property?
A. 5,000
B. 11,000
C. 13,000

Fantasmic!

Overview: In this spectacular combination of fireworks, dancing waters, lasers and a host of special effects, 7,000 guests enter the dream world of Mickey Mouse and soon witness an entertaining battle between good and evil. Classic Disney characters and film clips delight the audience before evil Disney villains such as Maleficent steal the show and unsuccessfully try to turn Mickey's positive energy into evil.

Thrill Time: 27 minutes

Be Aware of: The theater is located outdoors and is uncovered. This attraction closes during inclement weather such as thunder and lightning.

There are many appearances of Disney villains at the end of the show, such as Maleficent who transforms into a 40-foot tall dragon, as well as a larger-than-life snake. The moat surrounding the island will burst into flames during one portion of the show. Gunshots, fire, loud noises and many bright, flashing lights could frighten small children.

Because of the use of water screens, guests sitting in the front rows are likely to experience heavy misting water. Even guests in the back rows could feel a slight mist of water throughout the show. There is heavy smoke at the end of the show from the pyrotechnic display.

The seating for Fantasmic! is on long metal benches without back rests. To access most of the seating, you will have to climb shallow steps. If you cannot climb steps, ask a cast member to be seated in the disabled section, but you must arrive early because seating in this section is very limited.

Helpful Hints: Consult your Times Guide for performance times. Fantasmic! is extremely popular and even though the theater has a large capacity, guests who do not arrive early enough to claim a seat can be turned away. Ideally, you should arrive at least 60 minutes before the show begins to claim a seat, although seating is opened 90 minutes before show time.

Though the performance can be easily seen from any seat, the best seating is in the center section. Many guests attending the last performance of Beauty and the Beast - Live on Stage will immediately enter the Fantasmic! theater afterwards to secure seating. Be sure to arrive in the theater before the show ends to avoid the large crowd.

Though the theater is non-smoking, smoking is allowed in the courtyard area.

If you do not want to waste time by arriving at the Fantasmic! theater early to secure a seat, reserve a Fantasmic! dinner package available through Disney's dining reservations hotline or at Guest Services. For a set price, guests can enjoy a meal at the Hollywood Brown Derby, Hollywood and Vine or Mama Melrose's Ristorante and be guaranteed seating for Fantasmic!, however, the seating is in the far right section of the theater.

Restrooms, souvenir stands and a food service counter (hot dogs and drinks) are available within the theater. Be sure to bring a jacket or blanket to protect yourself from the cooler temperatures of this nighttime, waterfront show.

Guests exit the amphitheater the same way that they entered. There is only one exit for thousands of people, so the only way to avoid enormous crowds is to sit in the top rows of the center and right hand sections and exit immediately after the show. Otherwise, it might be wise to sit still within the theater at the end of the show and let the crowds subside. If Fantasmic! lets out after the Disney-MGM Studios has closed, everyone will be exiting the theme park at once so prepare yourself for lengthy waits in line for Disney transportation and trams to the parking lot. To pass the time, you might want to visit the shops along Sunset Boulevard which stay open later.

Disabled Access: Guests may remain in their wheelchair or motorized scooter and should stay to the right of the standard queue. Disney's assistive listening devices interact with this attraction. Reflective captioning is available.

• • • • • • • • • • • • • • • • • • •

1. What is a frightening dream called?

2. What Disney villain terrorizes the Three Little Pigs?

3. What Disney villain is a grasshopper?

4. What Disney villain loves fur coats and doesn't like dogs?

5. What Disney villain is a snake who serves as an advisor to a thumb-sucking prince?

6. What Disney villain is an evil boy who likes to tear apart toys?

7. What pair of Disney villains were sent to murder Hercules?

8. Is the Disney villain Maleficent in *Sleeping Beauty* a witch or a fairy?

9. Find the following Disney villains in the word search below: Frollo, Hades, Gaston, Captain Hook, Jafar, Maleficent, Ratcliffe, Ratigan, Scar, Stromboli and Ursula.

```
H P A F S T R O M B O L I F M J
U A J R H D O A M S H D A I A D
F L D C A P T A I N H O O K L M
R R I E L T R N M B O L T O E R
M A O G S T C G D P C G T C F I
C T S L K C S L U R S U L A I E
U I E T L F A H I J B I A J C F
H G A S T O N R P F D L N D E M
G A K B N Q C M J A F A R E N H
F N O A L D E A I K F E B G T C
```

10. Approximately how many gallons of water are in the moat surrounding the Fantasmic! island?
A. 900,000
B. 1.9 million
C. 5 million

11. Approximately how many gallons of water are sprayed each minute to create the three mist screens for the Fantasmic! show?
A. 20,000
B. 50,000
C. 80,000

12. The last time Walt Disney supplied the voice of Mickey Mouse in an animated feature was for which 1947 film?
A. *Fun and Fancy Free*
B. *Fantasia*
C. *Melody Time*

13. When was the first Mickey Mouse watch sold?
A. 1928
B. 1933
C. 1953

14. What is the name of Mickey Mouse's nephews?
A. He doesn't have any nephews
B. Rooney and Riley
C. Ferdy and Morty

15. Fantasmic! features Sorcerer Mickey who first appeared in the Disney animated film *Fantasia*. Though the film was comprised of many different animated shorts, the most memorable short was when Mickey Mouse borrowed the Sorcerer's hat to practice magic. When Mickey uses his newfound magical skills to make brooms with buckets of water dance, what happens?
A. The brooms clean Mickey's house
B. The buckets of water create a flood
C. The brooms take control of the village

16. True or False: *Fantasia* was the first time that Mickey Mouse appeared in a feature film.

17. In *Fantasia*, the Sorcerer's name is Yen Sid. Do you know what is significant about this name?

18. In *Fantasia*, Amilcare Ponchielli's "Dance of the Hours" is the background music for an animated short featuring what type of animals dancing in ballerina's tutus?
A. Hippos
B. Elephants
C. Cats

19. In *Fantasia*, the evil villain Chernabog loses his powers when he is exposed to what?
A. Daylight
B. Water
C. Kindness

20. When was *Fantasia* released?
A. 1938
B. 1940
C. 1949

21. *Fantasia* debuted in only 14 theaters because the film used a special stereo system created by the Disney Studios. What was the special system called?
A. DisneyDefinition
B. Animation Amplified
C. Fantasound

22. *Fantasia* premiered at The Broadway Theater (formerly The Colony Theatre) in New York. Which other famous Mickey Mouse cartoon was also released at The Broadway?
A. "Steamboat Willie"
B. "Mickey's Circus"
C. "The Klondike Kid"

23. What is Fantasia Gardens, which is located in the Walt Disney World® Resort?
A. A miniature golf course
B. A garden used primarily for weddings
C. A garden which grows vegetables for WDW Resort restaurants

24. A dream about falling typically indicates that you are experiencing what in life?
A. A loss of control or anxiety
B. Feelings of grandeur
C. Loneliness

25. If you have a dream about your teeth falling out, which of the following reasons is probably not the cause of your dream?
A. You feel unattractive
B. You are embarrassed of a situation
C. You frequently talk too much

Indiana Jones Epic Stunt Spectacular!

Overview: This behind the scenes look of how stunts are performed for motion picture films is inspired by the Indiana Jones film *Raiders of the Lost Ark*, with elements from the famous film and stunt doubles for Indiana and Marion. The theater seats 2,000 guests who experience a show-within-a-show as Indiana and Marion film action packed scenes and then stop to explain how fight scenes, gun chases and fiery explosions are all carefully choreographed and rehearsed to create realistic drama.

Thrill Time: 30 minutes

FASTPASS AVAILABLE

Be Aware of: This attraction closes during inclement weather such as thunder and lightning.

Seating for this show is on long metal benches with back rests. To access most of the seating, you will have to climb steps. If you cannot climb steps, ask a cast member to be seated in the disabled section, but you must arrive early because seating in this section is very limited.

Though this theater is covered, it is not air-conditioned. However, large fans throughout the theater usually keep the temperature comfortable.

The volume level of this attraction is very loud! No matter where you sit, the deafening sound track, combined with loud gun shots and explosions, will have you wishing there was a volume control. You will be able to feel the heat from the fire elements, and the closer you are to the stage area, the hotter it will be.

Helpful Hints: Consult your Times Guide for performance times.

It's easy to see the action from most seats in the theater because of the show's large props and the action which takes place at a considerable distance from the theater seating. However, arrive as early as possible to sit in the center of the theater close to the stage for the best views of the production crew who are as interesting to watch as the show. For easier exiting after the show, though, sit towards the back of the theater in either corner.

Before the show begins, extras are picked from the audience to be a part of the action. A casting director will come out about 10-15 minutes before show time to select audience members. If you would like to be an extra, you must be very enthusiastic. Sitting near the front helps in being selected, but it is not necessary. The casting director will ask for people who can either scream, laugh, or hold a pose which you will then be expected to do in front of an audience of 2,000 people before going to costuming and becoming part of the street scenes in the show.

At the end of the show, guests can sometimes have their picture taken with the actors who will be available at stage level.

Disabled Access: Guests may remain in their wheelchair or motorized scooter. Disney's assistive listening devices interact with this attraction.

• • • • • • • • • • • • • • • • • • •

🔊 **Listen For**: Music from the soundtracks of the Indiana Jones films are played in the theater before the show.

🔍 **Scavenger Hunt**: In the queue line, find: a shovel, a box labeled "Skeletal Remains," a blue ladle with white specks and clay jugs.

1. Indiana Jones is an archaeologist. What do archaeologists study?
A. The life and culture of ancient civilizations
B. The history and origin of the planet Earth
C. The science of living organisms, such as animals and plants

2. Indiana Jones is famous for battling his enemies with what?
A. A bullwhip
B. An antique dagger
C. A rifle

3. Indiana Jones hates snakes. What is the only continent that doesn't have snakes?
A. Asia
B. Africa
C. Antarctica

4. Which actor has portrayed Indiana Jones in the three Indiana Jones films?
A. Pierce Brosnan
B. Sean Connery
C. Harrison Ford

5. In which other Disney-MGM Studios attraction can you find a recreation of a scene from *Raiders of the Lost Ark*?
A. Star Tours
B. The Disney-MGM Studios Backlot Tour
C. The Great Movie Ride

6. Put the following Indiana Jones films in chronological order, from the earliest release to the most recent release date: *Indiana Jones and the Temple of Doom*, *Indiana Jones and the Last Crusade*, *Raiders of the Lost Ark*

7. Who directed all three of the Indiana Jones movies?
A. Steven Spielberg
B. George Lucas
C. Francis Ford Coppola

8. Steven Spielberg's wife, Kate Capshaw, appeared as Willie Scott in which Indiana Jones film?
A. *Raiders of the Lost Ark*
B. *Indiana Jones and the Temple of Doom*
C. *Indiana Jones and the Last Crusade*

9. What was originally going to be Indiana's last name before it was changed to Jones?
A. Walker
B. Smith
C. Utah

10. Which actor, now famous for his television role as a detective in Hawaii, was originally chosen to play the part of Indiana Jones?
A. Tom Selleck
B. Jack Lord
C. Roger Moore

11. Which of the following is not something that Indiana Jones is asked to find in the three Indiana Jones movies?
A. Ark of the Covenant
B. Magic stones
C. The Shroud of Turin

12. In *Indiana Jones and the Last Crusade*, Jones is searching for the Holy Grail. What 2003 bestselling book by Dan Brown also tells an exciting tale of the hunt for the Holy Grail?
A. *The Lovely Bones*
B. *The Da Vinci Code*
C. *Angels & Demons*

13. What is the importance of the Holy Grail?
A. It's believed to be the cup Christ drank from at the Last Supper
B. It's believed to contain secrets of the Egyptian pyramids
C. It's believed to be a cup that King Arthur drank from

14. What is the Ark of the Covenant, which Indiana Jones searches for in *Raiders of the Lost Ark*?
A. Another name for Noah's Ark
B. A wooden box that housed the Ten Commandments
C. The original hand written copy of the Koran

15. Unscramble the names of the following films which Harrison Ford starred in:

RAI RCOFE NOE
TRITOAP MAESG
TSNSEIW
GDRANREIG NRYEH
HTE IIVFETUG
IAABRSN
TWAH EILS NEEBHAT
RAST SWAR
MNAACIRE IAGRITFF
ETH SCOIRF IKD

Lights, Motors, Action! Extreme Stunt Show

Overview: This high action vehicle stunt show demonstrates how special effects are created in motion picture films with an emphasis on how cars, motorcycles and jet skis are modified to create heart pounding action. The show features a cast shooting an adventure film in the south of France who frequently stop to explain to the stadium of 5,000 guests how the special effects are carefully choreographed and rehearsed to create realistic drama.

Thrill Time: 32 ½ minutes

FASTPASS AVAILABLE

Be Aware of: This attraction closes during inclement weather such as heavy rain as well as thunder and lightning.

This attraction is very loud with lots of screeching tires, revving engines and gunshots. There are fire elements in the show and a stunt man in a protective suit is set on fire.

Seating for this show is on long metal benches without back rests. The front rows of the seating area could be splashed by water. To access most of the seating, you will have to climb steps. If you cannot climb steps, ask a cast member as you enter the queue line area to be seated in the disabled section, but you must arrive early because seating in this section is very limited.

Helpful Hints: Consult your Times Guide for performance times.

Restrooms are located on the lower level of the stadium. Be sure to watch the large screen in the middle of the set for trivia questions relating to cars and action-adventure films.

A volunteer from the audience is chosen during the show to drive a large remote controlled vehicle. The volunteer is generally picked from the lower center seating area.

Disabled Access: Guests may remain in their wheelchair or motorized scooter. Disney's assistive listening devices interact with this attraction.

• • • • • • • • • • • • • • • • • • •

Scavenger Hunt: In the movie set area, find: laundry on a clothesline, a bicycle, a cheese shop, the Tres Sportif store, a patisserie and the Earffel Tower.

1. If you put a hat on the Earffel Tower, the Disney-MGM Studios' water tower which can be seen beyond the stadium, what size would it be?
A. 128 ½
B. 289
C. 342 ¾

2. What 1980s television series featured a modified car named KITT which was customized with artificial intelligence and the ability to talk?
A. *MacGyver*
B. *Knight Rider*
C. *Miami Vice*

3. Which 1950s leather jacket-wearing television character was famous for driving a motorcycle?
A. Jack Tripper from *Three's Company*
B. Fonzie from *Happy Days*
C. Mork from *Mork and Mindy*

4. What television series featured two "good ol' boys" who routinely engaged in high speed car chases in the "General Lee"?
A. *The Dukes of Hazzard*
B. *Bosom Buddies*
C. *Cagney and Lacey*

5. In which film does Nicholas Cage star as a car thief who steals 50 cars, resulting in some amazing car chase scenes?
A. *Con Air*
B. *Face/Off*
C. *Gone in Sixty Seconds*

6. Which 1968 film stars Steve McQueen as a cop who is involved in a famous chase scene featuring Ford Mustangs?
A. *Bullitt*
B. *Smokey and the Bandit*
C. *The Getaway*

7. Which 1998 Robert De Niro film revolves around the retrieval of a suitcase and features spectacular car chase scenes?
A. *The Score*
B. *Ronin*
C. *Cop Land*

8. Which 2001 Vin Diesel film tells the fast action story of street racing gangs?
A. *The Fast and the Furious*
B. *Catch Me If You Can*
C. *The Italian Job*

9. Which 1977-1983 television series featured Ponch and Jon, two California Highway Patrol motorcycle officers?
A. *Street Hawk*
B. *CHiPS*
C. *Greatest American Hero*

10. Which television show chronicles the lives of Paul Senior and Paul Junior as they create custom motorcycles?
A. *Monster Garage*
B. *American Chopper*
C. *The O.C.*

11. At the Bobby Ore Motion Picture Stunt Driving School, movie stars, law enforcement officials and everyone else can get instruction in how to safely drive during exciting car chases. Where is this school located?
A. Washington, D.C.
B. New York City, NY
C. San Bernardino, CA

12. Lights, Motors, Action! originally debuted at the Walt Disney Studios theme park in Paris. When did the Walt Disney Studios theme park open?
A. April 1, 2001
B. March 16, 2002
C. September 12, 2003

Muppet*Vision 3-D

Overview: This funny film has the same type of antics and jokes of *The Muppet Show* television series combined with 3-D special effects. In the Muppet labs, Dr. Bunsen Honeydew and Beaker introduce the world to Waldo, the "Spirit of 3-D," who soon wrecks havoc on the Muppet's theatrical production. With Audio-Animatronics, a live character appearance, a ceiling full of fireworks and lots of special effects, the 580 guests in the theater feel as if they are truly part of a Muppets production gone awry.

Thrill Time: 15 minutes

Be Aware of: The pre-show area can get very crowded as hundreds of people enter the tiny room. Guests must wear 3-D glasses for the best experience of the show. Misting water and bubbles are elements of the show, as well as a few loud explosions.

Helpful Hints: A 15-minute pre-show film will keep you entertained before entering the theater. From the pre-show area, the doors on the far left will lead guests to the front of the theater and the far right doors lead to the back of the theater.

This is an attraction where you don't want to be at the front of the line heading into the theater. The best seats are in the center and left portions of the rows, but the first people to enter the theater must move to the far right of the rows. Try to sit in the center or the front of the theater for the best views of the Audio-Animatronics and the live appearance of the Muppet character Sweetums. Children who might be bothered by the 3-D effects can still enjoy the attraction without wearing the 3-D glasses.

Occasionally, Kermit or Miss Piggy will have character appearances in an area near the exit of the theater. Contact a cast member for a times schedule of their appearances.

Disabled Access: Guests may remain in their wheelchair or motorized scooter. Disney's assistive listening devices interact with this attraction. Reflective captioning is available. Disney's guest-activated video captioning devices interact with this attraction (pre-show only).

• • • • • • • • • • • • • • • • • • • •

👁 **Look For**: At the turnstile when you enter the Muppets building, there is a Security window to your right with a sign that says "Back in 5 minutes. Key under mat." If you pick up the rubber mat, there is a key embedded in the floor.

To the left of the turnstiles, look at the board with menu options, etc. There are some funny items on the board, including the cost of pea soup which is $2.95, but the cost to eat no soup is $3.95.

In the pre-show area, look for a rope net hanging from the ceiling which is full of what looks like gelatin cubes. It supposedly is a tribute to the Disney Mouseketeer Annette Funicello (if you say "a net full of Jell-O" really fast it sounds like "Annette Funicello").

☆ **Hidden Mickey Hunt**: From the outdoor queue line, look at the fountain just outside of the attraction entrance. Gonzo is standing on a flotation device which resembles Mickey Mouse.

In the outdoor queue line, there is a hidden Mickey on the "5 Reasons to Return Muppet*Vision 3D Glasses" poster to the left of reason number two. You'll have to be in an extremely long line in order to see this hidden Mickey while waiting in the queue.

🔍 **Scavenger Hunt**: In the pre-show area, find:
- A trunk of Miss Piggy's evening gowns
- Barrels of pickled herring
- A barrel of banana puree
- A crate with rubber toast and non-dairy cream pies
- Suitcases
- A drum
- A crate of emergency tuxedos for the Emperor Penguins

1. Which Muppet often gets hit with rotten tomatoes?
A. Fozzie the Bear
B. Pepe
C. Beaker

2. Which Muppet has a very bad temper?
A. Miss Piggy
B. Fozzie the Bear
C. Bean Bunny

3. Which Muppet used to be a tadpole?
A. Animal
B. Gonzo
C. Kermit

4. What type of animal is Gonzo?
A. A turkey
B. An anteater
C. No one knows

5. What type of animal is Rizzo?
A. Rat
B. Shrimp
C. Penguin

6. What are the names of the grumpy old men who sit in a theater box and heckle the Muppets?
A. Statler and Waldorf
B. Siskel and Ebert
C. Ropert and Rupert

7. Which of the following was the first movie that the Muppets starred in?
A. *The Muppet Movie*
B. *The Great Muppet Caper*
C. *The Muppets Take Manhattan*

8. Did you know that the characters on *Sesame Street* were created by Jim Henson, too? Unscramble the names of these famous residents of *Sesame Street*:

GBI RDBI   (Hint: He's yellow)
ERBT NAD NREEI   (Hint: They're friends)
CROSA EHT OUGHRC   (Hint: He's grumpy)
ICEKOO STREMON   (Hint: He likes sweets)
OEML   (Hint: He's red)
VERRGO   (Hint: He's a cute monster)
EZO   (Hint: She likes to dance)
UNOCT OVN CNTOU   (Hint: He likes to count)

9. In which year did the Walt Disney Company sign an agreement
with The Jim Henson Company to buy the Muppets?
A. 1999
B. 2001
C. 2004

Playhouse Disney - Live on Stage!

Overview: With lots of dancing, singing and bubbles floating
through the air, this stage show in a 600-guest theater is like a rock
concert for preschoolers. Your child's favorite characters from
Disney Channel shows such as *JoJo's Circus*, *The Book of Pooh*,
Stanley and *Bear in the Big Blue House* make appearances (Bear is
the only full size character - the rest are puppets rising from the
stage) as Tutter learns lessons in friendship as he tries to find the
courage to dance.

Thrill Time: 21 minutes

Be Aware of: This show is best appreciated by guests
traveling with preschool children.

There are no seats in this theater as families are encouraged to sit
together on the carpeted floor and occasionally get up and dance.
A few seats are available in the far right and left corners of the
theater, but they are far from the stage and can only accommodate
a couple families. There are flashing lights throughout the show.

Helpful Hints: Consult your Times Guide for performance times.

This is a great attraction for young kids who are tired of behaving and can't sit still any longer. Children are encouraged to scream, dance and wave their arms in the air. Try to sit close to the stage for the best views and interaction.

Disabled Access: Guests may remain in their wheelchair or motorized scooter. Disney's assistive listening devices interact with this attraction. Disney's handheld captioning devices interact with this attraction.

• • • • • • • • • • • • • • • • • •

Look For: In the large mural painted on the outside wall of the theater building, find Piglet, a big bear and a goldfish.

1. Playhouse Disney–Live on Stage! is a show about friendship. Name two of your friends.

2. In this show, Tutter tries to find the courage to dance. Show your friends and family your favorite way to dance.

3. What color are Pip and Pop from *Bear in the Big Blue House*?
A. Purple
B. Red
C. Blue

4. What is Bear from *Bear in the Big Blue House* famous for saying?
A. "T.T.F.N.!"
B. "Cha Cha Cha"
C. "Howdy, Partner!"

5. What does Bear from *Bear in the Big Blue House* love to do?
A. Eat
B. Sleep
C. Dance

6. What kind of animal is Treelo in *Bear in the Big Blue House*?
A. Lemur
B. Tiger
C. Ostrich

7. What is the name of Stanley's fish in the Disney Channel show *Stanley*?
A. David
B. Joey
C. Dennis

8. What kind of fish is in Stanley's fish bowl?
A. Goldfish
B. Jellyfish
C. Clown fish

9. Stanley and his fish like to learn about the animal kingdom by jumping into the *Great Big Book of Everything* and discovering fun facts about animals. If you could jump into the *Great Big Book of Everything*, which animal would you want to learn about?

10. In the television show *JoJo's Circus,* JoJo is a young clown who lives in Circus Town. What are some of the things that you might find at a circus? What kind of animals perform in a circus?

11. What is the name of JoJo's pet lion in *JoJo's Circus*?
A. Tiger
B. Oscar
C. Goliath

12. Have you ever watched *JoJo's Circus*? If you have, you know that JoJo likes to move around a lot. If you want to be like JoJo, try some of the following activities while you are standing in line (just make sure you don't hurt anyone around you!):

- Jump in place
- Stretch towards the sky
- Touch your toes
- Pretend you are juggling like a clown
- Pretend you are climbing steps

13. Who are Winnie the Pooh's friends in *The Book of Pooh*?

14. Which one of Winnie the Pooh's friends has a bow on his tail?
A. Eeyore
B. Tigger
C. Piglet

Sounds Dangerous – Starring Drew Carey

Overview: Follow the antics of Drew Carey as he portrays a TV show detective on an undercover assignment. When Drew puts the camera in his mouth, the 240-guest audience is plunged into darkness but they still hear every sound Drew makes as he tries to track down the criminals.

Thrill Time: 10 ½ minutes

Be Aware of: You must wear headphones to experience this attraction. The sound effects, such as buzzing bees and knives being thrown, are very loud and can be frightening. You will be misted with water.

This attraction has more than seven minutes of total darkness with loud sound effects. Though you can take off your headphones to escape the sound, you won't be able to see anything in the theater for an extended period of time, so exiting with a frightened child could be very difficult.

Helpful Hints: This is a great attraction to visit when you're tired and just want to sit down on an upholstered chair in a cool environment and rest your eyes. Because the theater is completely dark, no one will notice if you take a cat nap!

Video monitors in the queue line show trivia questions relating to ABC television shows. The queue lines to this attraction are longest after the parade and after each Indiana Jones Epic Stunt Spectacular! show which exits near this attraction entrance.

At the attraction exit, there is a lab where guests can play with sound effects. It's the perfect place for families to wait while other members of their party enjoy the show. Enter the lab to the left of the Golden Age Souvenirs shop at the attraction exit.

Parent/Guardian Switch option is available.

Disabled Access: Guests may remain in their wheelchair or motorized scooter. Disney's assistive listening devices interact with this attraction. Disney's handheld captioning devices interact with this attraction.

● ● ● ● ● ● ● ● ● ● ● ● ● ● ● ● ● ● ●

1. Sound is one of our five senses. What are the other four senses?

2. Find the following sounds in the word search below: bang, crash, buzz, hiss, beep, squeal, splat, creak, screech, howl, crunch and gurgle.

```
S E N H M A C J F R G I M S V C
M C G C L U G U R G L E B C B U
S I R N C H S I M P A N H N U E
B C M E M B P C O C E R S E Z L
S H C H E S E R H R Z C I M Z H
P B R D R C T E L U B A N G C R
L P A N B W H A P N F S P B A O
A C S E K C L K N C M N H O W L
T U H I S S S U I H Q A M R H F
A H M R F H N E S C S Q U E A L
```

3. If someone has lost their ability to hear sound and is considered deaf, how do they usually communicate with other people?
A. Braille
B. Sign language
C. Morse code

4. Drew Carey is known for wearing which distinctive accessory?
A. A diamond earring
B. Thick eyeglasses
C. Braces

5. In the television show *The Drew Carey Show*, what is the name of the character portrayed by Kathy Kinney who wears outrageous outfits and lots of blue eyeshadow?
A. Mimi Bobeck
B. Kellie Newmark
C. Kate O'Brien

6. Which of the following actors worked with Drew Carey on both *The Drew Carey Show* and *Whose Line Is It Anyway?*
A. Wayne Brady
B. Ryan Stiles
C. Colin Mochrie

7. In which city does *The Drew Carey Show* take place?
A. Memphis
B. Detroit
C. Cleveland

8. Put the following sounds in order from the least noisy to the noisiest according to decibel level:

- An airplane taking off
- Noisy squeeze toys
- A leaf blower
- A shotgun
- An ambulance siren
- A toilet flush
- Heavy traffic
- A balloon pop
- A telephone ring
- A stadium football game

9. When an aircraft breaks the sound barrier and flies faster than the speed of sound, what is the resulting sound called?
A. Sound blast
B. Cosmic crack
C. Sonic boom

10. Who was the first man to break the sound barrier?
A. Chuck Yeager
B. John Glenn
C. Alan Shepard

Voyage of The Little Mermaid

Overview: Puppeteers, live characters and a montage of film clips bring the story of the Disney animated film *The Little Mermaid* to life in this black light show. Brilliantly colored puppets and mesmerizing lighting effects will make you feel as if you've joined Ariel in her underwater world as you watch recreated scenes from the Disney film in the 400-guest theater.

Thrill Time: 15 ½ minutes

FASTPASS AVAILABLE

Be Aware of: The show is filled with bright, strobing lights and many laser effects. Because of the lighting effects, the theater is very dark. Expect to be misted with water.

The scene where Ariel gives up her voice to Ursula is very intense and could easily frighten small children because of the loud noises, flashing lights, and a 12-foot high Ursula that towers over Ariel.

Helpful Hints: Unlike other attractions, FASTPASS at this attraction is only valid for a ten minute time span. Be sure to look at the time frame that your ticket tells you to return to the show.

Expect longer queue lines for Voyage of the Little Mermaid immediately after a Playhouse Disney–Live on Stage! show exits.

In the indoor waiting area immediately before entering the theater, the doors to your left will lead to the back rows of the theater and the doors to your right will lead you to the very front rows. Because of the elevated stage, the better seats are in the middle to the rear of the theater.

Parent/Guardian Switch option is available.

Disabled Access: Guests may remain in their wheelchair or motorized scooter. Disney's assistive listening devices interact with this attraction. Reflective captioning is available.

• • • • • • • • • • • • • • • • • •

Scavenger Hunt: In the outside queue line, find pictures of Scuttle, Ursula, Flounder, Ariel and a French chef, as well as fish in the shrubbery.

In the indoor waiting area, find a starfish, a life preserver, an old diving suit, "Tinkerbell's Prison," a fuzzy fish and the typewriter that wrote *Old Man and the Sea*.

1. On what stage number is Voyage of The Little Mermaid located?

2. What kind of animal is Sebastian in Disney's *The Little Mermaid*?
A. Turtle
B. Shrimp
C. Crab

3. What color is Flounder in Disney's *The Little Mermaid*?
A. Orange and black
B. Yellow and blue
C. Red and white

4. In *The Little Mermaid* song "Under the Sea," Sebastian sings that the seaweed is always greener in somebody else's what?
A. Lake
B. Pond
C. Sea

5. In Disney's *The Little Mermaid*, what was Sebastian's job before King Triton told him to watch after Ariel?
A. Chef
B. Composer
C. King Triton's personal assistant

6. Which one of the following was not the name of one of Ursula's eels in Disney's *The Little Mermaid*?
A. Flotsam
B. Jetsam
C. Shellam

7. Which comedian was the voice of Scuttle in Disney's *The Little Mermaid*?
A. Buddy Hackett
B. Rodney Dangerfield
C. Gilbert Gottfried

8. What is the name of the 1984 film which featured Daryl Hannah as a mermaid who fell in love with Tom Hanks?
A. *Something's Fishy*
B. *The Human Fish*
C. *Splash*

9. Which marine animal was often mistaken for a mermaid by many early sailors, including Christopher Columbus?
A. Seahorse
B. Dolphin
C. Manatee

10. Disney's *The Little Mermaid* is based on a story written by which famous author?
A. Hans Christian Anderson
B. Shakespeare
C. Lewis Carroll

11. Which former Miss America and *Entertainment Tonight* reporter once portrayed Ariel in The Voyage of The Little Mermaid?
A. Leanza Cornett
B. Ericka Dunlap
C. Maria Menounos

12. Which famous filmmaker is known for his documentaries of life under the sea?
A. James Cameron
B. John Audubon
C. Jacques Cousteau

13. Which beloved Florida attraction has "live" mermaids that perform a show underwater?
A. Weeki Wachee Springs
B. Marineland
C. Fountain of Youth

EVERYTHING ELSE

Not every entertaining experience in the Disney-MGM Studios involves a queue line. The following attractions and entertainment do not require guests to stand in a queue line and typically do not involve a wait time.

- Much of the Disney-MGM Studios is modeled after **Hollywood's golden era** and many of the buildings and facades are patterned after structures that could once be found in southern California. The theme park's Hollywood Boulevard has a vintage feel while Sunset Boulevard is considered an old-time theater district. Be sure to look for the unique architecture and décor as you are walking through Disney-MGM Studios.

- Walking through the old-fashioned neighborhoods of the **Streets of America**, located near the Lights, Motors Action! Extreme Stunt Show, is like walking on a deserted studio backlot, with sound effects and plenty of authentic details against a backdrop of famous architecture.

- The **Disney Stars and Motor Cars Parade** is an old-fashioned motorcade of some of Disney's most beloved characters driving in uniquely decorated cars. See "Helpful Hints and Tips on Surviving Disney Queue Lines" for parade viewing information or enjoy the "Disney Entertainment Trivia" or "General Disney-MGM Studios Trivia" while you're waiting.

DISNEY ENTERTAINMENT TRIVIA

1. The Disney Channel show *Lizzie McGuire* stars which young celebrity who is also a movie actress and a recording artist?
A. Anne Hathaway
B. Hilary Duff
C. Ashley Simpson

2. Which Disney Channel show features a teenager from the year 2121 who has to adapt to life in this century?
A. *The Proud Family*
B. *Phil of the Future*
C. *Even Stevens*

3. What Disney Channel show features a high school girl who saves the world from evil villains?
A. *Kim Possible*
B. *That's So Raven*
C. *The Buzz on Maggie*

4. Match the following Academy Award winning songs with the Disney film that they appeared in:

"When You Wish Upon a Star"	*Song of the South*
"A Whole New World"	*Tarzan*
"Colors of the Wind"	*Mary Poppins*
"Can You Feel the Love Tonight"	*Pocahontas*
"Under the Sea"	*Dick Tracy*
"If I Didn't Have You"	*Aladdin*
"You'll Be in My Heart"	*Monsters, Inc.*
"Zip-a-Dee-Doo-Dah"	*Pinocchio*
"Sooner or Later"	*The Lion King*
"Chim Chim Cher-ee"	*The Little Mermaid*

5. Lindsay Lohan made her film debut in which Disney film?
A. *Freaky Friday*
B. *The Parent Trap*
C. *Confessions of a Teenage Drama Queen*

6. The Walt Disney Company acquired which major television network in 1996?
A. ABC
B. CBS
C. NBC

7. Which former *The Cosby Show* cast member and star of a Disney Channel show has a record deal with Hollywood Records, whose parent company is the Walt Disney Company?
A. Raven Symone
B. Phylicia Rashad
C. Malcolm-Jamal Warner

8. Which of the following cable television networks does the Walt Disney Company not own an interest in?
A. Lifetime
B. Nickelodeon
C. The History Channel

9. What was the first film produced by Touchstone Pictures, which was created by the Walt Disney Company in order to release adult movies, in 1984?
A. *Splash*
B. *Ghostbusters*
C. *Footloose*

10. Who are the "nine old men" in Disney history?
A. The nine executives who designed Disneyland
B. The nine songwriters who created Disney film soundtracks
C. Walt Disney's key animators from the 1950s

11. Which performer on the television show *Whose Line is it Anyway?* was a character performer at the Walt Disney World® Resort?
A. Drew Carey
B. Wayne Brady
C. Ryan Stiles

12. Which of the following performers was not a part of *The Mickey Mouse Club* before becoming a pop singing sensation?
A. Christina Aguilera
B. Justin Timberlake
C. Nick Lachey

13. Which of the following television shows is not produced by Touchstone Television, which is owned by the Walt Disney Company?
A. *Alias*
B. *Desperate Housewives*
C. *The Amazing Race*

14. Walt Disney has been nominated for and won the most Academy Awards of anyone in history. How many Oscars did he win?
A. 20
B. 26
C. 35

15. Which Disney animated film was the first to be primarily animated at the Walt Disney Feature Animation Florida studios which was located at the Disney-MGM Studios?
A. *The Little Mermaid*
B. *Tarzan*
C. *Mulan*

GENERAL DISNEY-MGM STUDIOS TRIVIA

1. Look at a Disney-MGM Studios guide map to find the following items: *(Note: Guide maps are subject to change)*

- A Kermit face on a hot air balloon
- A dinosaur
- Tiny Coca-Cola bottles
- A boat
- A guitar
- A dragon
- Ariel
- A fountain
- A green army truck
- An airplane

2. On what day did the Disney-MGM Studios open?
A. June 7, 1987
B. May 1, 1989
C. October 1, 1989

3. What was the price of an adult, one day passport ticket into a Walt Disney World® Resort theme park in 1989 when the Disney-MGM Studios opened?
A. $24.78
B. $30.65
C. $41.93

4. How tall is Mickey's giant Sorcerer's Hat, which has become the icon of the Disney-MGM Studios?
A. 100 feet
B. 200 feet
C. 300 feet

5. How many stars and moons are on Mickey's giant Sorcerer's Hat?

6. With a hat size of 606 7/8, how tall would Mickey Mouse have to be in order to wear this giant Sorcerer's Hat?
A. 50 feet tall
B. 200 feet tall
C. 350 feet tall

7. According to the Disney-MGM Studios dedication plaque located across from Keystone Clothiers near the giant Sorcerer's Hat, the theme park is "a Hollywood that never was–and _____."

8. Where in the Disney-MGM Studios can you find Mickey Mouse standing on top of a spinning globe?

9. Approximately how many pounds of pasta does Mama Melrose's Ristorante Italiano restaurant in the Disney-MGM Studios serve everyday?
A. 500
B. 720
C. 1,500

10. Approximately how many bags of popcorn are popped each year at the Walt Disney World® Resort?
A. 2 million
B. 5 million
C. 20 million

11. Approximately how many Cobb salads (the salad that the original Hollywood Brown Derby restaurant in California is famous for) are tossed each year at Disney-MGM Studio's Hollywood Brown Derby restaurant?
A. 7,000
B. 31,000
C. 100,000

12. Which of the following did not open on June 1, 1989, just one month after the opening of Disney-MGM Studios?
A. Pleasure Island
B. Typhoon Lagoon
C. Disney's Wide World of Sports

13. What do the initials MGM in MGM Studios stand for?
A. Movies Games Music
B. Metro Goldwyn Mayer
C. My Goodness Molly

14. Which animal is the "mascot" for MGM Studios?
A. Eagle
B. Tiger
C. Lion

15. Approximately how many cast members are employed at the Disney-MGM Studios?
A. 1,000
B. 5,000
C. 10,000

16. True or False: The idea for Disney-MGM Studios came from a concept designed by former Disney executive Michael Eisner's wife.

17. Before Disney-MGM Studios became a theme park, it was destined to be a pavilion with a ride-through attraction of great movie moments and another attraction about Disney animation. At which theme park was this pavilion going to be located?
A. Disneyland
B. Magic Kingdom
C. Epcot

18. Why is there a large dinosaur statue in Echo Lake?
A. It was a child's winning design for an ice cream stand
B. It represents the large monsters that were popular in early films
C. It pays tribute to Winsor McCay's historic animated dinosaur

19. What is the name of the large dinosaur that stands in Disney-MGM Studio's Echo Lake?
A. Mecho
B. Gertie
C. Atilla

20. Which of the following events is not held at the Disney-MGM Studios?
A. ABC Super Soap Weekend
B. Osborne Family Spectacle of Lights
C. Mickey's Not-So-Scary Halloween Party

DISNEY-MGM STUDIOS CHAPTER ANSWERS

Attractions
The Disney-MGM Studios Backlot Tour
1. C **2.** B **3.** C **4.** C **5.** A **6.** A **7.** B **8.** B **9.** B **10.** A **11.** C **12.** A
(Matlin won at 21 yrs old. Temple had won an honorary award
and O'Neal won for a supporting role) **13.** A (Tied with *All About
Eve*) **14.** *Forrest Gump* (1994), *Braveheart, The English Patient,
Titanic, Shakespeare in Love, American Beauty, Gladiator, A
Beautiful Mind, Chicago* (2002) **15.** *Good Morning, Vietnam; The
Sixth Sense; Cocktail; Pretty Woman; Signs; Ransom; Evita; G.I.
Jane; Coyote Ugly; Remember the Titans*

The Great Movie Ride
1. Purple **2.** Space **3.** John Wayne **4.** *Footlight Parade* **5.**
Casablanca **6.** Julie Andrews and Dick Van Dyke **7.** *Raiders of
the Lost Ark* **8.** *Fantasia* **9.** A **10.** C **11.** B **12.** A **13.** B **14.** Looking,
Kid **15.** A **16.** A **17.** C **18.** A **19.** C **20.** B **21.** True

Honey, I Shrunk the Kids Movie Set Adventure
1. A **2.** C **3.** C **4.** Swing; Slide; Seesaw; Sand Box; Rope ladder;
Playhouse; Merry-go-round; Monkey bars

The Magic of Disney Animation
1. Red **3.** C **4.** A **5.** Tinker Bell; Hercules; Bambi; Mowgli; Chip
and Dale; Woody **6.** C **7.** C **8.** C **9.** A

Rock 'n' Roller Coaster Starring Aerosmith
1. A **2.** C **3.** C **4.** A **5.** A **6.** C **7.** "Crazy;" "Jaded;" "Livin' on the
Edge;" "Walk this Way;" "Sweet Emotion;" "Dream On;" "Dude
(Looks Like a Lady);" "Angel" **8.** A (*Armageddon* Soundtrack) **9.**
"Walk Like an Egyptian" - Bangles (1986); "Blame It On the
Rain" - Milli Vanilli (1989); "What's Love Got to Do With It" -
Tina Turner (1984); "I Will Survive" - Gloria Gaynor (1979);
"Jive Talkin'" - Bee Gees (1975); "Let Me Love You" - Mario
(2005); "Getting' Jiggy Wit' It" - Will Smith (1998); "Emotions" -
Mariah Carey (1991); "Jessie's Girl" - Rick Springfield (1981); "I
Think We're Alone Now" - Tiffany (1987); "Hey Ya!" - OutKast

(2004); "Macarena" - Los Del Rio (1996); "Ice Ice Baby" - Vanilla Ice (1990); "I Write the Songs" - Barry Manilow (1976); "Eye of the Tiger" - Survivor (1982); "Genie in a Bottle" - Christina Aguilera (1999); "Dancing Queen" - ABBA (1977); "Hot in Herre" - Nelly (2002); "Sweet Child O' Mine" - Guns N' Roses (1988) **10.** A **11.** C **12.** B **13.** A **14.** B (18) **15.** A (16) **16.** B (20)

Star Tours
1. *The Phantom Menace, Attack of the Clones, Revenge of the Sith, A New Hope, The Empire Strikes Back, Return of the Jedi* **2.** B **3.** A **4.** Chewbacca **5.** A **6.** C **7.** B **8.** See the end of this chapter **9.** A **10.** A **11.** C **12.** James Earl Jones **13.** Ewoks **14.** A **15.** R2-D2 **16.** Alderaan **17.** False, he is her brother **18.** B **19.** *Monsters, Inc.* **20.** C **21.** B

The Twilight Zone Tower of Terror
Scavenger Hunt: HTH monogram above rock pillars in outside queue line; Hat and glasses on your right once inside the building **1.** 1917 – on plaque before entering building **2.** B **3.** Animal Kingdom Lodge, Beach Club Resort, Boardwalk Inn, Contemporary Resort, Grand Floridian Resort and Spa, Polynesian Resort, Wilderness Lodge, Yacht Club Resort, Walt Disney World Swan and Dolphin, Caribbean Beach Resort, Coronado Springs Resort, Port Orleans French Quarter, Port Orleans Riverside, All-Star Movies Resort, All-Star Music Resort, All-Star Sports Resort, Pop Century Resort, Boardwalk Villas Resort, Beach Club Villas, Old Key West Resort, The Villas at Disney's Wilderness Lodge, Fort Wilderness Resort and Campground, Shades of Green, Saratoga Springs Resort and Spa **4.** Wilderness Lodge **5.** A **6.** C **7.** C **8.** B **9.** B **10.** B **11.** A **12.** A **13.** C **14.** B **15.** B **16.** C **17.** Imagination; Sight; Substance; Ideas **18.** A

Walt Disney: One Man's Dream
1. Yes **2.** C **3.** B **4.** A **5.** C **6.** B **7.** A **8.** C **9.** B **10.** A

<u>Shows</u>
Beauty and the Beast - Live on Stage
Scavenger Hunt: *Wheel of Fortune* star is Vanna White; Gilligan's is Bob Denver; *Cheers* stars are George Wendt and Woody Harrelson; *Let's Make a Deal* host is Monty Hall;

Jeopardy host is Alex Trebek **1.** 58 **2.** C **3.** A **4.** Tea pot **5.** Candlestick **6.** Clock **7.** A **8.** B **9.** A **10.** C **11.** A **12.** B **13.** No **14.** B **15.** C **16.** C

Fantasmic!
1. Nightmare **2.** The Big Bad Wolf **3.** Hopper **4.** Cruella de Vil **5.** Sir Hiss **6.** Sid **7.** Pain and Panic **8.** An evil fairy **9.** See the end of this chapter **10.** B **11.** C **12.** A **13.** B **14.** C **15.** B **16.** True **17.** It's Disney spelled backwards **18.** A **19.** A **20.** B **21.** C **22.** A **23.** A **24.** A **25.** C

Indiana Jones Epic Stunt Spectacular!
Scavenger Hunt: Shovel is on the left side with point in the ground; "Skeletal Remains" is on the right; Blue ladle is on the left **1.** A **2.** A **3.** C **4.** C **5.** C **6.** *Raiders of the Lost Ark* (1981), *Indiana Jones and the Temple of Doom* (1984) and *Indiana Jones and the Last Crusade* (1989) **7.** A **8.** B **9.** B **10.** A **11.** C **12.** B **13.** A **14.** B **15.** *Air Force One*; *Patriot Games*; *Witness*; *Regarding Henry*; *The Fugitive*; *Sabrina*; *What Lies Beneath*; *Star Wars*; *American Graffiti*; *The Frisco Kid*

Lights, Motors, Action! Extreme Stunt Show
Scavenger Hunt: Cheese shop is titled Frommagerie on left **1.** C **2.** B **3.** B **4.** A **5.** C **6.** A **7.** B **8.** A **9.** B **10.** B **11.** C **12.** B

Muppet*Vision 3-D
Scavenger Hunt: Evening gowns are on the left wall looking towards the front of the room; Pickled herring in front of room; Banana puree and rubber toast are in the front left; Drum is near disabled theater doors; Emergency tuxedos are in the front right **1.** A **2.** A **3.** C **4.** C **5.** A **6.** A **7.** A **8.** Big Bird; Bert and Ernie; Oscar the Grouch; Cookie Monster; Elmo; Grover; Zoe; Count von Count **9.** C

Playhouse Disney - Live on Stage!
3. A **4.** B **5.** C **6.** A **7.** C **8.** A **11.** C **13.** Piglet, Tigger, Eeyore, Rabbit, Owl **14.** A

Sounds Dangerous – Starring Drew Carey
1. Touch, taste, smell and sight **2.** See the end of this chapter **3.** B **4.** B **5.** A **6.** B **7.** C **8.** Toilet flush (75 decibels), telephone ring,

heavy traffic, leaf blower, stadium football game, ambulance siren, noisy squeeze toys, airplane taking off, balloon pop, shotgun (170 decibels) **9.** C **10.** A

Voyage of the Little Mermaid
Scavenger Hunt: "Tinkerbell's Prison" and a fuzzy fish are on the left as you enter from the turnstiles; Typewriter is on the left as you enter the main theater **1.** 16 (on plaque next to turnstiles) **2.** C **3.** B **4.** A **5.** B **6.** C **7.** A **8.** C **9.** C **10.** A **11.** A **12.** C **13.** A

Disney Entertainment Trivia
1. B **2.** B **3.** A **4.** "When You Wish Upon a Star" - *Pinocchio* (1941); "A Whole New World" - *Aladdin* (1993); "Colors of the Wind" - *Pocahontas* (1996); "Can You Feel the Love Tonight" - *The Lion King* (1995); "Under the Sea" - *The Little Mermaid* (1990); "If I Didn't Have You" - *Monsters, Inc.* (2002); "You'll Be in My Heart" - *Tarzan* (2000); "Zip-a-Dee-Doo-Dah" - *Song of the South* (1948); "Sooner or Later" - *Dick Tracy* (1991); "Chim Chim Cher-ee" - *Mary Poppins* (1965) **5.** B **6.** A **7.** A **8.** B **9.** A **10.** C **11.** B **12.** C **13.** C **14.** B **15.** C

General Disney-MGM Studios Trivia
1. Dinosaur is in Echo Lake; Bottles are next to The Disney-MGM Studios Backlot Tour; Boat is in Echo Lake or the Disney Resort Boat Facility; Dragon is in Fantasmic! lake; Fountain is outside of Muppet*Vision 3-D, The Disney-MGM Studios Backlot Tour and Sounds Dangerous - Starring Drew Carey; Army truck is in Indiana Jones Epic Stunt Spectacular!; Airplane is in Indiana Jones Epic Stunt Spectacular! and The Disney-MGM Studios Backlot Tour **2.** B **3.** B **4.** A **5.** Six stars and two moons **6.** C **7.** Always will be **8.** On top of Crossroads of the World at the park entrance **9.** B **10.** B **11.** B **12.** C **13.** B **14.** C **15.** B **16.** False – It was one of Walt Disney's original ideas **17.** C **18.** C **19.** B **20.** C

312

Star Tours

```
STORMTROOPERSNCL
LAPCZMHKFWBNGAOF
WJNVEDAGOBAHICUD
KAHDRCPWTSWVEBNI
LUTXPNXMOSESPATG
ADBTWEGUKEPJMKDN
NCFKOCORUSCANTOE
DHAIROTPLDFSGROH
OGRAGRAMLHBYACKJ
WGELFSDJTEAUIWUD
```

Fantasmic!

```
HPAFSTROMBOLIFMJ
UAJRHDOAMSHDAIAD
FLDCAPTAINHOOKLM
RRIELTRNMBOLTOER
MAOGSTCGDPCGTCFI
CTSLKCSLURSULAIE
UIETLFAHIJBIAJCF
HGASTONRPFDLNDEM
GAKBNQCMJAFARENH
FNOALDEAIKFEBGTC
```

Sounds Dangerous

```
SENHMACJFRGIMSVC
MCGCLUGURGLEBCBU
SIRNCHSIMPANHNUE
BCMEMBPCOCERSEZL
SHCHESERHRZCIMZH
PBRDRCTELUBANGCR
LPANBWHAPNFSPBAO
ACSEKCLKNCMNHOWL
TUHISSSUIHQAMRHF
AHMRFHNESCSQUEAL
```

Travel to worlds you've likely only dreamed of at Disney's Animal Kingdom. Guests can experience an authentic safari ride in the wilderness preserves of Africa, explore the rainforests of Southeast Asia and travel back in time to the age of dinosaurs. You will encounter fascinating animals at every turn and learn about their struggle for survival in the world's shrinking wilderness. From thrill rides to stage shows to animal habitats along every path, a visit to Disney's Animal Kingdom is definitely a walk on the wild side!

Guest Information Board Location: Across from the Island Mercantile shop on Discovery Island. A smaller information board is located in Africa, as well, across from the Mombasa Marketplace shop, though this location has limited attractions listed.

Disney's Animal Kingdom

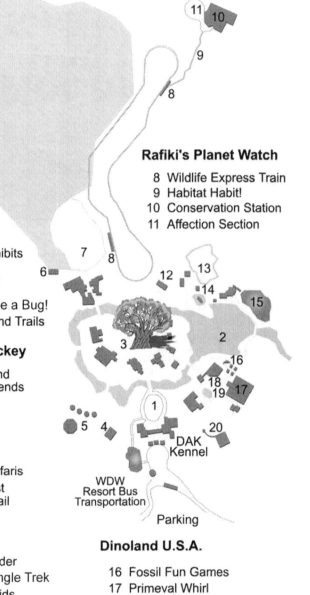

Oasis

1 The Oasis Exhibits

Discovery Island

2 It's Tough To Be a Bug!
3 Discovery Island Trails

Camp Minnie-Mickey

4 Pocahontas and
   Her Forest Friends
5 Festival of the
   Lion King

Africa

6 Kilimanjaro Safaris
7 Pangani Forest
   Exploration Trail

Asia

12 Flights of Wonder
13 Maharajah Jungle Trek
14 Kali River Rapids
15 Expedition Everest -
   Legend of the
   Forbidden Mountain

Rafiki's Planet Watch

8 Wildlife Express Train
9 Habitat Habit!
10 Conservation Station
11 Affection Section

Dinoland U.S.A.

16 Fossil Fun Games
17 Primeval Whirl
18 The Boneyard
19 TriceraTop Spin
20 DINOSAUR

Disney's Animal Kingdom Tips

- Disney's Animal Kingdom can become very hot in the warmer weather months. With so few enclosed, air-conditioned attractions and so many open-air attractions and animal trails, guests must be sure to drink plenty of water to prevent dehydration. Due to the nature of the attractions, rainstorms can pose a big problem, too, so be sure to check the weather report before heading to Disney's Animal Kingdom.

- A lesser known second entrance into Disney's Animal Kingdom can be found near the Rainforest Café restaurant. Guests can enter the Rainforest Café, which is located just outside of Disney's Animal Kingdom, and walk through the large gift shop to the opposite side where you will find a couple of entrance kiosks. Anyone can enter and exit the theme park from this secret location, not just guests who are eating at the restaurant.

- Because of the rugged pathways throughout much of Disney's Animal Kingdom, this theme park is more challenging for guests using strollers or wheelchairs.

- Children will enjoy the Kid's Discovery Club stations throughout the theme park. Kids are given a small booklet with animal fun facts and games and they can collect a different stamp in their booklet at each land's location. Booklets are provided at each station and Guest Relations.

- The core message of Disney's Animal Kingdom is conservation and reducing the Earth's waste is a major factor in animal conservation. You'll soon notice that quick service food locations don't put plastic tops on drinking cups and there are no plastic straws in the theme park. This isn't a cost cutting measure (although being friendly to the environment often saves money) but a way to protect animal habitats and reduce waste.

AFRICA

You'll feel as if you've been transported to the continent of Africa as you enter the bustling marketplace of Harambe, a coastal village on the edge of a wildlife reserve teeming with animals.

Kilimanjaro Safaris

Overview: On this authentic safari ride through the Harambe Wildlife Preserve, guests travel in open-air safari vehicles past giraffes, lions, elephants and other animals of Africa living in their natural habitats. The road gets rough, though, when you're called upon to help save a mother and baby elephant from poachers. Safari vehicles have eight rows which will each seat four adults or a combination of five adults and children.

Thrill Time: 20 minutes

FASTPASS AVAILABLE

Restrictions: Guests should be in good health and free from high blood pressure, heart, back or neck problems, motion sickness and other conditions that could be aggravated by the ride. Expectant mothers should not ride.

Be Aware of: This attraction closes during severe inclement weather such as thunder and lightning.

Videos shown in a portion of the queue line have images of dead animals killed by poachers.

This attraction can be very rough as the safari vehicles drive along primitive roads marred by potholes and deep ruts. There are no seat belts in the safari vehicles. Be sure to hold on tight to your camera, hats, etc. as you journey along the safari route. Personal items cannot be retrieved if they fall out of the vehicles.

Helpful Hints: Though animals can be seen throughout the day on this attraction, the best times to view the animals are during the early morning or late evening hours when they are most active. This is especially true during the warmer weather months.

Videos are shown in portions of the queue line which help pass the time. The outdoor queue is covered and has fans. Strollers are allowed through part of the queue line before cast members take them and park them at the attraction exit.

Because the animals are free roaming, no two safaris are ever alike. Consider experiencing the attraction twice in one visit for varied animal sightings. Animal identification guides are located above the seats.

Small mesh storage bags will secure your personal items along the rough ride. Be sure to have your camera ready to go as you board the safari vehicles. Picture taking opportunities start immediately after you begin your safari.

Parent/Guardian Switch option is available.

Disabled Access: Guests must transfer from a motorized scooter to the vehicle seat or a wheelchair that is provided at the attraction. Guests may remain in their wheelchair. Disney's assistive listening devices interact with this attraction. Disney's handheld captioning devices interact with this attraction. Disney's guest-activated captioning devices interact with this attraction (queue only). Guests with service animals should check with a host or hostess at this attraction.

• • • • • • • • • • • • • • • • • • • •

℗ *Scavenger Hunt*: In the queue line, find: a map of the Harambe Reserve, sleeping bags, pottery, oars, shovels and coolers.

1. In the beginning of the queue line, look towards the ceiling for signs that display the Swahili names of animals that you can find

in Africa. What is the Swahili name of a rhinoceros? What is the Swahili name of a cheetah?

2. Along the queue line, you will find the rules of the Harambe Conservation Code. What is Rule Number Two?

3. What color are baby flamingos?
A. Pink
B. Gray or white
C. Black

4. An elephant's trunk has how many muscles in it?
A. One
B. Around 5,900
C. Around 40,000

5. The male African elephant is the largest land mammal. How much can the elephant weigh?
A. 5,000 pounds
B. 15,000 pounds
C. 50,000 pounds

6. True or False: A rhino's skin protects it from sunburn.

7. Can a hippopotamus swim?

8. What does the word hippopotamus mean?
A. River horse
B. Floating pig
C. Water dog

9. Approximately how long is a giraffe's neck? (Their legs are approximately the same length, too.)
A. Four feet
B. Six feet
C. Eight feet

10. Approximately how long is a giraffe's heart?
A. 10 inches
B. 14 inches
C. 24 inches

11. Many animal species have scientific names for large groupings of that animal. For example, a group of antelope is called a herd. Match the following animals with the scientific names given to their large groups:

Apes   Bloat
Gorillas   Leap
Giraffes   Pride
Hippos   Band
Hyenas   Shrewdness
Leopards   Caravan
Lions   Corps
Camels   Zeal
Rhinoceroses   Crash
Zebras   Cackle

12. Wild elephants can eat how much vegetation in a day?
A. 10-30 pounds
B. 100-125 pounds
C. 220-440 pounds

13. How fast can a cheetah run?
A. Up to 20 mph
B. Up to 45 mph
C. Up to 70 mph

14. Find the following animals that live in Africa in the word search below: flamingo, monkey, ostrich, gorilla, crocodile, zebra, antelope, lion, tortoise and warthog.

```
P A C N E J H E O W A R T H O G
C F I R N D G O R I L L A Q A L
T A G D O M W B J C T Y I K G Z
B N E M V C R N E S F W D O W E
M T K O L T O R T O I S E R N B
H E J N D Q G D W L B P I C O R
S L A K M A O M I U E A D Y A A
F O T E I A F S F L A M I N G O
U P C Y C L B H O N E J H M D U
A E G W R O S T R I C H K A V E
```

321

15. The Kilimanjaro Safaris travel throughout an African savannah of approximately how many acres?
A. 25
B. 50
C. 100

16. How many tons of food are required to feed 1,000 animals each day at Disney's Animal Kingdom?
A. One
B. Three
C. Four

17. Lab technicians at Disney's Animal Kingdom have analyzed approximately how many samples of animal poop since the theme park opened?
A. More than 10,000
B. More than 100,000
C. More than one million

18. When laying out the landscape of Kilimanjaro Safaris, the landscape architect rode on what type of vehicle traveling at the same speed as the safari vehicles and created planting areas using a can of spray paint?
A. Riding lawn mower
B. Motorcycle
C. Segway Human Transporter

19. True or False: A female elephant is called a cow.

20. How many hours a day do lions sleep?
A. 3
B. 8
C. 21

21. Do all zebras have the same black and white stripe patterns?

ASIA

The mysterious and exotic animals and legends of Southeast Asia can be explored in this land which has two of Disney's Animal Kingdom's most thrilling attractions.

Expedition Everest - Legend of the Forbidden Mountain

Overview: Join a train journey that transports you up Mount Everest, a sacred mountain reportedly protected by the fearful Yeti. After beginning the ascent of the mountain, you soon discover that the train tracks have been torn apart by the Yeti. Suddenly, your 34-passenger train (17 rows each hold two guests) careens backwards, resulting in a high-speed thrill ride with one frightening 80-foot drop.

Thrill Time: 3 minutes

FASTPASS AVAILABLE

Restrictions: Passengers must be at least 44 inches (112 cm) tall. Guests should be in good health and free from high blood pressure, heart, back or neck problems, motion sickness and other conditions that could be aggravated by the ride. Expectant mothers should not ride.

Be Aware of: This attraction closes during severe inclement weather such as lightning. Portions of the queue line are outdoors and uncovered.

There are periods of pitch darkness during the ride.

The individual seats and safety harnesses of this attraction might not accommodate all body shapes and sizes.

Helpful Hints: If you want to reduce your wait time and don't have a FASTPASS time, utilize the singles line. The singles line takes individual guests from the queue line to fill empty single seats. You must be willing to split from your party and possibly ride the attraction at different times (though this is not always the case), but you will save a lot of time waiting in line.

Water fountains and fans are located in portions of the queue line.

The last portion of the queue line winds through a museum filled with artifacts and photographs of the Himalaya region with an emphasis on the legend of the Yeti.

There is a small mesh storage bag in each seat to secure your personal items during the ride.

Parent/Guardian Switch option is available.

Disabled Access: Guests must transfer from their motorized scooter or wheelchair to board this attraction. Service animals are not permitted on this attraction.

• • • • • • • • • • • • • • • • • •

☆ ***Hidden Mickey Hunt***: In the first air-conditioned building in the queue line, look into the display cases on the right-hand wall as you round the last corner before exiting the room. Among the small stuffed Yeti figures on the top shelf is one Yeti who is wearing a pair of Mickey Mouse ears.

♀ ***Scavenger Hunt***: Throughout the queue line, find: a lantern, snowshoes, an apple, socks, a GPS locator, a picture of a mountain lizard and a prayer flag.

1. True or False: The Yeti (also known as the Abominable Snowman) is covered with hair.

2. A creature similar to the Yeti is known as Bigfoot in the United States. What is this creature known as in Canada?
A. Mountie
B. Sasquatch
C. Apeman

3. The 2001 Disney-Pixar animated film *Monsters, Inc.* featured an Abominable Snowman character named Yeti who was voiced by which famous actor from the television series *Cheers*?
A. Ted Danson
B. Woody Harrelson
C. John Ratzenberger

4. The Abominable Snowman can be found in what Disneyland attraction?
A. Space Mountain
B. Matterhorn Bobsleds
C. Storybook Land Canal Boats

5. What is the name of the Abominable Snowman character in the classic Christmas television special *Rudolph, The Red-Nosed Reindeer*?
A. Bumbles
B. Mr. Freeze
C. Chilly

6. What is the name of the 1987 film starring John Lithgow in which a family lives with Bigfoot after accidentally hitting him with a car?
A. *Harry and the Hendersons*
B. *Look Who's Coming to Dinner*
C. *Bringing Home Bigfoot*

7. What is the Yeti known as in Australia?
A. Zixu
B. Hairini
C. Yowie

8. What is the Yeti known as in the Amazon?
A. Limal
B. Mapinguari
C. Nazzuu

9. Expedition Everest covers how many acres of land?
A. 2.8
B. 5.3
C. 6.4

10. How many species of shrubs were planted around Expedition Everest to recreate the look of the Himalayan environment?
A. 36
B. 87
C. 110

11. The mountain structure of Expedition Everest contains 1,800 tons of steel. That is approximately how much more steel than a traditional office building of the same size contains?
A. Twice as much
B. Six times as much
C. Twenty times as much

12. Approximately how many handcrafted items from Asia can be found throughout Expedition Everest?
A. 500
B. 2,000
C. 3,000

13. Worldwide fascination with the Yeti started in which year when Eric Shipton took photographs of large footprints that he discovered as he was trying to scale Mount Everest?
A. 1902
B. 1937
C. 1951

14. What is the name of the branch of science which studies rumored or mysterious animals that are thought to exist, such as the Yeti?
A. Cryptozoology
B. Mythology
C. Zoology

15. How did the Abominable Snowman get its name?
A. A reporter used the wrong word when describing its footprint
B. A child coined the phrase
C. Sir Edmund Hillary used the phrase to describe the creature

16. Mount Everest is part of the Himalayan mountain range which is the world's highest mountain system and stretches over several countries in Asia. Which of the following countries does not contain a portion of the Himalayan Mountains?
A. India
B. Bhutan
C. Vietnam

17. How tall is Mount Everest, the highest mountain in the world above sea level?
A. 20,812 feet
B. 29,035 feet
C. 35,786 feet

18. Mount Everest is located on the border between what two nations?
A. Nepal and Tibet (China)
B. India and Bangladesh
C. India and Nepal

19. Himalaya is a Sanskrit word which means what?
A. Heaven's peak
B. Abode of snow
C. Dangerous mountain

20. Sir Edmund Hillary and Tenzing Norgay are the first people known to have made a safe ascent and descent of Mount Everest. In which year was their historic climb?
A. 1953
B. 1967
C. 1971

21. What is reportedly the fastest ascent ever made to the summit of Mount Everest?
A. Eight hours and ten minutes
B. Two days and three minutes
C. Three days, five hours and nine minutes

22. In 1924, George Mallory made a famous attempt to climb Mount Everest. No one knows if he ever reached the summit because he was later found dead on the mountain. What was George Mallory's infamous reason as to why he wanted to climb to the top of the mountain?
A. "Because it is there."
B. "Why not?"
C. "What else do I have to do?"

Flights of Wonder

Overview: You won't find birds performing tricks or riding bicycles in this bird show, but there will be plenty of birds such as owls, macaws, toucans and the Bald Eagle exhibiting their natural behaviors on cue in the 1,000-seat theater.

Thrill Time: 27 minutes

Be Aware of: This attraction closes during inclement weather such as thunder and lightning.

Seating for this show is on long benches without back rests. The birds in the show fly over the crowd at very low levels, nearly skimming the tops of some guests' heads. A few large mice make an appearance on the stage during one portion of the show.

Helpful Hints: Consult your Times Guide for performance times. A cast member, accompanied by a live bird, presents a bird talk while guests are standing in the outside queue area before each show. The presentation is to the right of the entrance. Guests are encouraged to ask questions.

Where you sit during the Flights of Wonder show will make a big difference on what you are able to see throughout the presentation. Though cast members say that all seating locations are excellent because the birds fly through the air, only some of the birds in the show fly and those that fly only do so in certain areas. The front row seats will allow you to see the birds that make an appearance on stage as well as those that do not fly. Most of the birds that fly overhead follow the same path from the stage to the rear of the theater, flying over the aisle between the far left and center seating sections. The best seats are in the center section towards the left aisle. Since the birds typically fly to a trainer located in the rear of the theater, another good seating location is the very back rows of the far left and center seating sections, as well as the front rows of the tiered seating sections located in the left corner.

The open-air theater has a cover to reduce your exposure to the elements. Several large fans circulate air towards the back of the theater.

One child and several adult volunteers are asked to help with the bird presentations throughout the show. If you would like to be an adult volunteer, be sure to have a dollar bill (or any other denomination) in your hand or have a camera in your hand for when the host calls for volunteers.

After the show ends, guests are invited to come up to the stage and ask questions of the host or pose for pictures with the birds (You will be standing on ground level while the bird handler stays on stage level).

Disabled Access: Guests may remain in their wheelchair or motorized scooter. Guests using wheelchairs or motorized scooters must enter the theater from the right hand side of the queue line. Disney's assistive listening devices interact with this attraction.

● ● ● ● ● ● ● ● ● ● ● ● ● ● ● ● ● ● ●

1. Which of the following birds is able to fly long distances?
A. Ostrich
B. Penguin
C. Duck

2. In general, what is a group of birds called?
A. Flock
B. Team
C. Crowd

3. What is a group of geese called?
A. Google
B. Gaggle
C. Colony

4. Find the following birds in the word search below: puffin, tern, swan, heron, egret, ibis, partridge, cuckoo, nuthatch, goldfinch, wren, warbler and swallow.

```
F M B W J D U G L P Y H E R O N
A S W A L L O W M V U P G A O C
W R P N B S D R A I B F F L E S
A Y H T C U C K O O T K F W D W
R E L O E T G A P C J H V I S A
B L G J C R F Q E B Y W U L N N
L K I R O U N P A R T R I D G E
E A V P E W D N L E M E B H R I
R G B N U T H A T C H N I T C B
C S G O L D F I N C H E S K A F
```

330

5. Approximately how many species of birds are there worldwide?
A. 9,775
B. 29,678
C. 500,020

6. True or False: There are more pink plastic flamingos in the United States than there are real flamingos.

7. The dodo bird could only be found on the Indian Ocean island of Mauritius before it became extinct. Another Mauritius bird, the red hen, also became extinct on the same island when sailors started landing there in the 1600s. What was the unusual trait of the red hen that led to its extinction?
A. It liked the color red and the sailors hats were usually red
B. The red hens would fight each other to the death
C. The red hens were deathly allergic to human sweat

8. How many bird species have become extinct since the year 1500?
A. 27
B. 79
C. 131

9. Worldwide, approximately how many bird species are threatened with extinction?
A. 1 in 2
B. 1 in 5
C. 1 in 25

10. In 1986, only one breeding pair of California Condors, the largest flying land birds in North America, remained in the wild. Breeding programs have since slowly increased the number of the birds. Which of the following was not a reason why the California Condors, as well as many other bird species, nearly became extinct?
A. Lead poisoning from ingesting lead bullets in dead animals
B. DDT
C. Global warming

11. The pesticide DDT has been linked to the near extinction of many species of birds. How does a pesticide affect whether a bird species will become extinct or not?

12. What can you do to prevent more birds from becoming extinct?

Kali River Rapids

Overview: Your relaxing river ride through an Asian rainforest suddenly takes a terrifying turn as you encounter illegal loggers who are devastating the forest and the animals' habitats. This water adventure sends 12-person rafts (six pairs of two side-by-side seats) down the Chakranadi River which has one large descent that is sure to soak you!

Thrill Time: 4 ½ minutes

FASTPASS AVAILABLE

Restrictions: Passengers must be at least 38 inches (95 cm) tall. Guests should be in good health and free from high blood pressure, heart, back or neck problems, motion sickness and other conditions that could be aggravated by the ride. Expectant mothers should not ride.

Be Aware of: This attraction closes during inclement weather such as thunder and lightning.

You will get wet. Whether you just get wet or get soaked depends on your position in the raft. Shoes must be worn at all times.

To board the raft, guests must step onto a rotating platform and quickly step down three steps to get into the raft. If you are unable to board from a moving platform or feel you need extra time in boarding the rafts, ask a cast member about utilizing the disabled queue line where guests can board a raft that is not moving.

The rafts of this attraction spin uncontrollably as they head down the turbulent river. Guests who are prone to motion sickness could be affected by the spinning rafts.

There is smoke which accompanies the "fire" that illegal loggers have started. Each pair of seats accommodates two guests who must share one large seatbelt.

Helpful Hints: A waterproof compartment is located in each raft, however, the compartment tends to get wet as the day goes on. Be sure to secure any cameras, cell phones, etc. in a waterproof bag before putting them in the compartment which will only hold items the size of a video camera or smaller. Larger items and backpacks will need to be stowed before entering the queue line.

Hand grips surround the central waterproof compartment so that guests can hold on during the river ride.

During the hot weather months, everyone decides to experience Kali River Rapids during the afternoon to get a break from the heat. Therefore, the queue lines are unbearable during the afternoon. Be sure to experience this attraction in the early morning or as close to park closing as possible to avoid long queue lines.

This queue line is extensively decorated in beautiful artwork and items from Asia. Though the waits can be long, there are plenty of decorative items to enjoy while standing in line. There are fans in the covered outdoor queue line and a water fountain is located within the queue.

Parent/Guardian Switch option is available.

Disabled Access: Guests must transfer from their wheelchair or motorized scooter to board this attraction. The queue line is rather rough which makes maneuvering a wheelchair a little more challenging. There are three small steps leading down into the raft. Utilizing the disabled queue area allows guests to board a stationary raft rather than a moving raft that must be quickly boarded. Disney's assistive listening devices interact with this attraction (queue only). Service animals are not permitted on this attraction.

• • • • • • • • • • • • • • • • • • • •

♀ *Scavenger Hunt*: Throughout the queue line, find:

- A watermelon
- An orange
- A bicycle
- Bird cages
- A backpack
- Laundry hanging on a clothesline
- A large butterfly hanging from the ceiling
- A banana
- Pots and pans
- A headless statue
- A carving of a snake
- A fountain with water coming out of the mouth of a cobra

1. A football field-size portion of the world's forests disappears how often?
A. Every two seconds
B. Every minute
C. Every hour

2. If the amount of forest that disappears every minute equals the size of 30 football fields, calculate how many football fields of forest have been destroyed in the amount of time that you've been standing in the queue line for Kali River Rapids.

3. Approximately how much of the world's forests remain?
A. 10%
B. 20%
C. 35%

4. In the forests of Indonesia, approximately how much of the logging is illegal?
A. 40%
B. 73%
C. 88%

5. Why should anyone care if loggers get their wood either legally or illegally?

6. Is all illegal logging done only in South America and Asia?

7. Is there any type of good wood to buy?
A. No
B. Yes, any type of pine or oak wood
C. Yes, wood certified by the Forest Stewardship Council

8. The Forest Stewardship Council has created principles for managing forests around the world to ensure logging of wood that is done in a way that preserves the environment and protects the people that live near the forest. Over 50 countries are using these principles in approximately how many million hectares of forest? (One hectare is approximately 2 ½ acres)
A. 6
B. 17
C. 25

9. The Amazon rainforest is approximately the same size as which country?
A. United States
B. Japan
C. France

10. In the last 30 years, how much of the Brazilian Amazon rainforest has been lost?
A. An amount of land equal to the size of Connecticut
B. An amount of land equal to the size of Texas
C. An amount of land equal to the size of Western Europe

11. If you want to help preserve the world's rainforests, it's as simple as buying products that are not made from certain types of wood which are almost always illegally harvested. Find the

following types of wood in the word search below which you
should avoid buying: mahogany, red cedar, teak, hemlock, ramin,
abachi, merbau, iroko and sapelli.

```
H R D I S E A B A C H I S C B M
X E D Q B O L G M T Q J A S K W
B D T K A M C U F P E Y E A L I
O C R W N H Y B K D C A Y P H R
R E J A A E X I T N L P K E B O
F D L V M A H O G A N Y Q L P K
K A P G Z I U D J F N G C L V O
S R H E T O N Q A M K B L I I T
A M U C I D W S H E M L O C K O
N V M E R B A U H P E S J A G F
```

12. A typical four-square mile section of rainforest can contain
how many species of trees?
A. 5
B. 167
C. 750

13. Rainforests are home to what percentage of the world's plant
and animal species?
A. 33%
B. 50%
C. 80%

14. On average, how much rain does a rainforest receive in a year?
A. 30 inches
B. 60 inches
C. 800 inches

15. A typical four-square mile section of rainforest can contain
how many species of flowering plants?
A. 678
B. 1,239
C. 1,500

16. Unscramble the following types of animals that live in a tropical rainforest:

ZAILRD
TTFLYUERB
GTAORALIL
AREODPL
ROFG
NAKES
NYEKMO
GEITR
ILLOGRA
ACAMW

CAMP MINNIE-MICKEY

You'll find your favorite Disney characters in this Adirondack summer camp-inspired land which features shows and meet and greet areas.

Festival of the Lion King

Overview: This feel-good show features human performers depicting fanciful animals who have come to town for a celebration. The performers sing popular songs from the Disney animated film *The Lion King* amidst a raucous display of acrobatics, fire dancers, stilt walkers and colorfully costumed dancers. The theater will seat 1,400 guests.

Thrill Time: 31 minutes

Be Aware of: The queue line is entirely located outdoors with no cover. Misting fans are located in certain sections of the queue.

Be in line at least 30 minutes prior to show time to be assured seating for the show (Be in line at least 45 minutes prior to the show during peak attendance days).

Because of the popularity of the show, guests are not allowed to save seats. Make sure your entire party is together in the queue line before entering the theater. Seating for this show is on long benches without back rests. To access most of the seating, you will have to climb shallow steps. If you cannot climb stairs, contact a cast member at the entrance of the queue line.

Heavy smoke effects which rise from the floor are used throughout the show. Guests seated in the first few rows of each section will be engulfed in misting smoke during several periods of the show. Fire dancers perform during the show.

Helpful Hints: Consult your Times Guide for performance times.

This show is staged in the center of an intimate theater with guests sitting around the performance. The characters in the show are surprisingly close to the audience and guests seated in the first three rows of each section will receive a lot of attention, plus great views of the performance. However, the first two rows of each section are reserved for disabled guests. Disabled guests and their families will be seated before other guests, so any seating not being utilized can be claimed once all guests are allowed in the theater.

Children are invited to participate in portions of the show. The children are usually chosen from the first few rows of each section.

Guests are seated in four sections within the theater. Each section is given an animal name. As you enter the theater, the section immediately to your left is the giraffe section and the section immediately to your right is the warthog section. In the far left corner (to the left of the giraffe section) you will find the elephant section and in the far right corner is the lion section. Each section will be given an animal sound to make during the show. Your views during the show will also depend on which section you are seated in. The costumed character Timon spends most of his time in the area between the lion and warthog sections, where the float with Pumbaa is parked. The Simba float is parked between the lion and elephant section. All of the floats and character performers enter the theater between the lion and elephant sections. Though guests can easily see the entire performance regardless of which section you are seated in, sitting near the aisles of these sections (especially the aisles and front rows of the lion section) will give you a closer view of the characters.

This is a great attraction to visit during the middle of the day when you need an extended time to sit down and rest in an air-conditioned, darkened theater.

Guests can pose for pictures in front of the colorful floats after the performance.

Disabled Access: Guests may remain in their wheelchair or motorized scooter. Disney's assistive listening devices interact with this attraction. Disney's handheld captioning devices interact with this attraction.

• • • • • • • • • • • • • • • • • • •

1. In the Disney animated film *The Lion King*, what is the name of the young lion cub that is born at the beginning of the movie?
A. Simba
B. Ninja
C. Nala

2. In *The Lion King*, what is the name of the wise old baboon who blesses the young lion cub who will one day grow up to be king?
A. Shenzi
B. Banzai
C. Rafiki

3. In *The Lion King*, what is the name of the area that Simba's father, Mufasa, is king of?
A. Harambe
B. Pride Lands
C. Wild Africa

4. What is the name of Mufasa's brother who is bitter because he will not be king now that Simba has been born?
A. Scar
B. Jafar
C. Frollo

5. In *The Lion King*, who saves Simba from nearly being eaten by hyenas in the Elephant Graveyard?
A. Zazu
B. Mufasa
C. Scar

6. In *The Lion King*, what is the name of the female cub who is friends with Simba and whom he later falls in love with?
A. Nala
B. Sarabi
C. Zazu

7. Which child actor from the television series *Home Improvement* provided the voice for the young Simba in *The Lion King*?
A. Taran Noah Smith
B. Zachery Ty Bryan
C. Jonathan Taylor Thomas

8. Which Disney theme park used to have a show called Legend of the Lion King?
A. Magic Kingdom
B. Epcot
C. Disney-MGM Studios

9. Which actor provided the voice for the older Simba in *The Lion King*?
A. Matthew Broderick
B. Tim Allen
C. Rick Moranis

10. There have been two sequels to *The Lion King*, *The Lion King 1½* and *The Lion King II: Simba's Pride*. Which movie features Simba and Nala's daughter, Kiara, and which movie tells *The Lion King* story from Timon and Pumbaa's perspective?

11. Which famous recording artist helped write the songs for *The Lion King*?
A. Phil Collins
B. Elton John
C. Barry Manilow

12. Many of the character's names in *The Lion King* are Swahili words. What does Rafiki mean in Swahili?
A. Friend
B. Elder
C. Medicine man

13. What does Simba mean in the Swahili language?
A. Young boy
B. Lion
C. Arrogant

14. What does Pumbaa mean in Swahili?
A. Smelly
B. Beast
C. Silly or a simpleton

15. Where is the Swahili language spoken?
A. Eastern and Central Africa
B. Northern Asia
C. South America

16. In what year did *The Lion King* open on Broadway?
A. 1995
B. 1996
C. 1997

17. *The Lion King* story line shares common elements with which famous Shakespeare play?
A. Hamlet
B. Othello
C. Macbeth

18. Find the following characters, locations and phrases that appear in *The Lion King* in the word search below: Pride Rock, Sarafina, Zazu, Shenzi, Banzai, wildebeests, Sarabi and Circle of Life.

```
P N G E T A U J S E V Z A Z U H
O R M P H J Z C I P D Y U Q F X
F C I R C L E O F L I F E T B S
I D N D Q A O I N T B C K P G H
W K I S E V G E L S W M A L B E
A M T S A R A F I N A J O C A N
O H D P C U O P Q F W R P H N Z
E B J A S B M C H N D U A N Z I
L C I Q A K G V K O M E K B A S
F P W I L D E B E E S T S Y I J
```

Pocahontas and Her Forest Friends

Overview: Join Pocahontas, Grandmother Willow and live forest animals in a 400-seat outdoor theater as you learn how to protect the forest and its animals.

Thrill Time: 12 minutes

Be Aware of: This attraction closes during inclement weather such as thunder and lightning. This outdoor theater has a sheer cover, but the sun and rain can still pose a problem. The back rows of the theater and the far left and right sides are more exposed to the elements.

Seating for this show is on long plastic benches without back rests. Be sure to secure seats for this show before the Festival of the Lion King show empties as many of those guests will immediately head to Pocahontas and Her Forest Friends.

Snakes and rats are some of the animals that appear on stage.

Helpful Hints: Consult your Times Guide for performance times. A special animal training session is usually offered each day. Check your Times Guide for more information.

On less crowded days, it is often possible to enjoy this show immediately after exiting the Festival of the Lion King show. You might not get a front row seat, but you won't waste time waiting for the show to begin, either.

The front rows of the theater are reserved for guests 10 and under. Sit as close to the front as possible for views of the animals that make an appearance on stage.

After the show, children can come up to the stage to collect some of the paper leaves that Pocahontas uses during the show.

Disabled Access: Guests may remain in their wheelchair or motorized scooter. Disney's assistive listening devices interact with this attraction. Disney's handheld captioning devices interact with this attraction.

• • • • • • • • • • • • • • • • • • •

1. What is the name of the raccoon in the Disney animated film *Pocahontas*?
A. Meeko
B. Marlo
C. Mischief

2. What kind of animal is Flit in Disney's *Pocahontas*?
A. Hummingbird
B. Turkey
C. Deer

3. According to the song "Colors of the Wind" in *Pocahontas*, the rainstorm and what else are Pocahontas' brothers?
A. The river
B. The sun
C. The ocean

4. According to the song "Colors of the Wind" in *Pocahontas*, the wolf cries to what?
A. His brothers
B. The blue corn moon
C. The Native Americans' ancestors

5. Unscramble the following character names from the Disney film *Pocahontas*:

GOVRRNOE FFAERTCLI   (Hint: He's not a nice guy)
PYERC   (Hint: A pug dog)
SOMATH   (Hint: He kills an Indian brave)
FIECH WHAATNPO   (Hint: Pocahontas' father)
DMOGRANRHTE LLWWIO   (Hint: She's a tree spirit)
NAMAOK   (Hint: Pocahontas' best friend)

6. In *Pocahontas*, why was John Smith sentenced to die?
A. He wouldn't tell the others where the gold was hidden
B. He took the blame for killing an Indian brave
C. Chief Powhatan didn't like him being friends with his daughter

7. The real Pocahontas is famous for helping bring peace between the Algonquian Indians of Virginia and the English settlers who landed in which Virginia town?
A. Jamestown
B. Richmond
C. Roanoke

8. The real Pocahontas became very good friends with Captain John Smith, one of the English settlers. Did Pocahontas and John Smith ever get married?

9. True or False: *Pocahontas* was the first Disney animated film to be based on historical fact.

10. Where did the world premiere of the Disney film *Pocahontas* take place?
A. Jamestown, Virginia
B. A Cherokee Indian reservation
C. Central Park in New York City

11. Which actor supplied the voice of John Smith in *Pocahontas*?
A. Tom Cruise
B. Brad Pitt
C. Mel Gibson

12. What does Pocahontas' name mean?
A. Playful girl
B. Beautiful one
C. Soulful wanderer

13. Around what year was the real Pocahontas born?
A. 1389
B. 1595
C. 1801

DINOLAND U.S.A.

All of the attractions in this land are dinosaur themed, including Chester & Hester's Dino-Rama! with fun carnival games.

The Boneyard

Overview: Kids can be kids in this oversized playground with a dinosaur discovery theme. Slides, ropes and plenty of objects to crawl on can be found in The Boneyard along with a dig site where kids can unearth dinosaur fossils hidden under layers of sand.

Thrill Time: Allow an average of 15-30 minutes.

Be Aware of: This attraction closes during inclement weather. This entire attraction is located outdoors. Anyone in the fossil dig site must remove their shoes.

Helpful Hints: This attraction typically doesn't have a queue line. The playground is best experienced by children age 4-10 years old. Water fountains are located inside the playground.

Disabled Access: Many portions of this attraction are not accessible to guests with disabilities. Guests may remain in their wheelchair or motorized scooter.

• • • • • • • • • • • • • • • • • •

1. What is a fossil?
A. Ancient writings found on rocks
B. The remains of an animal or plant which are preserved in rock
C. Pottery from an ancient era

2. Have you ever touched a fossil?

3. Have fossils ever been found underwater?

4. What is the name of a scientist that studies fossils?
A. Paleontologist
B. Meteorologist
C. Psychologist

5. True or False: An animal's bones and its fleshy parts are usually preserved in a fossil.

6. Which of these tools usually isn't used in fossil hunting?
A. Shovel
B. Hammer
C. Screwdriver

7. Some fossils are wood, bones or teeth that have become petrified. What does petrified mean?
A. An object has turned to stone
B. An object has turned to liquid
C. An object is really frightened

8. What is Florida's official state fossil?
A. The fossilized remains of sea urchins
B. The fossilized remains of manatees
C. The fossilized remains of palm trees

DINOSAUR

Overview: Travel 65 million years back in time on a 12-passenger Time Rover (three rows of four guests each) to the Cretaceous period and help a scientist bring back a live Iguanodon before an asteroid impact promises both the dinosaur's and your extinction.

Thrill Time: 4 minutes

FASTPASS AVAILABLE

Restrictions: Passengers must be at least 40 inches (102 cm) tall. Guests should be in good health and free from high blood pressure, heart, back or neck problems, motion sickness and other conditions that could be aggravated by the ride. Expectant mothers should not ride.

Be Aware of: This is an extremely rough ride with jerky movements and sharp turns. Due to the nature of this attraction, children could be frightened by the towering Audio-Animatronic dinosaurs that seem very real to life. The attraction is very loud with moments of pitch darkness, smoke and plenty of bright, flashing lights.

The individual seats on this attraction are narrow and might not accommodate all body types. A seat belt must be worn by all passengers.

The standard queue line requires guests to climb down a flight of stairs. If stairs will pose a problem for you, ask a cast member to utilize the elevator immediately after you exit the pre-show.

Helpful Hints: Unlike many of Disney's Animal Kingdom attractions, DINOSAUR has an enclosed, air-conditioned queue line that is a welcome respite during humid weather and afternoon rain showers. The queue line has many dinosaur fossils to look at and an informative audio presentation.

Sit in the front of the vehicle for a slightly less turbulent ride.

Guests waiting for the rest of their party to experience the DINOSAUR attraction can wait in the air-conditioned gift shop area at the exit or in a shaded seating pavilion outside.

Disabled Access: Guests must transfer from their wheelchair or motorized scooter to board this attraction. Disney's assistive listening devices interact with this attraction (pre-show only). Disney's guest-activated captioning devices interact with this attraction (pre-show only). Service animals are not permitted on this attraction.

● ●

☆ **Hidden Mickey Hunt**: After entering the building entrance, find a tree in the far left side of the mural on the right side of the queue line which has a hidden Mickey on its trunk.

♀ **Scavenger Hunt**: In the indoor queue line, find: a duck eating a fish, a picture of an asteroid impact, dinosaur fossils, the skeleton of a dinosaur, a picture of a waterfall and a Carnotaurus skeleton.

1. Could dinosaurs swim?

2. True or False: Most baby dinosaurs were hatched from eggs.

3. Did all dinosaurs walk on two legs?

4. Approximately how many kinds of dinosaurs have been discovered?
A. 48
B. 190
C. 350

5. This attraction is loosely based on the 2000 Disney film *Dinosaur*. What was the name of the main character, the Iguanodon, in the film?
A. Aladar
B. Iggie
C. Dina

6. In *Dinosaur*, where does the Iguanodon live before a meteor shower forces him to leave and look for food and shelter?
A. Under the ocean
B. On an island of lemurs
C. At the base of Mount Everest

7. Bill Nye the Science Guy presents an audio history of the dinosaur age in the queue line. What other Walt Disney World® Resort attraction, which also features dinosaurs, does Bill Nye the Science Guy help host?

8. Did Iguanodons eat meat or plants?

9. What does the name Iguanodon mean?
A. Mighty warrior
B. Iguana tail
C. Iguana tooth

10. True or False: The fossils of the Iguanodon were one of the first dinosaur fossils to be discovered.

11. A full sized Iguanodon could grow to what length?
A. 10 feet long
B. 30 feet long
C. 50 feet long

12. What does the word dinosaur mean?
A. Large monster
B. Frightful beast
C. Terrible lizard

13. Find the following dinosaurs in the word search below:
Alioramus, Raptor, Styracosaurus, Carnotaurus, Parasaurolophus, Pterodactyl and Saltasaurus.

```
C A R N O T A U R U S T H A C M
N H L P C M Y G J I D R L S E H
E K B I L P T E R O D A C T Y L
R A Q M O F U D E T N P F N B O
F W D C O R I H S A J T Q G M P
U P A R A S A U R O L O P H U S
L B N J T D R M W G C R L E Y K
E S A L T A S A U R U S P J A O
O G S T Y R A C O S A U R U S R
A R H M C P F S K U N B L H D G
```

14. Dinosaurs can be classified according to the type of hip structure that they had. Which one of the following animals does not have a hip structure that has been found in dinosaurs?
A. Bird
B. Lizard
C. Dog

Primeval Whirl

Overview: This spinning roller coaster is a dizzying ride back in time to the dinosaur age. The carnival-themed attraction features four-passenger circular time machines (two benches each seat two guests) which travel over dips, turns and curves while spinning in a random pattern throughout the ride.

Thrill Time: 3 ½ minutes

FASTPASS AVAILABLE

Restrictions: Passengers must be at least 48 inches (122 cm) tall. Guests should be in good health and free from high blood pressure, heart, back or neck problems, motion sickness and other conditions that could be aggravated by the ride. Expectant mothers should not ride.

Be Aware of: The entire attraction is located outdoors with no cover. This attraction closes during inclement weather such as thunder and lightning.

Primeval Whirl is a very rough ride with jerky movements which often cause guests to slam against each other as they travel around the curves. At the beginning of the attraction your time machine will bump against other time machines waiting in line (like bumper cars) before starting your journey.

The time machine's seating is very low to the ground and boarding the vehicle could be difficult for anyone with slow movement or difficulty in bending at the knees. Each pair of guests in the time machine must share one large shoulder harness.

Helpful Hints: There are fans in the covered queue line. Parent/Guardian Switch option is available.

Disabled Access: Guests must transfer from their wheelchair or motorized scooter to board this attraction. The wooden grooved ramps throughout the queue line make pushing a wheelchair more challenging. Service animals are not permitted on this attraction.

• • • • • • • • • • • • • • • • • • •

☆ **Hidden Mickey Hunt**: In the meteors on the attraction sign above the entrance to the covered queue line, some of the craters form hidden Mickeys.

⚲ **Scavenger Hunt**: In the covered queue line, find: a scientist with a Yea! pennant and a gauge with an arrow that points to "Older Than Dirt."

1. If you could travel back in time to the age of dinosaurs, would you? Why or why not?

2. The Hanna-Barbera cartoon *The Flintstones* took place in the Stone Age and shows humans and dinosaurs living and working together. Did humans exist when dinosaurs were on the Earth?

3. The Flintstones lived in what town?
A. Bedrock
B. Flagstone
C. Sheetrock

4. What were the names of the members of the Flintstone family?

5. Who were the Flintstones' neighbors?

6. What was Fred Flintstone's occupation?
A. He was a dinosaur hunter
B. He was a scientist
C. He worked in a quarry

7. Jim Henson Productions created a television show about a working family of blue-collar dinosaurs that aired on ABC from 1991-1994. What was the name of the show?
A. *Dinosaurs*
B. *Fraggle Rock*
C. *Dinotopia*

8. Dinosaurs lived in the Jurassic and Cretaceous periods. Which period came first?

9. Both the Jurassic and Cretaceous periods were part of a larger part of history called the Mesozoic era, which was from 65 to 250 million years ago. What is this era commonly called?
A. Age of Reptiles
B. Age of Discovery
C. Age of Large Animals

10. Dinosaurs are believed to have become extinct approximately how long ago?
A. 20 million years ago
B. 65 million years ago
C. 140 million years ago

11. Which of the following is not a likely reason why the dinosaurs became extinct?
A. There was a large volcanic eruption
B. A large asteroid crashed into Earth
C. The dinosaurs' food supply vanished overnight

12. Though not all scientists can agree on the specific event that caused the dinosaurs' extinction, the extinction has been determined to be largely caused by what?
A. A worldwide climate change
B. A change in the dinosaurs' DNA
C. A widespread illness

13. The oldest known dinosaurs date back to how many millions of years ago?
A. 230 million years
B. 500 million years
C. 720 million years

14. The 1993 movie *Jurassic Park* was based on the novel *Jurassic Park* written by which famous author?
A. Stephen King
B. Janet Evanovich
C. Michael Crichton

15. In the film *Jurassic Park*, live dinosaurs were being used for what purpose?
A. To start a war
B. They were part of a theme park
C. They were being used in medical research

16. How did scientists bring dinosaurs back to life in the film *Jurassic Park*?
A. They used dinosaur DNA taken from ancient fossilized insects
B. They found a dinosaur living in the wild and cloned him
C. They mutated the DNA of lizards to create dinosaurs

17. The sequel to the *Jurassic Park* book and film was *The Lost World* which was based on a 1912 book by the same name written by Sir Arthur Conan Doyle. Sir Arthur Conan Doyle is famous for creating which famous literary character?
A. Perry Mason
B. Sherlock Holmes
C. James Bond

TriceraTop Spin

Overview: Enjoy a gentle flight through the air aboard a Triceratops dinosaur vehicle. Each of the 16 dinosaurs has two rows which can each accommodate two guests.

Thrill Time: 1 ½ minutes

Be Aware of: This entire attraction is located outdoors with no cover. This attraction closes during inclement weather such as thunder and lightning. Guests must step up and then down into the vehicle.

Helpful Hints: Guests sitting in the front row can use a lever to tip the dinosaur vehicle forwards or backwards. Guests in the back row can use a lever to move the vehicle higher or lower.

Parent/Guardian Switch option is available.

Disabled Access: Guests must transfer from a motorized scooter to a wheelchair that is provided at the attraction. Guests may remain in their wheelchair on the attraction. Service animals are not permitted on this attraction.

• • • • • • • • • • • • • • • • • •

Scavenger Hunt: Find a dinosaur balancing a ball on its nose and a dinosaur balancing a ball on its feet.

1. How many stars can you count on the large spinning top in the center of the attraction?

2. How many comets can you count on the large spinning top in the center of the attraction?

3. How many horns are on each of the dinosaur's faces?

4. What other animal living in Disney's Animal Kingdom has large horns on its face? (Hint: It's large and grey)

5. The dinosaurs on this attraction fly through the air. Could real dinosaurs fly?

6. Have you seen a dinosaur in any other Disney theme park?

7. What is the name of the large purple dinosaur who has his own television show and likes to say "Super-dee-duper!"

8. Barney has two friends who are also on the *Barney & Friends* show. Which of the following characters is not the name of a dinosaur that is friends with Barney?
A. Baby Bop
B. BJ
C. Barnyard Billie

9. What are the lyrics of the famous song that is sung at the end of every *Barney & Friends* show?

10. On the Hanna-Barbera cartoon series *The Flintstones*, what was the name of the Flintstones' pet dinosaur?
A. Pebbles
B. Hoppy
C. Dino

11. The dinosaur vehicles in this attraction are inspired by a dinosaur named Triceratops. What does the name Triceratops mean?
A. Three-horned face
B. Baby dinosaur
C. Flying dinosaur

12. Though the Triceratops dinosaurs in this attraction are cute and small, real Triceratops were the opposite. How tall could a Triceratops grow?
A. 5 feet high
B. 10 feet high
C. 25 feet high

13. Do you think that Triceratops ate meat or plants?

14. The two horns near a Triceratops' eyes could grow to be three feet long. What do you think these horns were used for?
A. Attracting females
B. Gathering plants
C. Fighting

15. Where did the Triceratops mainly live in the United States?
A. In the western U.S.
B. In Alaska
C. In Florida

16. The Triceratops could grow to be up to 30 feet long. Being such a large animal, the Triceratops could weigh as much as how many cars?
A. Three
B. Seven
C. Nine

DISCOVERY ISLAND

Home to Disney's Animal Kingdom's icon, the Tree of Life, this island encircled by Discovery River is at the hub of the theme park with paths (or spokes) radiating outwards towards the other lands.

It's Tough To Be A Bug!

Overview: Become an honorary bug and learn about how hard it is to be an insect in this comical 3-D film emceed by Flik from the Disney-Pixar film *A Bug's Life*. Flik and his bug friends produce a hilarious variety show which portrays the good things that bugs do for the planet while at the same time appealing to the 428-guest audience to stop killing the insect population.

Thrill Time: 8 ½ minutes

FASTPASS AVAILABLE

Be Aware of: Though this attraction features the cute characters from *A Bug's Life*, it can be very frightening to children and adults. The show takes place in a darkened theater and many of the special effects, such as large spiders dropping from the sky, heavy smoke and the feel of bugs crawling under your seat, are too intense for many guests. Additional effects such as misting water, 'stingers' in your back, a foul smell, puffs of air and a menacing, larger-than-life Hopper character are guaranteed to send at least one mother and screaming child towards the exit.

This outdoors queue line has no cover and can become very warm in the Florida heat. The queue line meanders through landscaped paths which surround the Tree of Life and it could be very difficult to catch up with members of your party who have gone ahead of you.

Guests must wear 3-D glasses for the best experience of the show.

Helpful Hints: Strollers are allowed through a brief portion of the queue line. Cast members will take your stroller at a designated point and park it near the attraction exit.

The last portions of the queue line are fun to walk through as they pass by the root systems of the Tree of Life. Some of the animals carved into the tree can be seen while standing in line.

This is an attraction where you don't want to be at the front of the line heading into the theater because the best seats are in the center of the theater. To sit in the center of the theater, allow several guests to enter a row before you because the cast members will instruct everyone to move to the far end of the row before sitting down.

Children who might be bothered by the 3-D effects can still enjoy the attraction without wearing the 3-D glasses.

Parent/Guardian Switch option is available.

Disabled Access: Guests may remain in their wheelchair or motorized scooter. Disney's assistive listening devices interact with this attraction. Reflective captioning is available. Guests with service animals should check with a host or hostess at this attraction.

• • • • • • • • • • • • • • • • • •

☆ ***Hidden Mickey Hunt***: Look on the rock wall to the left of the disabled entrance into the theater. Towards the top of the rock next to a spotlight is a small, dark impression of a hidden Mickey.

♀ ***Scavenger Hunt***: In the outdoor queue line, find: a Bung Brothers poster, a Claire de Room poster and carvings of an elephant, rhinoceros, pelican and ape in the Tree of Life.

In the indoors waiting area, find the following posters: *The Dung and I*, *Web Side Story*, *Antie*, *Beauty and the Bees*, *A Stinkbug Named Desire* and *Barefoot in the Bark*.

1. In the Disney-Pixar film *A Bug's Life*, what is the name of the princess ant that Flik falls in love with?
A. Atta
B. Lulu
C. Terma

2. In *A Bug's Life*, what is the name of the youngest and smallest princess who is impatiently waiting for her wings to grow so that she can fly?
A. Speck
B. Spot
C. Dot

3. When Flik leaves the island in *A Bug's Life*, who does he find to help fight off the grasshoppers?
A. An army of centipedes
B. A colony of birds
C. Circus bugs

4. In *A Bug's Life*, the colony of ants works all year to harvest food for the grasshoppers. Why do they spend all of their energy feeding the grasshoppers?
A. So the grasshoppers will protect the ants from larger insects
B. The ants have been put under a spell to obey the grasshoppers
C. The grasshoppers are the ants' friends and they share food

5. In *A Bug's Life*, what do the ants do to stop the grasshoppers from harassing them anymore?
A. Ask a group of cockroaches to eat the grasshoppers
B. Build a bird to scare away the grasshoppers
C. Moved to another ant hill to hide from the grasshoppers

6. At the end of *A Bug's Life*, what happens to Hopper, the mean grasshopper?
A. He is voted off of the island
B. He gets lost in a field of grass
C. He gets eaten by a bird

7. Match the following characters from *A Bug's Life* with the type of insect that they are:

Francis   Moth
Heimlich   Walking stick
Tuck and Roll   Pill bugs
Slim   Black widow spider
Gypsy   Caterpillar
Rosie   Male ladybug

8. Unscramble the following types of insects:

DEIPSR
EEEBTL
AYIPRNG MANSIT
OOUIMSQT
YFL
APSW
EFLA
FLYAONGDR

9. Which of the following is not a reason why bees are beneficial to humans?
A. They pollinate plants
B. They make honey
C. They eat rotten wood

10. A caterpillar will turn into what kind of insect after shedding its skin?
A. Butterfly
B. Spider
C. Termite

11. True or False: Butterflies can taste things with their feet.

12. How many beneficial insects are released each year at the Walt Disney World® Resort to control pests on plants?
A. 2.7 million
B. 9.8 million
C. 12.5 million

13. What is a large group of grasshoppers called?
A. Annoying
B. Swarm
C. Cloud

14. What is a large group of cockroaches called?
A. Intrusion
B. Disgusting
C. Army

15. How many noses does a slug have?
A. 1
B. 4
C. 16

16. How many eggs can a queen bee lay each day?
A. 500
B. 2,000
C. 10,000

17. Approximately how many lenses are in each eye of a dragonfly?
A. 500
B. 15,000
C. 30,000

RAFIKI'S PLANET WATCH

Rafiki's Planet Watch is all about the care and conservation of animals. Guests learn how to conserve animal habitats and can see some of Disney's animal care experts preparing food or performing medical checkups. A petting zoo full of barnyard animals is fun for the little ones who have been anxious to touch the animals they have seen all day.

Wildlife Express Train

Overview: The Wildlife Express Train is the only way to and from Conservation Station and Affection Section. The 250-passenger trains take guests through some backstage animal areas of Disney's Animal Kingdom before arriving at Rafiki's Planet Watch.

Thrill Time: 4 minutes each way

Be Aware of: The Wildlife Express Train begins operating later than normal park operating hours and the last train departure occurs shortly before Disney's Animal Kingdom closes. Consult the Times Guide for operating hours. This attraction closes during inclement weather such as lightning.

Helpful Hints: Both train stations in Africa and Rafiki's Planet Watch are covered and have fans. Trains typically leave every 5-7 minutes. The train station at Rafiki's Planet Watch for the return trip to Africa has limited seating.

The seats on the train all face outwards towards the open windows. Sit in the front row for unobstructed views of the landscape.

Collapsible strollers can be brought onboard the Wildlife Express Train. If you are traveling with small children, you will want to have a stroller with you for the walk along Habitat Habit! which leads to Conservation Station and Affection Section.

Disabled Access: Guests may remain in their wheelchair or motorized scooter. Disney's handheld captioning devices interact with this attraction.

• • • • • • • • • • • • • • • • • • •

1. Many birds are losing their homes because so many trees are being cut down. What can you do in your own backyard to create a place where birds can live?

2. Do bats do anything but hang around and look scary?

3. How many worms are fed to the animals each week at Disney's Animal Kingdom?
A. 500
B. 10,000
C. 40,000

4. About how many animal wellness checkups are performed each year at Disney's Animal Kingdom?
A. 125
B. 600
C. 1,000

5. True or False: Disney's Animal Kingdom veterinarians have given an injured lion an artificial eye.

6. Disney's Animal Kingdom's veterinarians have performed a surgery to remove what from a snake found at a Disney golf course?
A. A golf ball
B. A pair of Mickey Mouse ears
C. A stuffed Minnie Mouse doll

7. How many times a day is the water that comes into contact with animals filtered at Disney's Animal Kingdom?
A. One
B. Two
C. Five

8. The Florida panther is one of the most endangered animals in the world because they are losing their homes due to overdeveloping in the state. Approximately how many Florida panthers remain in the wild today?
A. Fewer than 10
B. Fewer than 100
C. Fewer than 1,000

9. Pandas are also considered an endangered species. About how many pandas remain in the wild today?
A. 16
B. 160
C. 1,600

10. According to the 2004 Red List of Threatened Species produced by the IUCN, the World Conservation Union, which country had the most animals who have become extinct, are critically endangered or are facing a high risk of extinction?
A. Australia
B. The United States
C. Mexico

11. According to the IUCN, how many of the world's turtles are threatened and could become extinct one day?
A. About 30% of all freshwater turtles
B. About 50% of all freshwater turtles
C. About 80% of all freshwater turtles

12. In 1993, the Walt Disney Company purchased 8,500 acres of land and gave it to The Nature Conservancy, whose mission is to preserve plants and animals. Visitors are welcome to explore the Disney Wilderness Preserve which is located where?
A. Atlanta, Georgia
B. Cleveland, Ohio
C. Orlando, Florida

13. Approximately how much of the land at the Walt Disney World® Resort has been set aside as a wilderness preserve and will not be built on?

A. One fourth of the land
B. One third of the land
C. One half of the land

EVERYTHING ELSE

Not every entertaining experience in Disney's Animal Kingdom involves a queue line. The following attractions and entertainment do not require guests to stand in a queue line and typically do not involve a wait time.

- The **Oasis Exhibits** are hidden among the dense foliage and meandering trails that you encounter immediately after entering Disney's Animal Kingdom. Take either path (left or right) to make your way to Discovery Island, but be sure to take time to find the giant anteater, colorful birds and other animals that call The Oasis their home. Cast members are often stationed at the animal habitats to answer questions.

- The **Discovery Island Trails** house even more animal habitats hidden among a section of the theme park that most visitors often overlook. Enjoy a peaceful walk along the base of the Tree of Life (try to spot some of the animals carved into its trunk) and discover Galapagos tortoises, lemurs and other wildlife. Cast members are often stationed at the animal habitats to answer questions.

- Africa's **Pangani Forest Exploration Trail** is a walk through the forest with several animal habitats along the way. This is where you'll find gorillas who stare back at you through large observation windows in their habitat. An underwater hippo viewing area, naked mole rats, plenty of birds (be sure to pick up a birds guide along the trail) and large observation windows looking into small lakes of fish can all be found in this African forest. The entire outdoor trail is uncovered and its rough terrain makes pushing strollers and wheelchairs somewhat challenging. For guests with a wheelchair, motorized scooter or stroller, there are many doors leading into and out of animal habitats which are difficult to maneuver without the assistance of a second person opening the door. Allow a minimum of 15 minutes.

367

- Asia's **Maharajah Jungle Trek** is a beautiful nature walk through the Anandapur Royal Forest. With colorful ancient buildings and exotic animals around every turn, you'll definitely feel as if you've traveled around the world to a foreign land. This walking trail is where you'll find magnificent tigers, bats (you can easily bypass the open-air bat house if you would like), Komodo dragons and plenty of birds. Be sure to pick up an animal guide at the entrance to the trail, as well as at the bird area, so that you know what animals you are looking at. The entire outdoor trail is uncovered and its rough terrain makes pushing strollers and wheelchairs somewhat challenging. Limited bench seating and water fountains are along the trail, as are plenty of cast members to answer your questions. Allow a minimum of 15 minutes.

- **Habitat Habit!** in Rafiki's Planet Watch is a forest trail that guests walk along to reach Conservation Station and Affection Section. Along the path you will see animals and learn about ways that you can protect the environment by creating habitats at home for wildlife.

- **Conservation Station** in Rafiki's Planet Watch is an air-conditioned exhibit area with plenty of interactive ways to learn about the animal world. Live animal presentations, videos, sound booths and interactive computer displays all teach guests about wildlife. Take a peek inside the world of Disney's Wildlife Tracking Center and watch scientists at work, talk to an animal nutritionist assistant as they prepare the animals' meals or even watch an animal medical checkup in Disney's Animal Hospital. Contact Guest Relations for a listing of scheduled medical checkups taking place throughout the day (usually in the morning) if you are interested in watching a medical procedure.

- **Affection Section** in Rafiki's Planet Watch is a petting zoo with typical barnyard animals. A hand washing station is located within the petting zoo for the health and safety of guests. For the safety of the animals, any guests who have traveled outside of North America in the past five days are asked not to visit the petting zoo to prevent possible transmission of Foot and Mouth Disease.

- The **Fossil Fun Games** in DinoLand U.S.A. are typical carnival redemption games with a dinosaur theme. Guests must pay to play these games which range from $2 to $6 per play.

- **Mickey's Jammin' Jungle Parade** is a wild street party starring your favorite Disney animal characters and plenty of abstract animals portrayed by humans in colorful costumes. The parade route begins near the Tusker House Restaurant in Africa and winds its way around Discovery Island before returning to the Tusker House. Want a great view of the parade without having to wait at a viewing spot for a lengthy period of time? Since the parade starts and ends at the Tusker House Restaurant, the majority of people waiting near that location will leave once the parade has passed through. Arrive at the same location about 15 minutes after the parade has started and you'll find far fewer guests and possibly get a front row seat while enjoying the same floats and characters. See "Helpful Hints and Tips on Surviving Disney Queue Lines" for more parade viewing information or enjoy the "Disney's Animal Kingdom Trivia" or "Animal World Trivia" sections while you are waiting.

ANIMAL WORLD TRIVIA

1. How many hours a day do pandas spend eating?
A. 2
B. 14
C. 20

2. Do any snakes live in the bitterly cold regions of the Arctic Circle?

3. Marsupials are animals that live where when they are young?
A. In their mother's pouches
B. In trees
C. Under water

4. What kind of plant are giant pandas famous for eating?
A. Eucalyptus leaves
B. Cactus
C. Bamboo

5. What is the difference between most frogs and toads?
A. Frogs have bumps that look like warts and toads don't
B. Frogs have longer legs than toads
C. Toads are more likely to live by water than frogs

6. Many animal species have specific names for large groupings of that animal. For example, a group of cattle is called a herd while a group of seagulls is called a colony. Match the following animals with the scientific names given to their large groups:

Goldfish	Lounge
Flamingos	Troop
Peacocks	Stable
Beavers	Parliament
Horses	Family
Bears	Pride
Monkeys	Troubling
Lizards	Stand
Owls	Barrel
Baboons	Sloth

7. Each species of animal has a special name given to babies of the species. For example, a baby tiger is called a cub. Match the following types of animals with the names given to their baby animals:

Whale	Pup
Turtle	Chick
Spider	Gosling
Sheep	Squeaker
Seal	Joey
Pigeon	Fledgling
Pig	Tadpole
Koala	Piglet
Hawk	Spiderling
Goose	Hatchling
Eagle	Kitten
Frog	Lamb
Bobcat	Colt
Zebra	Calf

8. What do horned lizards squirt from their eyes to scare away predators?
A. Blood
B. Water
C. Urine

9. What is the only kind of plant that koalas can eat?
A. Eucalyptus leaves
B. Maple leaves
C. Lettuce

10. What is the difference between most turtles and tortoises?
A. Turtles can crawl out of their shell and tortoises cannot
B. Turtles primarily live in water and tortoises live on land
C. Turtles do not have webbed feet and tortoises do

11. What is the difference between alligators and crocodiles?
A. Alligators live in fresh water and crocodiles live in saltwater
B. An alligator's teeth are visible outside of their mouth
C. Alligators' snouts are pointed and crocodiles' snouts are round

12. A crocodile can hold its breath underwater for approximately how long?
A. 30 minutes
B. 60 minutes
C. 24 hours

13. Both deer and rabbits share the same name for the males and females in their species. What is the name of a male deer or rabbit? What is the name of a female deer or rabbit?

14. What is the name of a male chicken? (Hint: He makes a lot of noise in the morning)

15. What is the name of a female chicken?

16. Can a reptile stay cool when it is in the sun with no shade?

17. The largest animal on Earth is the blue whale. The largest recorded specimen of a blue whale was as long as a building how many stories high?
A. 5
B. 9
C. 11

18. An animal that eats both plants and animals is called a what?
A. Herbivore
B. Carnivore
C. Omnivore

19. Do leopards like to swim?

20. Can lions climb trees?

21. Can a crocodile move its tongue?

22. Do lions like catnip?

23. How many hearts does an octopus have?
A. One
B. Two
C. Three

GENERAL DISNEY'S ANIMAL KINGDOM TRIVIA

1. Look at a Disney's Animal Kingdom guide map to find the following items: *(Note: Guide maps are subject to change)*

- A dinosaur
- A safari vehicle
- Pictures of animals
- A waterfall
- A train
- A really large tree

2. When did Disney's Animal Kingdom theme park open?
A. April 22, 1998
B. May 5, 1998
C. November 1, 1998

3. What was significant about the opening day of Disney's Animal Kingdom?
A. It was also Arbor Day
B. It was also Earth Day
C. It was also Walt Disney's birthday

4. Approximately how many animals live at Disney's Animal Kingdom?
A. 900
B. 1,300
C. 1,500

5. Approximately how many animal species are represented in Disney's Animal Kingdom?
A. 93
B. 175
C. 250

6. During the construction of Disney's Animal Kingdom, how many dump trucks full of dirt were delivered to the site each day for two years?
A. 20
B. 40
C. 60

7. How tall is the Tree of Life?
A. 145 feet
B. 160 feet
C. 187 feet

8. The Tree of Life has how many leaves that actually blow in the wind?
A. 103,000
B. 179,000
C. 2 million

9. How many animals are carved into the Tree of Life?
A. 175
B. 295
C. 325

10. Artists had what amount of time to carve the animals into the Tree of Life before the plaster hardened?
A. One to two hours
B. Six to ten hours
C. Two to three days

11. The first animal birth at Disney's Animal Kingdom was what type of animal species?
A. African antelope
B. African elephant
C. Black rhino

12. Disney's Animal Kingdom's animals eat approximately how many specially ordered crickets each month?
A. 600
B. 80,000
C. 1 million

13. What was the original working name of Disney's Animal Kingdom theme park?
A. Wild Kingdom
B. Lands of the Wild
C. Wild Life

14. The Walt Disney Company was busy expanding their empire in 1998. Not only did they open their fourth theme park, but they launched several other new Disney ventures. Which of the following did not premiere in 1998?
A. DisneyQuest
B. Disney Cruise Line's *Disney Magic*
C. Disney's Wide World of Sports Complex

15. Disney's Animal Kingdom is the largest of all four theme parks. How many acres of land are in the theme park?
A. 400
B. 500
C. 1,000

16. Would the Magic Kingdom, Epcot and Disney-MGM Studios all fit within Disney's Animal Kingdom at the same time?

17. True or False: A themed land based on mythical animals was planned when Disney's Animal Kingdom first opened, but the land was never built.

18. Disney Imagineers traveled over 500,000 miles around the world to capture the look and feel of life in the wild in order to make Disney's Animal Kingdom as authentic as possible. That is a distance equal to circling the globe how many times?
A. 20
B. 30
C. 40

19. Approximately how many different plant species can be seen throughout the Walt Disney World® Resort?
A. 1,900
B. 2,500
C. 10,000

20. The Disney Wildlife Conservation Fund, which was established in 1995 when plans for Disney's Animal Kingdom were announced, has donated approximately how much money to non-profit groups for the conservation of endangered animals and their habitats?
A. $2 million
B. $10 million
C. $18 million

21. The Walt Disney World® Resort has always had a location where visitors could learn about endangered and rare animal species. From 1974 to 1999, guests could visit an 11-acre island near the Magic Kingdom that had over 500 animals, including a large bird population. What was the name of this island that closed a year after Disney's Animal Kingdom opened?
A. Treasure Island
B. Discovery Island
C. Wild Oasis

22. What kind of animals were bred on Discovery Island which were trained to assist disabled individuals?
A. Monkeys
B. Parrots
C. Dogs

DISNEY'S ANIMAL KINGDOM CHAPTER ANSWERS

Africa
Kilimanjaro Safaris
Scavenger Hunt: The sleeping bags and pottery are located in the rafters. **1.** Kifaru; Duma **2.** Litter can seriously injure wildlife **3.** B **4.** C **5.** B **6.** True **7.** No **8.** A **9.** B **10.** C **11.** Apes - Shrewdness; Gorillas - Band; Giraffes - Corps; Hippos - Bloat; Hyenas - Cackle; Leopards - Leap; Lions - Pride; Camels - Caravan; Rhinoceroses - Crash; Zebras - Zeal **12.** C **13.** C **14.** See the end of this chapter. **15.** C **16.** C **17.** A **18.** B **19.** True **20.** C **21.** No - each has a unique pattern.

Asia
Expedition Everest - Legend of the Forbidden Mountain
1. True **2.** B **3.** C **4.** B **5.** A **6.** A **7.** C **8.** B **9.** C **10.** C **11.** B **12.** B **13.** C **14.** A **15.** A **16.** C **17.** B **18.** A **19.** B **20.** A **21.** A **22.** A

Flights of Wonder
1. C **2.** A **3.** B **4.** See the end of this chapter. **5.** A **6.** True **7.** A (Sailors easily caught the birds and ate them all) **8.** C (An additional 21 species are probably extinct) **9.** B **10.** C **11.** When birds ingest DDT, their eggs have shells which are so thin that they crack under the weight of the parents. **12.** Limit pesticide use, build bird habitats, protect natural resources by recycling and reducing waste and donate to wildlife funds.

Kali River Rapids
1. A **3.** B **4.** C **5.** Illegally logged trees are obtained by using logging practices which waste much of the wood and devastate the environment, which causes animal and plant species to become extinct, including medicinal plants which help in pharmaceuticals and drug research. Trees are not replaced, centuries old trees are cut down and the indigenous cultures which live near forests are negatively affected. **6.** No (It happens around the world, even in North America where a lot of illegal logging occurs in the

377

northwest U.S. and Canada. **7.** C **8.** C **9.** A **10.** B **11.** See the end of this chapter. **12.** C **13.** B **14.** B **15.** C **16.** Lizard; Butterfly; Alligator; Leopard; Frog; Snake; Monkey; Tiger; Gorilla; Macaw

Camp Minnie-Mickey
Festival of the Lion King
1. A **2.** C **3.** B **4.** A **5.** B **6.** A **7.** C **8.** A **9.** A **10.** *Lion King 1 ½* tells the *The Lion King* story from Timon and Pumbaa's perspective. **11.** B **12.** A **13.** B **14.** C **15.** A **16.** C **17.** A **18.** See the end of this chapter.

Pocahontas and Her Forest Friends
1. A **2.** A **3.** A **4.** B **5.** Governor Ratcliffe; Percy; Thomas; Chief Powhatan; Grandmother Willow; Nakoma **6.** B **7.** A **8.** No **9.** True **10.** C **11.** C **12.** A **13.** B

DinoLand U.S.A.
The Boneyard
1. B **3.** Yes **4.** A **5.** False - soft fleshy parts of animals don't preserve well so most fossils are bones and hard shells. **6.** C **7.** A **8.** A

DINOSAUR
1. No **2.** True **3.** No, some walked on four legs **4.** C **5.** A **6.** B **7.** Ellen's Energy Adventure at Epcot **8.** Plants **9.** C **10.** True - The teeth were the first dinosaur fossil to be found, but were the second to be scientifically classified in the same year after the Megalosaurus. **11.** B **12.** C **13.** See the end of this chapter. **14.** C

Primeval Whirl
2. No **3.** A **4.** Fred, Wilma, and Pebbles **5.** Barney and Betty Rubble and their son Bamm Bamm **6.** C **7.** A **8.** The Jurassic period, which was first, was 149-152 million years ago while the Cretaceous period was 65-144 million years ago. **9.** A **10.** B **11.** C **12.** A **13.** A **14.** C **15.** B **16.** A **17.** B

TriceraTop Spin
2. Four **3.** Three **4.** Rhinoceros **5.** No, but their cousins, the pterosaurs, could. **6.** Dinosaur Gertie is by the lake in Disney-MGM Studios and there are dinosaurs in Ellen's Energy Adventure at Epcot. **7.** Barney **8.** C **9.** "I love you, you love me,

we're a great big family, with a great big hug and a kiss from me to you, won't you say you love me, too." **10.** C **11.** A **12.** B **13.** Plants **14.** C **15.** A **16.** A

Discovery Island
It's Tough To Be A Bug
1. A **2.** C **3.** C **4.** A **5.** B **6.** C **7.** Francis - Male ladybug; Heimlich - Caterpillar; Tuck and Roll - Pill bugs; Slim - Walking stick; Gypsy - Moth; Rosie - Black widow spider **8.** Spider; Beetle; Praying mantis; Mosquito; Fly; Wasp; Flea; Dragonfly **9.** C **10.** A **11.** True **12.** C **13.** C **14.** A **15.** B **16.** B **17.** C

Rafiki's Planet Watch
Wildlife Express Train
1. Plant trees and bushes and put out birdhouses. **2.** Yes, they eat many rodents and insects that humans try to get rid of. **3.** C **4.** B **5.** False, but they have put an artificial eye in a fish. **6.** A **7.** C **8.** B **9.** C **10.** B (The U.S. has 903, Australia has 565 and Mexico has 487) **11.** B **12.** C **13.** A

Animal World Trivia
1. B **2.** Yes, one species. **3.** A **4.** C **5.** B **6.** Goldfish - Troubling; Flamingos - Stand; Peacocks - Pride; Beavers - Family; Horses - Stable; Bears - Sloth; Monkeys - Barrel; Lizards - Lounge; Owls - Parliament; Baboons - Troop **7.** Whale - Calf; Turtle - Hatchling; Spider - Spiderling; Sheep - Lamb; Seal - Pup; Pigeon - Squeaker; Pig - Piglet; Koala - Joey; Hawk - Chick; Goose - Gosling; Eagle - Fledgling; Frog - Tadpole; Bobcat - Kitten; Zebra - Colt **8.** A **9.** A **10.** B **11.** A **12.** B **13.** Buck; Doe **14.** Rooster **15.** Hen **16.** No - Reptiles must stay in warm spots to be warm and in cool spots to stay cool. **17.** C **18.** C **19.** Yes **20.** Yes **21.** No **22.** Yes **23.** C

General Disney's Animal Kingdom Trivia
1. Dinosaur - outside of DINOSAUR attraction and in DinoLand U.S.A.; Safari vehicle - Kilimanjaro Safaris; Waterfall - Rainforest Café; Train - Wildlife Express Train **2.** A **3.** B **4.** C **5.** C **6.** C **7.** A **8.** A **9.** C **10.** B **11.** A **12.** B **13.** A **14.** C **15.** B **16.** Yes **17.** True **18.** A **19.** B **20.** B **21.** B **22.** A

379

Kilimanjaro Safaris

```
PACNEJHEOWARTHOG
CFIRNDGORILLAQAL
TAGDOMWBJCTYIKGZ
BNEMVCRNESFWDOWE
MTKOLTORTOISERNB
HEJNDQGDWLBPICOR
SLAKMAOMIUEADYAA
FOTEIAFSFLAMINGO
UPCYCLBHONEJHMDU
AEGWROSTRICHKAVE
```

Kali River Rapids

```
HRDISEABACHISCBM
XEDQBOLGMTQJASKW
BDTKAMCUFPEYEALI
OCRWNHYBKDCAYPHR
REJAAEXITNLPKEBO
FDLVMAHOGANYQLPK
KAPGZIUDJFNGCLVO
SRHETONQAMKBLIIT
AMUCIDWSHEMLOCKO
NVMERBAUHPESJAGF
```

Flights of Wonder

```
FMBWJDUGLPYHERON
ASWALLOWMVUPGAOC
WRPNBSDRAIBFFLES
AYHTCUCKOOTKFWDW
RELOETGAPCJHVISA
BLGJCRFQEBYWULNN
LKIROUNPARTRIDGE
EAVPEWDNLEMEBHRI
RGBNUTHATCHNITCB
CSGOLDFINCHESKAF
```

DINOSAUR

```
CARNOTAURUSTHACM
NHLPCMYGJIDRLSEH
EKBILPTERODACTYL
RAQMOFUDETNPFNBO
FWDCORIHSAJTQGMP
UPARASAUROLOPHUS
LBNJTDRMWGCRLEYK
ESALTASAURUSPJAO
OGSTYRACOSAURUSR
ARHMCPFSKUNBLHDG
```

Festival of the Lion King

```
PNGETAUJSEVZAZUH
ORMPHJZCIPDYUQFX
FCIRCLEOFLIFETBS
IDNDQAOINTBCKPGH
WKISEVGELSWMALBE
AMTSARAFINAJOCAN
OHDPCUOPQFWRPHNZ
EBJASBMCHNDUANZI
LCIQAKGVKOMEKBAS
FPWILDEBEESTSYIJ
```

CHARACTER MEET AND GREETS

If you're like many Disney visitors, you just can't wait to get your picture taken with Mickey Mouse or Donald Duck or any of the other Disney characters that you have come to love. The good news is that there are plenty of opportunities to meet the Disney gang regardless of which park you visit. However, the locations, times and schedules of characters change rapidly throughout all four theme parks. For up to date information, be sure to check the Times Guide when you enter each park or ask any character escort.

Character Meet and Greet Tips

- Have your autograph book open to a clean page with a pen easily available and make sure your camera is ready to go with the lens cap off, the lens in focus and the battery levels checked. In case you're in line when the character is whisked away for a break, they might grab an autograph book and sign while they are walking or pose for a quick snapshot, but they sure won't do it if you've got to fumble around for the supplies.

- Costumed characters have big hands with little mobility and some characters have an extremely tough time signing their autographs. Be sure to have a large pen, pencil or marker for the characters to use instead of a golf size pencil or crayon.

- If you need a character escort to take a picture for you, be sure to ask ahead of time and not when you get up to the character. You will find that the escorts often disappear and you will be left without a snapshot.

- If you are bringing small children to the Walt Disney World® Resort for the first time, you might want to let them get acclimated to seeing the characters before actually meeting them. Because the characters are so much larger in life than they are on the television screen, your child could be easily frightened and refuse to visit any characters for the rest of your trip (which can really put a dent into your vacation photo plans). To prevent your child from being frightened at his or her first character meet and greet, you might want to spend your first day or two in the parks simply looking at the characters from afar before actually visiting with them.

- If you want to know where to find any character at any theme park, simply ask a character escort. If they don't instantly know, they can radio the CHIP hotline which will let them know the precise times and locations of where the Disney characters can be located across the property. Character escorts aren't the only cast members who are able to access this information. Almost any cast member (especially Guest Relations cast members) who has the time and a phone or radio can call the CHIP hotline.

- If you find yourself left in a queue line after a character departs, be sure to ask the escort if they will be reappearing again or can be found in other locations in the park. Sometimes there is just a five minute wait for the character to reappear, but sometimes it could be an hour or more.

- Keep an eye on little ones during character meet and greets. Because of a character's line of vision, they often cannot see anything that isn't directly in front of them, including small children who have run up to the character from behind or from the side. A character can accidentally step on a child or trip over them because they cannot see the child.

Disney Character Fun

1. Match the following famous Disney character pairs:

Mickey	Dale
Chip	Tramp
Beauty	Daisy
Timon	Tweedledum
Lilo	Panic
Lady	Hound
Aladdin	Stitch
Tweedledee	Minnie
Donald	Jasmine
Pain	Pumbaa
Fox	Beast

2. Which Disney characters are white with black spots and have a lot of brothers and sisters?

3. Which Disney character has a nose that grows whenever he tells a lie?

4. Which Disney characters are very rich kittens?

5. Which Disney character is a loveable deer?

6. Which Disney characters like to eat bugs?

7. What Disney character flies through the air and wears green-colored clothes?

8. What is Sleeping Beauty's real name?

9. Which Disney characters like to gather nuts and live in a tree?

10. Which forgetful Disney character thinks she can talk with whales?

11. What Disney character wears a bow on her head and is Minnie's friend?

12. Which Disney character is a snake who lives in the jungle?

13. Which Disney characters are Hades' assistants?

14. Which Disney character is Jafar's pet bird?

15. Which Disney monster scares children in order to make electricity?

16. Which Disney mother has arms that stretch?

17. Find the following Disney character names in the word search below: Alice, Ariel, Bambi, Captain Hook, Cinderella, Cruella de Vil, Dumbo, Esmeralda, Flik, Gaston, Genie, Goofy, Hades, Hercules, Hopper, Jafar, Jasmine, Jiminy Cricket, Kaa, Maleficent, Mowgli, Mulan, Mushu, Peter Pan, Pinocchio, Quasimodo, Pocahontas, Pluto, Robin Hood, Scar, Sleeping Beauty, Snow White, Tinker Bell and Ursula.

```
M O W G L I W U M U L A N P R E
J H A D E S M E R A L D A I R C
I A C Q L M B Q I S K M U N O H
M F I S R A L P U O C A Q O B O
I W N N G L R N P A V A A C I P
N K D O C E K I J A S L R C N P
Y A E W B F P B E G H I Z H H E
C J R W D I R E U L E G M I O R
R A E H U C A P T A I N H O O K
I F L I M E H L I E S W I E D Q
C A L T B N N O I H R L P E A O
K R A E O T B D I C E P L U T O
E R T O H E R C U L E S A D Q R
T K C P O C A H O N T A S N U J
I N K C R U E L L A D E V I L A
S L E E P I N G B E A U T Y M S
F N M U S H U A B U R S U L A M
D L G J S T I N K E R B E L L I
T S I G O O F Y B A M B I W G N
U C R K W G A S T O N U M I G E
```

CHARACTER MEET AND GREETS CHAPTER ANSWERS

1. Mickey - Minnie; Chip - Dale; Beauty - Beast; Timon - Pumbaa; Lilo - Stitch; Lady - Tramp; Aladdin - Jasmine; Tweedledee - Tweedledum; Donald - Daisy; Pain - Panic; Fox - Hound **2.** 101 Dalmatians **3.** Pinocchio **4.** The Artistocats **5.** Bambi **6.** Timon and Pumbaa **7.** Peter Pan and Fauna **8.** Aurora **9.** Chip and Dale **10.** Dory **11.** Daisy **12.** Kaa **13.** Pain and Panic **14.** Iago **15.** Sulley **16.** Elastigirl **17.**

```
MOWGLIWUMULANPRE
JHADESMERALDAIRC
IACQLMBQISKMUNOH
MFISRALPUOCAQOBO
IWNNGLRNPAVAACIP
NKDOCEKIJASLRCNP
YAEWBFPBEGHIZHHE
CJRWDIREULEGMIOR
RAEHUCAPTAINHOOK
IFLIMEHLIESWIEDQ
CALTBNNOIHRLPEAO
KRAEOTBDICEPLUTO
ERTOHERCULESADQR
TKCPOCAHONTASNUJ
INKCRUELLADEVILA
SLEEPINGBEAUTYMS
FNMUSHUABURSULAM
DLGJSTINKERBELLI
TSIGOOFYBAMBIWGN
UCRKWGASTONUMIGE
```